The Essence of Success

Earl Nightingale

With a foreword by W. Clement Stone

This book is a transcription of the original

Audio Cassette: The Essence of Success 10 Volumes
By Earl Nightingale

Description

Drawing upon a total of more than 700 hours of recordings, it was identified the themes that continued to fascinate Earl Nightingale over the years, and it was fashioned a two-cassette album around each of these fundamental ideas:

1. Attitude and excellence
2. Courage and self-esteem
3. Creativity
4. Opportunity and goal setting
5. Personal Growth
6. Interpersonal communication and relationships
7. The Mind
8. Writing and public speaking
9. Success
10. Happiness

Table of Contents

Foreword

I first met Earl Nightingale more than four decades ago. Napoleon Hill and I had just begun an association which was to last ten years and carry us around the globe spreading the message that every individual could achieve lasting success by following a set of established principles that Hill had first written about in his all-time best seller Think and Grow Rich. Nightingale, at the time, had his own radio program on WGN in Chicago.

Dr. Hill and I had been discussing ways to promote his new book, How to Raise Your Own Salary, when Nightingale paid us a visit. "Your book, Think and Grow Rich, completely changed my life," he said. "I believe I knew all the principles before I read the book. But in Think and Grow Rich, they were in crystallized form. I could see them clearly. I decided to employ them: specifically, to double my earnings within a period of two weeks. I wrote my definite objective on a piece of paper and my earnings doubled in two weeks.

"I felt this might have been a coincidence. So I again decided to double my earnings and set a specific date. When I achieved this objective before the date set, I said to myself, 'This is no coincidence. Here I have a formula for success.'"

He looked at Napoleon Hill and continued: "I want to show my gratitude to you for Think and Grow Rich. I am here to help you all I can in any way."

Nightingale amazed me with the offer that followed. He would publicize How to Raise Your Own Salary at no cost to us. We decided to try him out to see if he was sincere. He was, and he did a magnificent job of publicizing the book. Sales were coming in volume.

Before the week was over, I called Nightingale, complimented him and said, "I don't want something for nothing. We will pay you your regular rate beginning with your second week of broadcasting for us." Through Nightingale's efforts, we sold more copies of How to Raise Your Own Salary than through all other advertising and promotional media combined.

Nightingale and I and Napoleon Hill became great friends and we met often to discuss our common love of helping others learn to apply the principles of success in their own lives. It was one of the greatest experiences of my life to work with these outstanding individuals who were dedicated to the achievement of such noble objectives and to helping each other reach our own personal goals. It was at one of those meetings that I suggested to Nightingale that he reach out to hundreds of thousands more people than he was already reaching by multiplying himself.

Nightingale did multiply himself with the same intensity that he applied to reaching every goal he set for himself. He formed a partnership with Lloyd Conant to establish Nightingale-Conant to produce motivational recordings and special courses for listeners around the world. Their company literally pioneered the development, production, design and marketing of motivational programs.

Nightingale-Conant was itself built upon fundamental principles of success. Their partnership was what I call a Master Mind Alliance in which they worked together in a spirit of perfect harmony, toward a common purpose. Each had skills that complimented the other's. Conant was the business and marketing brain, and Nightingale was the company's spokesperson. Conant ran the operation and Nightingale chaired the board of directors. Together they made the company highly successful.

They had one goal: to publish the best recorded self-help material available anywhere. Though they have both passed away, the Nightingale-Conant legacy is a company built upon principles, values, and ethics so strong that it survives them, and the organization that bears their names has set the standard for and become synonymous with quality in motivational recordings.

Earl Nightingale was in many ways a "river person," a term he often used to describe other great men. River people, he believed, recognize their life's purpose early on. "They are born to spend their lives in great rivers of the most absorbing interest, and they throw themselves into those rivers wholly," he said. He used Wolfgang Amadeus Mozart and Leonardo da Vinci as examples of river people.

Nightingale's destiny, the river that swept him to great heights, was to convey the principles of success to millions of listeners in a style that was uniquely his own. No one who ever heard his distinctive gravelly voice as he recounted his own brand of insightful inspiration or read the wise words that flowed from his pen will ever forget Earl Nightingale. His profound thoughts touched and changed the lives of millions.

One of my favorite Earl Nightingale recordings is his account of Carl Sandburg's story about the Kansas farmer (Earl called him a sodbuster) who, as he contemplated the great mysteries of life, was asked by a passing stranger in a covered wagon, "What kind of people live around here?" To which the farmer replied, "Well, stranger, what kind of folks were there in the country you come from?" "Well, there was a mostly low-down, lying, thieving, gossiping, backbiting lot of people," said the stranger. And the farmer replied, "Well, stranger, I guess that's about the kind of folks you'll find around here."

The first wagon was hardly out of sight when another newcomer interrupted the farmer's reverie with the same question: "What kind of folks was there in the country you came from?" the farmer asked again. "Well," said the stranger, "there was mostly a decent, hardworking, law-abiding, friendly lot of people." And again the farmer replied, "Well, I guess stranger, that's about the kind of folks you'll find around here."

In Nightingale's own inimitable way, he tells us that the reality we experience will be that of our own creation. "Our individual worlds," he said, "will respond to us in the way in which we see them. They will become for us that which we expect of them. We are the creators of our own surroundings."

The book is organized in an easy-to-use format that offers several lessons on twenty-five topics, each with a success message that you can adopt and apply in your own life. Each is a combination of the most profound thoughts of some of the world's greatest thinkers, plain old common sense, and unique insight into what motivates us to great achievement. It is singularly Earl Nightingale.

Nightingale believed that we are not all born river people. It takes some of us longer to find our river —our own specific, individual purpose in life. We must somehow set about discovering what it is within ourselves, Nightingale wrote, "with the patience and assiduity of a paleontologist on an important dig."

The stories included in this book may hold the key to helping you better understand yourself as you attempt to find your own river. You will know you have found it when your purpose in life demands fulfillment just as Nightingale's mission to carry his inspirational message of success to others led him to multiply himself a thousandfold through writing and recording. Your river will become your burning desire in life and it will fill you with energy and enthusiasm.

Earl Nightingale's writings and recordings shine as brightly today as they did when they were first created. They are yours to read and enjoy, and to help light the way in your own life.

W. Clement Stone

Succeeding in life with Goal-Setting

The Strangest Secret

Why do men with goals succeed in life, and men without them fail? Well, let me tell you something which, if you really understand it, will alter your life immediately. You'll suddenly find that good luck just seems to be attracted to you. The things you want just seem to fall in line. And from now on you won't have the problems, the worries, the gnawing lump of anxiety that perhaps you've experienced before. Doubt, fear...well, they'll be things of the past.

Here's the key to success and the key to failure: We become what we think about. Now, read that again. We become what we think about.[!]

Throughout all history, the great wise men and teachers, philosophers and prophets have disagreed with one another on many different things. It is only on this one point that they are in complete and unanimous agreement.

Marcus Aurelius, the great Roman emperor, said: "A man's life is what his thoughts make of it."

Benjamin Disraeli said, "Everything comes if a man will only wait. I have brought myself by long meditation to the conviction that a human being with a settled purpose must accomplish it, and that nothing can resist a will that will stake even existence for its fulfillment."

Ralph Waldo Emerson said, "A man is what he thinks about all day long."

My old friend, Dr. Norman Vincent Peale, put it this way: "This is one of the greatest laws in the universe. Fervently do I wish I had discovered it as a very young man. The great law briefly and simply stated is that if you think in negative terms you will get negative results. If you think in positive terms you will achieve positive results. That is the simple fact," he went on to say, "which is the basis of an astonishing law of prosperity and success. In three words: Believe and succeed."

Well, it's pretty apparent, isn't it? And every person who discovered this (for a while) believed that he was the first one to work it out. We become what we think about.

Now, how does it work? Why do we become what we think about? Well, I'll tell you how it works, as far as we know. Now to do this, I want to tell you about a situation that parallels the human mind.

Suppose a farmer has some land, and it's good, fertile land. Now, the land gives the farmer a choice; he may plant in that land whatever he chooses. The land doesn't care; it's up to the farmer to make the decision.

Now, remember we're comparing the human mind with the land because the mind, like the land, doesn't care what you plant in it. It will return what you plant, but it doesn't care what you plant.

Now, let's say that the farmer has two seeds in his hand—one is a seed of corn, the other is nightshade, a deadly poison. He digs two little holes in the earth and he plants both seeds—one corn, the other nightshade. He covers up the holes, waters and takes care of the land, and what will happen? Invariably the land will return what is planted. As it's written in the Bible, "As ye sow, so shall ye reap."

Remember, the land doesn't care. It will return poison in just as wonderful abundance as it will corn. So up come the two plants—one corn, one poison.

The human mind is far more fertile, far more incredible and mysterious than the land, but it works the same way. It doesn't care what we plant: success, failure, a concrete, worthwhile goal, or confusion, misunderstanding, fear, anxiety and so on. But what we plant, it must return to us.

You see, the human mind is the last great, unexplored continent on earth. It contains riches beyond our wildest dreams. It will return anything we want to plant.

Now you might say, well, if that's true, why don't people use their minds more? Well, I think they've figured out an answer to that one, too. Our mind comes as standard equipment at birth. It's free. And things that are given to us for nothing, we place little value on. Things that we pay money for, we value.

The paradox is that exactly the reverse is true. Everything that's really worthwhile in life came to us free—our minds, our souls, our bodies, our hopes, our dreams, our ambitions, our intelligence, our love of family and children and friends and country. All these priceless possessions are free.

But the things that cost us money are actually very cheap and can be replaced at any time. A good man can be completely wiped out and make another fortune. He can do that several times. Even if our home burns down we can rebuild it. But the things we got for nothing, we can never replace.

The human mind isn't used because we take it for granted. Familiarity breeds contempt. It can do any kind of job we assign to it, but generally speaking, we use it for little jobs instead of big, important ones. Universities have proved that most of us are operating on about 10% or less of our abilities.

So decide now. What is it you want? Plant your goal in your mind. It's the most important decision you'll ever make in your entire life.

You see, the very law that gives us success is a two-edged sword. We must control our thinking. The same rule that can lead a man to a life of success, wealth, happiness and all the things he ever dreamed of for himself and his family—that very same law can lead him into the gutter. It's all in how he uses it: for good or for bad. This is the Strangest Secret in the World!

Sailing to a Port of Call

I had the good fortune to be raised near a harbor on the sea. As a kid, I used to spend hours down on the docks, watching the ships loading and unloading. They'd bring in cargoes from the distant and romantic ports all over the world, and I used to stand there with a faraway look in my eyes, envying those sailors who were so fortunate to travel to all those places. They traveled over the distant horizon to places I could only imagine or read about in my geography books.

I hung around so much that some of the mates and skippers finally recognized me and actually invited me aboard. I guess you can imagine the heaven that was for me. They'd take me from the engine room to the forecastle and finally to the place I liked best—the navigation bridge. The bridge had the best view—but it was much more than that. It was there that the ship was controlled and steered into all those distant places I dreamed of. (Once I was even invited to lunch, and I didn't get over that for months!)

It's strange how something like that can have such an overwhelming fascination for a youngster and exert such an influence over his life. As soon as I was old enough, I was on a ship, and I sailed to quite a few of those distant, deep-water ports. No matter how long the trip, I never got tired of sailing and watching the sea in all its different moods. Entering a distant port, even if I'd been there before, was always a brand new thrill.

Over the years, I've tried to figure out why I like ships so much. I believe I've come up with the answer. Ships operate the way people ought to, I believe—but so few do. Maybe you've never given it much thought, but at any given moment, a ship has a direction. That is, either she's sailing to a predetermined port of call, or she's in port, getting ready to sail to another one. You can climb up to the navigation bridge of a big, far-sailing ship and ask the captain where he's going. He can tell you instantly—and in one sentence.

How many people do you know who can do the same thing? It seems that most people want so many different things—or at least they think they want them—that they're unable to focus their efforts, their minds, their hearts on anything specific. And all this leads to are doubt and confusion. They're like the guy who jumped on a horse and rode off in all directions at once. They don't recognize how vital it is to pick one port that's important, then sail to it, rest and refit for a little while and then sail to another port. In this way, in not so many years, a person can set and reach his goals, one by one, until finally he has a tremendous pile of accomplishments in which he can take pride—the has all the things he wants, just because he had sense enough to realize he could do well with only one thing at a time.

There's another analogy that fits here, and maybe it makes the most important point of all. If a ship tied to a dock for some reason had no place to go, she would stay there until she fell apart from rust and disuse. A ship's engine isn't started until she has some place to go. Here again, it's the same with people. This is why it's so important that each of us has a port of call we want to reach—a goal—a place to get to that we feel will be better than the place in which we now find ourselves. If we don't—why, we might never cast off. We might never start our engines and know the thrill of sailing a charted course to a place we can't see for fully 99% of the journey. But we know it's there, and we know that if we keep sailing toward it, we'll reach it.

If someone came up to you today and asked you what your next port of call is—that is, where you're going—could you answer him in one sentence, as could the captain on the bridge of his ship? If not, maybe you'd like to give it some thought.

Tips for Setting Goals

A Clinical Associate Professor of Psychiatry, Dr. Ari Kiev, writes, "In my practice as a psychiatrist, I have found that helping people to develop personal goals has proven to be the most effective way to help them cope with problems. Observing the lives of people who have mastered adversity, I have noted," he writes, "that they have established goals and sought with all their effort to achieve them. From the moment they decided to concentrate all their energies on a specific objective, they began to surmount the most difficult odds."

So writes Dr. Kiev in his book, A Strategy for Daily Living. He writes, "The establishment of a goal is the key to successful living. And the most important step toward achieving an objective is first to define it. I'm sure you have at least thirty minutes a day in which to list your thoughts about possible goals. Set aside such a period each day for a month. At the end of that time, choose from the possible objectives you have listed the one that seems most important, and record it separately on a single card. Carry this card with you at all times. Think about this objective every day. Create concrete mental images of the goal, as if you've already accomplished it."

The doctor points out, "You can determine your special talents or strengths in a number of ways, ranging from psychological tests to an analysis of the unexpressed wishes in your dreams. No one method works for everyone. You might start, for example, by clipping and posting newspaper articles that interest you. After thirty days, see if there isn't some trend suggestive of a deep-seated interest or natural inclination. Keep alert to the slightest indications of any special skills or talents, even when they seem silly or unimportant.

"From this exercise, you should be able to get some sense of potential strengths. Whenever you discover a strength or talent, think of five possible ways to develop it. Write these down on a card as well, and check them periodically to keep them fresh in your mind.

"Focus on one objective at a time. Like a servo-mechanic, the brain, set on a target, will call into play those mental processes that will bring your efforts to fruition. Your actions will conform to your expectations, thereby bringing about the event. If you believe that you will reach your objective, you will continue to work at a task until you have accomplished it."

And he suggests that we be aware of situations that generate the five great enemies of peace: avarice, ambition, envy, anger and pride. Petrarch said, "If those enemies were to be banished, we should infallibly enjoy perpetual peace."

Old advice—perennial advice—and perennially forgotten. It has been said that we need reminding as much as we need educating. Even Petrarch in the fourteenth century knew all about this subject. Dr. Kiev got the idea of writing his book because of a young businessman who visited his office saying he needed a set of guidelines to follow that would let him function without professional help, in the face of considerable confusion and despair caused by serious personal problems.

So take the good advice of the psychiatrist, Dr. Ari Kiev. And don't be afraid of failure. As Herodotus wrote, "It is better by noble boldness to run the risk of being subject to half of the evils we anticipate than to remain in cowardly listlessness for fear of what may happen."

Finding Your Great Motivating Desire

Desire is prayer

The key that unlocks energy is 'Desire.' It's also the key to a long and interesting life. If we expect to create any drive, any real force within ourselves, we have to get excited.

Did you ever wonder where those human dynamos, those people who can pack as much work into one day as most of us do in two, get all the energy and drive that makes them go? Well, the source of drive and energy in human beings is known. It's the personal excitement that comes from a great motivating desire.

If you ask most people why they get out of bed in the morning and slug away all day on the job, they'll probably have to think about it a while before coming up with an answer. When they do, it's usually along the line of "Oh, to pay the rent" or "To put food on the table." Answers like these aren't exciting. I belong to the group that thinks life is far too short to be dull. Shelter and food are things we need, but unless we're living out in the street or starving to death, we're not up to getting too excited about a place to sleep or something to eat.

Those who have no exciting reason for getting out of bed in the morning may be fine people, but they never seem to accomplish anything out of the ordinary, and they miss a lot of fun and a lot of rewards they could be enjoying. They haven't the drive to become outstanding because they don't have a great motivating desire.

The key that unlocks energy is "Desire." It's also the key to a long and interesting life. If we expect a person to do something we want him to do, we have to get him excited. And if we expect to create any drive, any real force within ourselves, we have to get excited. We have to decide upon something we desire very much—a goal that fires our imagination with a mental picture of having something, doing something or being something.

In a company I once surveyed, one of the men had won the admiration of all the others. I noticed that he had thorough knowledge of his company, its products, markets and competitors.

He took pains to understand his customers and their problems. These things, along with an easy manner and a good personality, marked him as an outstanding employee. We asked him about all this and he said, "When I came with this company a few years back, I decided to shoot for a manager's job in one of our districts. I'm doing everything I can to be the kind of man who would have that job."

Well, that explained it. In his mind he was already running his own district. The rest of him was merely carrying out the motion that would soon propel him into the job he wanted. Meanwhile, he was enjoying himself tremendously. The mental image of being a district manager so appealed to him that he found all the enthusiasm, energy and drive he was going to need to achieve that position. Everything he said and did in his current job had to conform to the image he held in his mind. He was outstanding because nothing less than his best would fit with the goal he'd picked out.

Of course he'll get that district managers job and all that goes with it. People with unusual drive and energy, people who excel, are the ones who have given themselves a mental picture, a goal to work toward. And the amount of drive they possess will always be in exact proportion to the strength and their desires to make that mental picture a reality, to reach that goal.

14

We don't have to worry about setting a goal we can never reach; that's the strange and wonderful thing about humans, something that most people seem to miss. We never seriously desire anything we can't possibly have. If you get all fired up over something—whether it's an executive position in your company, or the income you feel you and your family need to do and have the things you want —if you can clearly envision how it will feel to satisfy your desire, well, then it can be yours.

Arnold Bennett wrote that the kind of desire that triggers drive and energy within us isn't some vague hankering, some undefined wish. The productive kind of desire is real, it's concrete; it's a mental picture that will never leave us alone. It's always there in front of our minds, prodding and poking, goading us on. It's an obsession, a whip. It has no mercy and we'll never be satisfied until we've achieved that which we truly desire.

Well, how about you? What's your goal? What is it that gets you fired up every time you think about it? If you have such a goal you'll never have to worry about the drive and energy you'll need to achieve it. But if you find that you lack drive, that you're short on energy, give it some thought. Decide upon the dream that's more important to you than any other. Then begin to make that dream a reality. You can, and you'll find that you've got all the drive you need, all the energy you want.

Long-Range and Short-Range Goals

Aman, hunting tigers in India, was suddenly surprised by a huge Bengal tiger—it was almost on top of him. The man raised his rifle and fired, but he overshot and missed. The tiger, frightened by the man and thrown off stride by the noise of the gun, leaped toward the hunter. But the leap was too wide, and he missed his prey.

The man returned to camp and spent several hours perfecting his aim for short distances and quick firing. On the following day, he again stalked the tiger. Finally, he spotted the beast at some distance. The tiger was practicing short leaps.

It's a charming little story, and it started me thinking about a subject it seems we can't say too much about—goals.

Did you ever sit down and make a list of everything you want? It's a very interesting experiment, and you'll make some surprising discoveries. You might find that you have already managed to get most of the things you have wanted seriously. Or if you don't have most or all of them, chances are you're now in the process of getting them.

If your list contains some items you want very much but don't have, you might ask yourself why you've failed to get them. Chances are that you haven't tried very hard. Or perhaps you felt, for one reason or another, that these things are completely beyond your ability to achieve. But on second look, they might make very worthwhile goals.

At any rate, it's a good idea to have two lists of things you want. The first list would include those bigger goals that relate to your career or the overall good of your life or your family. These might include the position and/or income you're working toward, perhaps a higher educational degree, a certain amount of money in your savings account, a plateau of business success or that beautiful home you've had your eye on.

The other list could be a fun list. It might include the car you want for no good reason except it's the car you happen to want, redecorating the house, getting new furniture, traveling to some special place —perhaps abroad— buying a new wardrobe. This is a list of things you want just because you want them.

Now here's where the story of the tiger comes in. We all should have long-range goals. These should be on our number one list, and each of them should be numbered in the order of importance to us. These are goals that might take five years or longer to achieve. They're extremely worthwhile to us, and we should be working toward them daily. These are the goals that give meaning and direction and substance to our lives.

But we also need short-range goals. These are the goals that add zest and interest to our lives, and fun, and break up the monotony of the long haul for the long-range goals. We need to practice these short jumps, too.

If you're honest with yourself about the things you want—not idle, will-o'-the-wisp wishes that change from day to day but things you're serious about—you'll find that they all can be yours, and in a surprisingly short time, if they're taken one at a time.

It's been said that, "People can have anything they want." The trouble is that they don't know what they want. Get off by yourself for a quiet hour or two, and make up your two lists. It's fun and very rewarding.

What Happens When You Run Out of Goals

Here are some interesting questions for you. You might want to try answering them. One: If you could completely change places with any other person in the world, would you do it? And who would that person be? Two: If you could work at any job you could choose, would that work be different from the work you're now doing? Three: If you could live in any part of the country you want to live in, would you move from where you're now living? Four: If you could go back to age 12 and live your life from that point over again, would you do it?

Studies indicate that the great majority of people, even though they have a certain amount of dissatisfaction with their present lives and don't seem to be as happy as they might be, will answer "no" to all four questions. What brought this to mind is an attorney friend of mine who confided that now that he's accomplished everything he's worked and struggled for so long to achieve, he finds himself depressed more and more of the time. He has a fine practice and an excellent income, a beautiful home, a wife and children to whom he's devoted. In fact, everything is finally just as he'd planned it for so many years. And for no reason that he can put his finger on, all the fun and enthusiasm has strangely disappeared. He's listless and unhappy and he can't think of a single reason why.

This has become a common modern malady, and it's what so often happens when a person runs out of goals. This is when the game of life begins to go to pot, and the person needs to remind himself of the basic rules for successful, enthusiastic living. And the first rule is that a human being must have something worthwhile toward which he's working. Without that, everything else, even the most remarkable achievements of the past and all the trappings of worldly success tend to turn sour. Achieving our life goals can be compared to opening our presents on Christmas morning and watching those we love open theirs. We look forward to the day and plan and work toward it. Suddenly it's there. All the presents have been opened and then what?

Well, we must then turn our thoughts and attention to other things. The successful novelist begins planning his next book before he completes the one he's working on. The scientist always has something new and challenging to turn to when he completes a project. The teacher has a new class coming up. The young family has children to raise and get through school, the new home to buy, the promotion to work for.

But for millions who reach their 40's and 50's and find they've done all they set out to do and that there are no new challenges to give them stimulus and direction, there often comes the most trying time of their lives—the search for meaning, for new meaning, and it must be found if the old interest and vitality are to be restored to their lives, if they're to achieve renewal as persons.

If they understand this, even the search for new meaning can bring new interest into their lives. They've got to say to themselves, "All right, I've done what I've set out to do. Now I must find something new and interesting to do."

Getting back to our questions, the thought of going back to age 12 fills most people with a dread bordering on horror. They wouldn't do it for anything. And the upshot of the whole thing is that most people are living lives they themselves have fashioned and have, or are getting, what they really want, or at least what they're willing to settle for.

And when this is brought to their attention, they often begin to get a lot more enjoyment from the life they've got. They begin to enjoy themselves more and realize that things aren't so bad after all.

Do you appreciate the life you have fashioned for yourself?

When was the last time you assessed your long-term goals?

Are you prepared to create new goals after you have accomplished your current goals?

The River or the Goal

If you're going to be a big success as a human being, you have to fit into one of two groups, or belong to both of them, it seems to me. So let's talk about these two groups of very successful men and women.

The first group belongs to what I call "the river." These are men and women who have found, often early in life, although not always, a great river of interest into which they throw themselves with exuberance and abandon. They are quite happy to spend their lives working and playing in that river.

For some, the river may be a particular branch of science, for others, one of the arts. There are some physicians, for example, who are so wrapped up in medicine that they hate to leave it; even after a sixteen- hour day, they can't wait to get back to it. For others, quitting time comes as a welcome reward when they can indulge themselves in other interests.

There are some people who are happiest and most alive when they're in their river—in whatever business or career or profession it happens to be. And success comes to such people as inevitably as a sunrise. In fact, they are successes the moment they find their great field of interest; the worldly trappings of success will always come in time. Such people don't have to ask, "What will I do with my life?" Their work is a magnet for them, and they can't imagine doing anything else.

We all know such people, or about such people. Doing what they do is even more important to them than the rewards they earn for doing it. So much for the river people.

The second group of successful people are those who are goal-oriented. These people have not found a particular river, necessarily, and can be quite happy doing a number of things. It's the goals they set that are important to them, and they're quite aware that there are many roads that can lead to their goals.

Someone once said, "Americans can have anything they seriously make up their minds to have. The trouble is that most of them never make up their minds about anything." Goal-oriented people do make up their minds about what they want, and they keep their eyes and their enthusiasm on the goal they've established until it becomes a reality in their lives. Then they set a new goal, if they're wise.

One of the problems with this latter group is that after achieving a number of goals and becoming quite successful, they can run out of goals and become listless and unhappy. But not the river people. Their interest in what they're doing never fades.

So if you're going to be a big success, chances are you need to be a river person or a goal-oriented person, or both—the two groups, you see, are not mutually exclusive.

It's Not the Destination

"So the person who knows what he wants—knows what he must become, and he then fixes his

17

attention on the preparation and development of himself."

I read the great Greek poem by Constantine Cavafy titled Ithaka, and in it we're reminded that it is the voyage and the adventures on the way that count, not the arrival itself. Cervantes said the same thing.

This seems to be a most difficult truth to understand. This is not to say that a person's goal in life is unimportant. On the contrary, it's vital. For without a goal, a distant destination, we would not begin the trip at all. Instead, we'd run around in circles, endlessly following the shoreline around and around our tiny island. Every person needs a great and distant goal toward which to strive. But in traveling toward it, he should try to keep in mind that the fabled land he seeks has shores much like the one he left behind, that its purpose is not so much a resting place but, rather, the reason for the trip.

Where a person goes is not nearly as important as how he gets there. That a house is built is not all that important. It is the manner in which it is built that makes it great, average or poor. That we live is not nearly as important as the manner in which we live.

I think that it's misunderstanding this that often keeps people in a state of unhappiness and anxiety. They forget to enjoy the trip. They forget what they're really looking for, or what they should be looking for: the discovery of themselves. This is the island toward which everyone should journey. It's a difficult journey, beset, like the travels of Ulysses, with many dangers and hardships. But it gives real meaning to life, and there are many rich rewards to be found along the way—all kinds of serendipitous benefits.

It means asking the questions that are hard to answer: Where am I going? Why am I going there? What do I really want, and why do I want it? Am I gradually realizing my potential? Am I discovering my best talents and abilities and using them to their fullest? Am I living fully extended in my one chance at life on earth? Am I really living? Who am I?

These are the questions everyone must ask himself and answer. As Emerson said, "Though we travel the world over to find the beautiful, we must carry it with us, or we find it not."

Whatever you're looking for must first be found within you, whether it be peace, happiness, riches or great accomplishments. Everything we do outwardly is only an expression of what we are inwardly. To ask for anything else is as absurd as looking for apples on an oak tree.

So the person who knows what he wants—knows what he must become, and he then fixes his attention on the preparation and development of himself. As he grows toward the ideal he holds in his mind, he finds interest, zest and joy on the journey. He looks forward to tomorrow, but he also enjoys today, for it is the tomorrow he looked forward to yesterday. He knows that if he cannot find meaning and value in his present, he will very likely be missing it in his future. Today is the future of five years ago. Are you enjoying it as much as you thought you would? Have you progressed to the point you wanted then to reach?

These are the questions that make us think.

The Secret to Perseverance

The Flame of Hope

When a child is born, he or she comes equipped with certain basic drives that psychologists have been listing for us for many years. And to my mind, one of the most interesting of these basic drives is the one we might call the drive to go on—the virtually indestructible tendency on the part of a human being to keep going, to wait for one more sunrise, to try just one more time and then once more again and again.

No matter how crushed, how defeated, how demoralized, when all hope seems gone, there is, in the healthy person, a small, inextinguishable flame of hope—like a faint but persistent pilot light—that stays alight, much like the fire ancient man used to carry with him as he moved from place to place.

It's been seen in the faces of men, women and children escaping from behind the Iron Curtain, and refugees from countries such as Vietnam, Cambodia, and Afghanistan. It was still smoldering in the shrunken faces of the victims of Hitler's death camps when they were liberated by the Allied soldiers at the close of World War II. It's what causes a person to keep putting one foot in front of the other on what seems like an endless road with no destination in sight. And it's this natural drive to go on, to keep trying, that's responsible for man's progress through the long centuries.

Almost everyone comes to a place in life when going on seems futile, even ridiculous—when he seems overwhelmed by a suffocating mattress of events and situations, and desires just to sit down in the middle of the road and let the world and everything in it go to blazes.

So he sits down for a while. But then the vibration of the world seems to make itself felt in his bones. Pretty soon, he raises his head and begins to look around. After a while, he takes a couple of deep breaths, gets slowly, painfully, to his feet, wobbles there for a minute or two, and then he starts out again. Often as not, around the next bend in the road, he'll find the reason he kept going. And he'll shudder at the thought of how close he came to giving up.

His hope lies in movement and time. If he doesn't get up and start moving again, he's done for. But he has this natural drive to keep moving along the road. As long as he keeps heading for what he's looking for, what seemed like the end of the world for him will be nothing more than a bad dream, and a part of the preparation he needed to qualify for the achievement his perseverance has brought.

Movement, time and the law of averages. I remember reading about the manager of a major-league ball club who kept a rookie on the team and in the lineup because even though he wasn't hitting anywhere near what was expected of him. When he struck out, he struck out swinging. He wasn't just standing there watching strikes go by. And, as the manager expected, he soon started getting wood on the ball and bringing his average up to where it belonged.

Discouragement seems to be a part of life, but the reason people prevail is because of this built-in drive to keep going.

The Cure for Procrastination

A person carrying a heavy weight is all right as long as he keeps moving. The minute he stops, puts the weight on the ground and sits down to rest, the weight seems to become heavier, the distance to be traveled, greater, and the work, just that much more unpleasant.

Have you ever noticed that the longer you look at something you should be doing, the more difficult it seems to appear? That the longer you put off something you should do, the more difficult it is to get started? A good deal of frustration and unhappiness could be avoided if people would just do what they know they should do.

The great newspaper editor, Arthur Brisbane once wrote, "Don't exaggerate your own importance, your own size or your own miseries. You are an ant in a human anthill. Be a working ant—not a ridiculous insect pitying yourself." Strong language, maybe, but there's a lot of sense in it.

A person carrying a heavy weight is all right as long as he keeps moving. The minute he stops, puts the weight on the ground and sits down to rest, the weight seems to become heavier; the distance to be traveled, greater; and the work, just that much more unpleasant.

Sometimes it must seem to everyone that things have piled up so high there's just no way of digging out. But there is. Pick the thing that's most important to do, and simply begin doing it. Just by digging in, you'll feel better, and you'll find that it's not nearly as bad as you thought it would be. Keep at it, and before long, that pile of things to do that seemed so overwhelming is behind you— finished.

What overwhelms us is not the work itself. It's thinking how hard it's going to be. It's seeing it get larger every day. It's putting it off and hoping that somehow, through some miracle, it will disappear. The Chinese have a saying that a journey of a thousand miles begins with but a single step. And that step accomplishes two things. First, it automatically shortens the distance we still have to travel, and second, and just as important, it makes us feel better, more hopeful—it strengthens our faith. And if a person will just keep putting one foot in front of the other, he will be taken into new and exciting places, see new and interesting things, and think thoughts that never would have come to him if he'd remained at the starting point. And then the journey is finished. He wonders how or why he could ever have sat so long and worried and stewed about the time and trouble it would involve to do what he knew he should do.

If you'll think back, you'll remember that you've always been happiest, most contented, after having finished a difficult project or faced up to a responsibility you were worried about. It's never as bad as you think it's going to be, and the joy that will come with its accomplishment makes it more than worthwhile.

Work never killed anyone. It's worry that does the damage. And the worry would disappear if we'd just settle down and do the work.

As Calvin Coolidge put it, "All growth depends upon activity. There is no development physically or intellectually without effort, and effort means work. Work is not a curse; it is the prerogative of intelligence, the only means to manhood, and the measure of civilization."

Falling Isn't Failing

Mary Pickford used to say, "Don't look at the sudden loss of a habit, or a way of life, as the end of the road; see it instead as only a bend in the road that will open up all sorts of interesting possibilities and new experiences. After all, you've seen the scenery on the old road for so long, and you obviously no longer like it."

The breaking of a long-time habit does seem like the end of the road at the time—the complete cessation of enjoyment. Suddenly dropping the habit so fills our minds with the desire for the old habitual way that, for a while, it seems there will no longer be any peace, any sort of enjoyment. But that's not true. New habits form in a surprisingly short time, and a whole new world opens up to us.

For those who have tried repeatedly to break a habit of some kind, only to repeatedly fail, Mary Pickford said, "Falling is not failing, unless you fail to get up." Most people who finally win the battle over a habit they have wanted to change have done so only after repeated failures. And it's the same with most things.

So don't think of it as the end of the road but as a bend in the road. And falling is not failing, unless we fail to get up again.

I remember in Arthur Miller's play The Price, the father lost everything during the stock market crash of 1929 and, for the rest of his life, sat in a room in the attic of a relative. That's failing. It seems some people lack the stamina, the energy, to do it all over again or to make a new start. For them, it's just the end of the road, and they've come to a full stop. Many lead such superficial lives, have so little depth of mind and spirit, that the sudden loss of income or material things is too much for them, and they jump out a window or retreat into insanity.

I remember hearing the story of the little boy who wanted to get over the backyard fence. He stood for a long time looking at the fence, and then slowly, with many falls and failures, he dragged a box to the fence. After many more attempts and falls, he managed to get to the top of the box. But he still couldn't reach the top of the fence. He set to work once again, this time getting a small box to place on the top of the big one. Again, he fell many times and had to get back on his feet. After much tugging, pushing, lifting, and dropping, he got the small box on top of the big box, laboriously clambered to the top of it, grasped the top of the fence and flopped over.

So if you've been trying to start in a new direction, you might do well to remember the advice of Mary Pickford; it isn't the end of the road, it's just a bend in the road. And falling isn't failing, unless you don't get up.

The Secret to Perseverance

Many years ago, I discovered Professor William James' wonderful little book On Vital Reserves. In it, he says that everyone knows what it is to start a piece of work, either intellectual or physical, feeling stale. And everyone knows what it is to warm up to his work. The process of warming up is particularly striking in the phenomenon known as "second wind."

Now, usually, most people stop working at the first sign of fatigue. They say, "Boy, I'm bushed," and that's it for the day. As Dr. James put it, "We have then walked, played or worked enough, so therefore we desist." We simply quit. This sort of fatigue forms a kind of wall inside of which, as a rule, we work and live our lives.

But if an unusual necessity forces us to press onward, a surprising thing occurs. The fatigue gets worse up to a certain critical point, then gradually or suddenly it passes away, and we are fresher than before. We have evidently tapped a level of new energy that had, until then, been masked by the "fatigue barrier" we usually obey. In fact, we may have discovered that we have third and fourth winds.

This phenomenon occurs in mental activity as well as physical, and in some cases we may find, beyond the fatigue point, stores of energy that we never dreamed we possessed. Evidently, we stockpile reserves of energy we don't ordinarily use. And these reserves will go to work only when we demand enough of ourselves.

Only a few exceptional persons make any serious demands of themselves. The great majority of us miss the far greater accomplishments of which we are capable—and the greater joy in living this would bring to us—because we quit and sit down, gasping at the first sign of fatigue.

I remember one Sunday when I knew I had to write ten radio shows, all in one day. I got started at 9 o'clock in the morning, and by 5 o'clock that afternoon, I was so bushed, I could hardly think. But I still had five shows to write, so I kept at it.

All of a sudden, I felt better and had more energy than I had previously. And by 1:30 the next morning, when I finally finished, I felt great. After 16 ½ hours of steady mental work, I was as fresh as a daisy! But I had felt like quitting after only 7 or 8 hours.

The next time you get tired, and you're doing something important, stay with it and see what happens. Each of us has a tremendous second wind, mental and physical. Passing through the fatigue barrier to draw upon our idle reserves can make the difference between existing and really living.

Emerson said, "Vigor is contagious; and whatever makes us either think or feel strongly adds to our power and enlarges our field of action."

The Value of Active Patience

"Every time a person admits to himself—usually much later—that he has made a fool of himself, he can trace it to a lack of patience; if he had only waited a while, everything would have been all right."

To a child, waiting five minutes for the motion picture to begin, or counting the minutes until the family arrives at Grandmother's house, can seem like an eternity. To talk to children in terms of months—to say nothing of years—is to boggle their impatient little minds.

But as the years pass, a good measure of maturity can be said to be the degree of a person's patience. And the older and, hopefully, wiser a person becomes, the more he comes to realize the importance of patience. He learns that it's little short of amazing when it comes to the size and number of problems that can be solved by the passage of time.

It's as though everyone is riding on the outer edge of a great wheel that turns very slowly but that will, in time, bring everyone to his turn of great good fortune, if he's doing things right.

Often, crimes of violence can be traced to nothing more than a lack of patience. And the number of broken marriages that could be heaped upon this same cause must number in the many millions. And how many times do parents later wish they had not acted or spoken so quickly at something their child had done?

Every time a person admits to himself—usually much later—that he has made a fool of himself, he can trace it to a lack of patience; if he had only waited a while, everything would have been all right.

It's been said that everything comes if a person will only wait. And it was Benjamin Franklin who said, "He that can have patience, can have what he will." And Horace Bushnell wrote, "It is not necessary for all men to be great in action. The greatest and most sublime power is often simple patience." And De Maistre said, "To know how to wait is the great secret of success." Not to leave out Shakespeare, who wrote, "How poor are they who have not patience! What wound did ever heal but by degrees."

But patience is not passive and should never be confused with idleness and a phlegmatic insensibility. On the contrary, it is active; it is concentrated strength; it is perseverance—it is knowing that to persevere is to prevail.

Aristotle wrote that patience is so like fortitude that she seems either her sister or her daughter. And Rousseau said, "Patience is bitter, but its fruit is sweet."

A great life, a great home and family, a great career, a great business, a great accomplishment of any kind—all these come with patience—patience with others, with the world and with ourselves.

It is said that every day begins a new year for each of us. If you're in the mood for a little self-improvement—for turning over a new leaf—write the word patience some place where you'll see it every day for the next, oh, say, 50 or 60 years. You'll be amazed what this one word can do for your life.

There is as much difference between genuine patience and sullen endurance as there is between the smile of love and the malicious gnash of teeth. If your turn has not yet come, keep at it, and be patient.

Participating in Your Personal Evolution

Wiping Away Negativity

"The mature person strives for strength—strength of purpose, strength of mind and strength of character. Only these can give us peace and serenity, joy and accomplishment."

I remember as a child in school watching my teacher write the word ain't on the blackboard. Then she had all of us look at the word for a long time. Finally, very slowly, she erased it. As she did, she told us to erase it from our minds, never to use it again. As the word disappeared from the blackboard, it disappeared from our minds. I've never forgotten the incident and how effective it was.

From time to time, we all need to clean the slate of our lives—to face up to and then wipe away certain emotions and unrewarding habits of thinking and behavior that hold us back. Some of these things that need to be wiped away can sour and spoil our lives and rob us of the success we seek.

I read a story once about a man who decided to do something about an enormous piece of granite that rose up out of the ground near his house. He got a chisel and a hammer, and before long he had carved an excellent reproduction of an elephant. His neighbors and passersby were amazed, because it looked for all the world like a real elephant grazing in his yard.

A friend asked the amateur sculptor how he ever managed to so faithfully reproduce the form of an elephant without a model to go by. The man replied, "I just chipped away everything that didn't look like an elephant."

For a person to build a rich and rewarding life for himself, there are certain qualities and bits of knowledge that he needs to acquire. But there are also things—harmful attitudes, superstitions, emotions—that he needs to chip away. A person needs to chip away everything that doesn't look like the person he or she most wants to become.

The mature person strives for strength—strength of purpose, strength of mind and strength of character. Only these can give us peace and serenity, joy and accomplishment.

In cutting things away, an excellent place to begin is with animosity toward others. Getting rid of hatred and animosity is like putting down a hundred-pound weight. We may hurt no one else by hating, but we do serious damage to ourselves. It shows in the face, in the attitude and in the person's life. Ulcers, high blood pressure, colitis and heart disease are physical ailments that can often be traced to hate and even minor resentments. Beyond that, these harmful emotions can strangle a person's creative ability and will to win.

It is the unfailing mark of the little person—the person who has failed to grow—to spend his life dreaming and plotting to "get even" for real or fancied injuries. History shows that a person who wants revenge brings it only upon himself.

Lincoln was famous for not holding a grudge. He put his political enemies, Stanton, Seward and Chase, into his presidential cabinet.

Benjamin Disraeli, England's brilliant prime minister, did favors for many who bitterly opposed him. He said, "I never trouble to be avenged. When a man injures me, I put his name on a slip of paper and lock it up in a drawer. It is marvelous to see how the men I have so labeled have a knack of disappearing."

In cleaning the slate of our lives, we should do all in our power to get rid of hate, self-pity, guilt and remorse. All that we have is the present moment and the future. They can be anything we want them to be.

We Invent Ourselves

Have you given much thought to the fact that you create yourself? You do, to an altogether unsuspected extent, simply by the choices you make; by the things you decide to do, or decide not to do.

As Kierkegaard said, "The self is only that which it is in the process of becoming." So it is that an adult can stand in front of a full-length mirror and take a good long look at what he's created.

We leave home and we form ourselves into new people and we learn, as Thomas Wolfe learned, that we can't go home again, that we don't fit as well as we used to. We wonder, after a visit, as we leave to regain our own lives, what happened, if something is wrong, what the strangeness was. It is simply that we are different now, and going back home again is like trying to get a two-year-old shoe on a teenager. It's not going to fit anymore.

We have shaped ourselves into new people. And we have done so by our own decisions. There's no going back, of course, and I guess most of us wouldn't want to if we could, even though we're acutely conscious of mistakes we've made. We have to remember that each of us is new at this business of living and content ourselves with the fact that most of us have plenty of time to make good decisions in the future.

If there's a rule in making decisions, I suppose it would be to listen to that inner voice and try to make decisions that tend to be growth-oriented. There's really no standing still, even if we'd like to.

I wonder how many mothers in poor families have said to their children, "I want you to get an education and make something of yourselves." The old term, "Make something of yourself" carries with it the clear message that we invent, that we make ourselves.

I do think, however, that most try to play it safe—that is, select those decisions which seem to carry the least risk of failure and by so doing live out their lives well below their real potential as persons. Sayings such as "I'm not going to stick my neck out" and "Don't rock the boat"—to say nothing of the popular "Take it easy" and "Never volunteer" all indicate a reluctance to live fully extended, or at the leading edge of life. In business, every time a suggestion is made that involves any sort of innovation, some old-timer will ask, "Who else is doing it?" He needs reassurance that the idea is not completely new, that it's been tested by someone else before he'll venture a "yes" vote.

Professor Sidney Hood writes, "...my observations lead me to the conclusion that human beings have suffered greater deprivations from their fear of life than from its abundance."

Developing Two Great Factors

"If we would develop heart and mind, learn to love greatly and think clearly, everything else would be added to us...everything we want and more than we need."

There's a small paperback book, edited by Erich Fromm, titled The Nature Of Man in which appears the following statement:

"People tend to achieve their human potential insofar as they develop love and reason." It might be a good time to ask ourselves how well we're doing in those departments. To the extent that we develop love and reason, will we realize our potential as persons. These are the faculties that are uniquely human and on which you and I must depend, if we're to achieve what we were designed to achieve.

We tend to think of developing human potential along lines more closely associated with kinds of work or sports, and perhaps that's part of it. But it's the development of heart and mind that can raise us to new levels of humanness. If we would develop heart and mind, learn to love greatly and think clearly, everything else would be added to us— everything we want and more than we need. Most importantly, there would be peace and loving kindness in all our relations with others.

If you'll think about it, you'll realize that those whose lives are marked by lack in the midst of abundance, are those who have not discovered, who have not developed in themselves, the capacities for love and reason.

And if someone should ask you, "How does a person develop his or her potential?" you can reply, "By developing love and reason." With those two capacities alone, the fulfillment is there. We have only to think of the truly great people we have known personally: the great teacher, perhaps a relative, a friend, a parent, a fellow worker...or the stranger who appeared out of nowhere to help us out of a bad situation and who then quietly disappeared leaving only the memory of a smile and that calm willingness to help.

When we think of the person who has developed love and reason to an uncommonly high degree in his or her life, we invariably think of someone who has a calm, even serene way of looking at things, studying things, before making a decision. Such people give of themselves freely, unstintingly and they reap an abundant harvest in return. They tend to be quiet people, although they can laugh and enjoy themselves as much as anyone. More, really, because they see more in their surroundings, notice more about the people with whom they associate. They are more understanding, more forgiving and look for the reasons behind events, rather than just at the events themselves.

"People tend to achieve their human potential insofar as they develop love and reason." People with closed minds, on any subject, are stuck somewhere along the way.

Maximizing Your Potential

I'd like to quote something to you from George B. Leonard's excellent book Education and Ecstasy. He asks, "Who is this creature we would educate so joyfully? What are his capacities? Can he really be changed? Will great efforts yield us great gains? History tells us more than we want to know about what is wrong with man, and we can hardly turn a page in the daily press without learning the specific time, place and name of evil.

"But perhaps the most pervasive evil of all rarely appears in the news. This evil, the waste of human potential, is particularly painful to recognize, for it strikes our parents and children, our friends and brothers, ourselves."

James Agee wrote: "I believe that every human being is potentially capable, within his 'limits,' of fully 'realizing' his potentialities; that this, his being cheated and choked of it, is infinitely the ghastliest, commonest and most inclusive of all the crimes of which the human world can accuse itself. I know only, that murder is being done against nearly every individual on the planet."

To doubt is less painful than to rage. Throughout much of history, the safe, the authoritative, the official viewpoint has pronounced man limited, flawed and essentially unchangeable. Each age has found ways of comforting men with pessimism. Accept limits, the wise men say, to keep from overreaching yourselves or going mad with hope.

But hope and the awareness of wasted potential have never really faded from consciousness. Ever since the race of man first learned to wonder, men have been haunted by this irrepressible dream: that the limits of human ability lie beyond the boundaries of the imagination; that every human being uses only a tiny fraction of his abilities; that there must be some way for everyone to achieve far more of what is truly his to achieve. History's greatest prophets, mystics and saints have dreamed even more boldly, saying that all men are somehow one with God. The dream has survived history's failures, ironies and uneven triumphs, sustained more by intuition than by what our scientific-rationalist society calls "facts."

Now, however, the facts are beginning to come in. Science has at last turned its attention to the central questions of human capability, has begun the search for a technology as well as a science of the human potential. Men in varied fields, sometimes unknown to each other, sometimes disagreeing on method, philosophy and even language, are coming to startlingly similar conclusions that make pessimism about the human prospect far more difficult than before. These men—neurologists, psychologists, educators, philosophers and others—are making what may well be the century's biggest news. Almost all of them agree that people now are using less than 10% of their potential abilities; some put the figure at less than 1%. The fact of the matter is that anyone who makes a responsible and systematic study of the human animal eventually feels the awe that moved Shakespeare to write, "What a piece of work is a man! How noble in reason! How infinite in faculty!"

The Number One Quality for Success

In talking about ideas that we want to pass along to our kids, in school and more importantly in the home, of all the qualities that parents can instill in children, which would you say is the most important? Some time back, the editors of a business magazine conducted a survey on what qualities it takes to be successful. They didn't indicate what they meant by successful, but since the survey was by the editors of a business magazine, it was naturally assumed that what was meant is success in business.

Well, interestingly enough, the same number one quality emerged for success in business that came up for success as a father or mother. And do you know what that single quality is? One word: Integrity.

There are millions today who will laugh at that but the odds are good that neither they nor their youngsters are doing too well.

Children who are taught the importance of integrity never seem to lose it. It becomes a part of their being, their way of doing things, and more than anything else, it will guarantee their success in life as persons. Integrity is what a man wants in his wife and she in him.

That's what we look for and hope for in a doctor or dentist, the man who designs and builds our home, the man we work for, and the people who work under us. It's what we want more than anything else in a politician or an appointed official, in judge and police officers.

Integrity is honesty, but much more than the superficial kind of honesty that keeps a person from stealing or cheating. Integrity is a set of mind and character that goes all the way through like good solid construction.

And integrity, or the lack of it, is generally taught in the home, in little as well as big things. In business or in life, the number one quality is integrity.

For most people it would seem getting through life is a matter of managing a compromise between integrity and expediency. Integrity is all well and good, and everybody would like to have the word apply to her, but there are times it is usually thought when it's perhaps best to wink at integrity and indulge in a little larceny or remain silent, when speaking one's mind might result in a loss of popularity or ostracism of some kind.

As Ortega tells it, "The human creature is born into the world in a natural state of disorientation. He's the only creature on earth who is not at home in his environment. He must and he does, in a God-like fashion, create his own life, his own world."

Now that's an awesome thing to think about. The responsibility is onerous, frightening. To present a white knight-like facade of unblemished and unsoiled integrity is not only difficult; to most people, I'm sure, it's also a little ridiculous. The old battle cry of the mob is, "Everybody does it. Why shouldn't I?" And that's exactly why the person of integrity doesn't do it. They will ask, "What are you trying to be, a boy scout?" What's wrong with being a boy scout? Why shouldn't we go straight in a time when such an attitude needs all the recruits it can get?

Integrity in business is the surest way on earth to succeed. Sometimes it might seem that what you're doing is going to cut into profits, but it inevitably ends by increasing profits.

When we put the well-being of people in first place, we'll never make a mistake. People first, profit last. And the more you do it, the bigger and better your profits become. It's the old law of cause and effect. In my opinion, there should be courses in integrity. Someone once wrote that if honesty didn't exist, it ought to be invented as the best means of getting rich.

But kids don't learn integrity when they see their father bringing home loot from his place of employment, or bragging about how he cheated on his income tax, or lifting towels and other loose impedimenta from a hotel or motel room.

In a product, a service or a human being, integrity is priceless and can only lead to success in the long run. We've all played golf with people who conveniently forget strokes. They fool no one, least of all the other club members, and they become objects of derision. And every week we read in the newspapers of men, quite often in high places, whose lack of basic integrity has landed them in trouble with the law, with the resulting damage to themselves and the members of their family. They were not taught the importance of integrity as youngsters and failed to mature and learn the importance of it as adults.

How to Act Like a Pro

My old friend, Herb True, dropped into my office with some exciting thoughts. There are some people you just can't sit down with, without getting all fired up—people who are interested in ideas and people.

He said that the pro, in whatever field he happens to work, doesn't follow standards; he sets them! And the first step toward becoming a pro in anything you want very much to do is to learn the rules.

He went on to say that the amateur is the person who doesn't know the rules, and what's even worse - he doesn't know that he doesn't know the rules.

The amateur, when he fails at what he does, says, "Well, that's the way the cookie crumbles." He finds ways of finding exterior reasons for his failures. We tend to look inside of ourselves to explain our successes and outside of ourselves to explain our failures.

But the pro accepts responsibility for his act. There's the story of the football coach whose team had won four games in a row. When asked by reporters for his secret, the coach went into detail as to his superior methods of coaching, choosing men and scouting. The following week, his team lost. When asked why, he said, "It rained." And one reporter asked, "Just on your team?"

The real pro would have said, "They fielded a better team than we did today." But the amateur is always scrambling for excuses. He spends the time looking outside of himself for reasons for his failures that could easily be used to bring about success the next time if he decided to turn pro and learn the rules.

The next mark of the real pro is that he has a definite code of conduct. This code is all set up and working. Whenever he comes upon a situation that violates his code, he passes it up. But he doesn't have to sit around and think about it, or try to rationalize it or find excuses for doing something he knows very well he should not do. He's got a code of conduct and he sticks by it.

For example, let's say he's in politics or on the police force. His code is that he will not accept bribes of any kind. If someone offers him a bribe, he instantly refuses it because it is a bribe. The amount of the bribe then becomes totally unimportant. Whether it's five dollars, or five million dollars, makes not the slightest difference.

Another mark of the pro is that he tries always to distinguish between the urgent and the important. Something may be, or may appear to be very urgent but is it really important? Is it important in a permanent, meaningful way? Or is its seeming urgency little more than a needless time consumer? Every act we perform during the day is goal-achieving, tension-relieving, or unnecessary. The pro keeps an intelligent balance. He does this by making sure that the time he's supposed to be working, he's working. He enjoys his work and he enjoys his leisure.

Yes, the real pro, in whatever he has chosen to do, does not follow the standards set by others—he sets his own. He knows that the precedents he sets will be broken some day just as he breaks those that have been established before.

Do you possess the characteristics of the "pro"?

Do you:

 -accept responsibility for your acts?

-have a definite code of conduct?

-distinguish between the urgent and the important?

When was the last time you set standards in your behavior?

Eight Words to Live By

Ever since people have been able to communicate, they have compiled words to live by. But the world is still troubled. Take these words: honesty—workmanship—ambition—faith—education—charity—responsibility—courage. Chances are 4.5 billion people won't agree to live their lives by them. But think how much better your life would be if just one person does. You.

With those eight words—eight concepts, really—you'd have about all the good advice you'd ever need to live a productive, rewarding, satisfying life. Let me go over the words once more.

Honesty. It means honesty in everything we do or say. Honesty as a way of life. It's saying, "If it isn't honest, I won't have anything to do with it."

Workmanship. Workmanship is not a male or female word even though it contains the word "man' in the middle of it. It means doing a job as well as we can do it without becoming neurotically obsessed with it. It's the kind of work one expects from a top professional. It's saying, "Everything I do, I will do to the best of my ability."

Ambition. Ambition is a good thing. It means striving toward something we believe to be worthwhile. Ambition keeps us on the most interesting of journeys, and as we'll find when we fulfill our ambition, the journey is better than the accomplishment. Ambition is the desire to do something and human beings are at their best when they're doing things. Succeed at what you're now doing, and then move on to your next ambition.

As for the idea of faith, the fourth word in the list, we could talk about that all day. Faith makes everything work, and faith in ourselves and what we believe in is the driving power of our ambition.

And next comes—education. A very big word that means many things. Certainly not limited to schooling—although that's important, too. The better our education, the broader, the more comprehensive our knowledge—the better, the richer, the more interesting our lives become. And the more we'll understand the true meaning of the words we're discussing here today.

The next one is charity, which is a lot more than giving to the United Way—although that's part of it. It's having an attitude of charity; understanding that the more we share, the more we get. The more we help and lift up others, the more we are helped and lifted up ourselves.

Responsibility means responsibility for ourselves and our lives. If something's wrong in our lives, chances are we're a big part of the problem.

And, of course: courage. Courage turns the darkness into bright daylight, problems into possibilities.

Improving Your Ability to Cope

How to React to Stress

Two young boys were raised by an alcoholic father. As they grew older, they moved away from that broken home, each going his own way in the world. Several years later, they happened to be interviewed separately by a psychologist who was analyzing the effects of drunkenness on children in broken homes. His research revealed that the two men were strikingly different from each other. One was a clean-living teetotaler, the other a hopeless drunk like his father. The psychologist asked each of them why he developed the way he did, and each gave an identical answer, "What else would you expect when you have a father like mine?"

That story was revealed by Dr. Hans Selye, internationally renowned Canadian physician and scientist known as the father of stress. A medical pioneer, he devoted the majority of his years to the exploration of biological stress. And he related the story of the two sons of the drunken father in an article for New Realities.

And the story demonstrates a cardinal rule implicit in stress, health and human behavior. According to R. H. Schuller, "It is not what happens to you in life that makes the difference. It is how you react to each circumstance you encounter that determines the result. Every human being in the same situation has the possibilities of choosing how he will react—either positively or negatively."

Thus, stress is not necessarily caused by stressor agents; rather, it is caused by the way stressor agents are perceived, interpreted, or appraised in each individual case. Outside events and people upset some more than others, because they are looked upon and dealt with in entirely different ways. The stressors may even be the same in each case, yet the reaction will almost always be different in different people. So what is the cause of our stress? The outside agents and people, or the perception and interpretation each person brings to a given situation? If a microbe is in or around us all the time and yet causes no disease until we are exposed to stress, what is the cause of our illness—the microbe or the stress?

Basowitz, Persky, Korchin and Grinker, in their book Anxiety and Stress, have this to say about the cause of stress:

"The stress accruing from a situation is based...on the way the affected subject perceives it; perception depends upon the multiplicity of factors, including the genetic equipment, basic individual needs and longings, earlier conditioning influences and a host of life experiences and cultural pressures. No one of these can be singled out for exclusive emphasis. The common denominator of 'stress disorders' is reaction to circumstances of threatening significance to the organism."

Armed with that kind of information, it would seem that we can greatly improve our reactions to stressful situations. What seems to be a cruel world to one person might be filled with challenge and opportunity to another. It is our reaction that makes the difference.

Only 8% of Worries Are Worth It

According to the Bureau of Standards, "A dense fog covering seven city blocks, to a depth of 100 feet, is composed of something less than one glass of water." That is, all the fog covering seven city blocks, at 100 feet deep could be, if it were gotten all together, held in a single drinking glass. It would not quite fill it. And this could be compared to our worries. If we can see into the future and if we could see our problems in their true light, they wouldn't tend to blind us to the world, to living itself, but instead could be relegated to their true size and place. And if all the things most people worry about were reduced to their true size, you could probably put them all into a water glass, too.

It's a well-established fact that as we get older, we worry less. We learn that with the passing of the years and the problems each of them yields, that most of our worries are not really worth bothering ourselves about too much, and that we can manage to solve the important ones.

But to younger people, they often find their lives obscured by the fog of worry. Yet, here's an authoritative estimate of what most people worry about: Things that never happen—40%. That is, 40% of the things you worry about will never occur anyway. Things over and past that can't be changed by all the worry in the world—30%. Needless worries about our health—12%. Petty, miscellaneous worries—10%. Real, legitimate worries—8%. Only 8% of your worries are worth concerning yourself about. 92% are pure fog with no substance at all.

The wife or husband will nurse and cling to things which have happened or have been said in the past and keep exhuming them like desiccated corpses. If the collection gets large enough, and it could easily get large enough in even the best of households, if a person never forgets every little slight or oversight or word spoken in impatience or anger, the marriage will wind up on the rocks.

The largest cause of all arguments in the home, incidentally, is worry about money. And this wouldn't be such a problem, in fact it could be a source of gratification, if we could just learn to live within our means and save a part of every dollar we earn. It isn't easy, but it will get rid of the worries and most of the arguments about money.

Ben Franklin said there are two ways of solving money problems. Augment your means. That is, make more money. Or diminish your wants. Either will do. But the best plan of all is to do both at the same time. Think of ways to earn more money and diminish your wants. In this way you'll live well within your means and always have a nice surplus of money.

Nurture Your Ability to Laugh

"I have found it a good rule of thumb to be slightly suspicious of anyone who takes himself too seriously. There's usually something fishy there someplace:"

One of the enriching blessings of growing older all the time is that it has a way of improving one's sense of humor—or at least it should. The person without a good sense of humor is a person to avoid as though he were a known carrier of the plague.

Horace Walpole once said, "I have never yet seen or heard anything serious that was not ridiculous." And Samuel Butler said, "The one serious conviction that a man should have is that nothing is to be taken seriously." It has been said that seriousness is the only refuge of .the shallow. Oscar Wilde said, "It is a curious fact that the worst work is always done with the best intentions, and that people are never so trivial as when they take themselves very seriously."

I remember that when I was in the service, one of the toughest jobs I had was to keep from laughing at the wrong times—during an admiral's inspection, for example. There is nothing funnier than the seriousness of the military, especially high-ranking military. The fancy costumes, the panoply, the shining sabers, the serious faces—it was all, to me, hilariously funny.

We can be serious about situations. When a youngster is ill or hurt, or someone insults your spouse, you can get very serious about the situation in a hurry. But that's not taking ourselves seriously. That's different.

The thing that bothered me about Hemingway, as much as I admired his work, was that I thought he tended to take himself too seriously. He didn't seem to be able to laugh at himself. And I think he suffered from this flaw in his character.

I have found it a good rule of thumb to be slightly suspicious of anyone who takes himself too seriously. There's usually something fishy there someplace. I think this is why we love children so much; life is a game to them. They will do their best at whatever work is given them, but they never seem to lose their ebullient sense of humor; there is always a sparkle of humor in their eyes. When a child lacks this, he is usually in need of help.

Dictators are famous for their lack of humor. The mark of a cruel person is that he doesn't seem to be able to see anything funny in the world. And, a sense of humor was what was so great about Mark Twain. No matter how serious the subject, he could find the humor in it and bring it out. So could Will Rogers. All the great comedians have this ability to see what's funny in the so-called serious situation. They can poke fun at themselves. There are those who believe that a sense of humor is the only thing that has kept the human race from totally extinguishing itself.

People who are emotionally healthy, with a sense of proportion, are cheerful people. They tend to look upon the bright side of things and see a lot of humor in their daily lives. They're not Pollyannas, they know what's going on and that a lot of it's not at all funny, but they don't permit the dark side of things to dominate their lives. To my mind, when a person lacks a sense of humor, there's something pretty seriously wrong with him.

Samuel Butler said, "A sense of humor keen enough to show a man his own absurdities as well as those of other people will keep a man from the commission of all sins, or nearly all, save those that are worth committing."

It took a sense of humor to write that, and only people with blank spaces where their senses of humor should be will find it offensive. There's something so healthy about laughter, especially when it's directed at ourselves. This form of humor was what made Jack Benny and Bob Hope such durable and successful comedians, along with many others, going clear back to Charlie Chaplin.

I remember the wonderful ending to that really fine motion picture, Treasure of Sierra Madre. After months of backbreaking toil and the constant danger of death from bandits, the characters find they have lost all the gold; that they're right back where they started from. And suddenly they begin to laugh. They almost faint from laughter. And you realize they've seen themselves in their true perspective, the ludicrousness of the situation and their former greed. And just as suddenly, you realize that everything is all right again as they part and go their separate ways.

There are times for all of us when all the laughter seems to be gone, but we should not permit these periods to last too long. When we've lost our sense of humor, there isn't very much left. We become ridiculous. We must then go to war against the whole world and that's a war we've got to lose.

The 12 Things to Remember

Here are 12 things to remember. The author is unknown:
1. The value of time;
2. The success of perseverance;
3. The pleasure of working;
4. The dignity of simplicity;
5. The worth of character;
6. The power of example;
7. The influence of life;
8. The obligation of duty;
9. The wisdom of economy;
10. The virtue of patience;
11. The improvement of talent; and
12. The joy of originating.

Good list, isn't it? It could be the kind of checklist that a person might carry with him to glance at from time to time. None of us is smart enough to remember all he knows, as Will Rogers once said. We all need reminding.

The value of time: At first you might think that applies to working, which it does for a part of the time; but it also applies to time spent not working—time spent thinking, or dreaming, or relaxing, or reading, or walking, or indulging in a favorite hobby. The value of time—not to waste it on things that do nothing to help or bring enjoyment

The success of perseverance: Perseverance can accomplish anything. My friend W. Clement Stone tells the story of Tom, who was born without half of a right foot and only a stub of a right arm. As a boy, he wanted to engage in sports as the other boys did. He had a burning desire to play football, of all things. Because of this desire, his parents had an artificial foot made for him. It was made of wood. The wooden foot was encased in a special stubby football shoe. Hour after hour, day after day, he would practice kicking the football with his wooden foot. He would try and keep on trying to make field goals from greater and greater distances. He became so proficient that he was hired by the New Orleans Saints. Now, just offhand, what would you say a person's chances of playing professional football were, if he were born without half of a right foot and a withered arm? But the screams of 66,910 football fans would be heard throughout the entire United States when Tom Dempsey, with his crippled leg, kicked the longest field goal ever kicked in a professional football game within the last two seconds of the game, to give the Saints a winning score of 19 to 17 over the Detroit Lions. "We were beaten by a miracle," said Detroit coach Joseph Schmidt. But they were beaten by perseverance.

The pleasure of working: Often the pleasure that comes from working only comes after the work has been finished—but it's pleasure you can't find any other way.

The dignity of simplicity: If only more people could learn to keep things simple, straightforward, honest. It's best in everything from architecture to living.

The worth of character goes without saying. It is the one thing each of us can build for himself that gives value to his life and himself.

The power of example: The example set by parents will have a much greater influence on the life of a child than all the schooling in the world. The secret is: don't tell him; show him.

The obligation of duty gives meaning to our lives.

The wisdom of economy: This ties in with the dignity of simplicity.

The virtue of patience: Half the problems of the world could be prevented by patience. Give it a little time and it will usually come out fine.

The improvement of talent: That's how we grow and mature at whatever we have chosen, of our own free will, to do with our lives.

And the joy of originating: Great list: 12 things to remember.

A Short Memory Is Good and Bad

Everything in nature has two sides: a good and a bad, a positive and a negative. In philosophy, this message goes back thousands of years, to the Chinese yin and yang. The yang is the good, the sunny side of the hill; and the yin is the dark side. There is a dualism in everything in the universe. The rain that waters and fertilizes the crops also brings floods; the fire that warms our homes and cooks our meals causes widespread havoc when it's out of control.

And have you ever thought about the good and the bad sides of memory?

Each of us really has a very short memory. Sure, the subconscious remembers everything, but our conscious minds forget. We forget the bad, and that's good. We forget our failures, our mistakes, our foolishness, the pain we've caused, the opportunities we've missed, the love we've failed to give when it was needed. These things pass from our conscious memory as though from a filter to which they cling for a while and then are cleansed away by time.

But we also forget—to our pain—the good, and that's bad. We forget the principles, the systems which, if we will but live by them daily, will result in our achieving the things we want to achieve. We literally forget how to live successfully.

If, through some diabolical device, we were constantly reminded of all of our past failures and mistakes, we would live in a state of constant depression, fear and sorrow—a hell on earth. But instead, our conveniently forgetful minds save us from this.

But if, through some wonderful agency, we could be constantly reminded only of the good, of those principles and systems that we know work to our benefit and the benefit of society, we would live in a state of optimism, enthusiasm and hope. We would go from one success to another.

Well, it's a fact that the world's most successful people manage to accomplish this latter state. They manage to arrange their minds so that they constantly remind themselves of what they're doing and where they're going. They know for certain that if they'll just do certain things in a certain way, every day, they will be led to the goals toward which they're striving.

Most news seems to be bad. Our newspapers and newscasts are not filled with all the good that's going on in the world. That would be kind of silly, I suppose. They report all the news, and the great majority of it seems to be on the negative side: wars, murders, crime, disasters, accidents, swindles, scandals. Additionally, most people are so constituted, or so lacking in the proper education, that they, too, seem to act and talk rather on the negative side, and we're influenced by them. If we live then in accordance with our environment, we'll tend to forget the good and dwell on the bad the majority of the time. This means we will live most of our lives on the dark side of the ancient Chinese hill.

What's the solution?

It is to find a way to remind ourselves every day, as do the really successful, of those things that lead to success, to the good. Otherwise, we'll forget the good, along with the bad.

A Definition of the Self-Actualized Person

What would it be like to be a fully mature, self-actualizing, fully functioning human being? This is the ideal, busy, happy person with all his faculties smoothly functioning in perfect cooperation. No wars going on inside; no hang-ups, no neuroses...the ideal, productive person.

Dr. Abraham Maslow has made a study of self-actualized people, and they stack up this way:

First, these superior people have the ability to see life clearly, to see it as it is rather than as they wish it to be. They are less emotional and more objective about their observations. They are far above average in their ability to judge people correctly and to see through the phony or the face. Usually, their choice of marriage partners is far better than average, although by no means perfect.

These self-actualized people are more accurate in their prediction of future events; they see more fully and their judgment extends to an understanding of art, music, politics and philosophy.

Yet they have a kind of humility, the ability to listen carefully to others, to admit they don't know everything and that others can teach them. This concept can be described as a childlike simplicity and lack of arrogance. Children have this ability to hear without preconception or early judgment. As the child looks out upon the world with wide, uncritical, innocent eyes, simply noting or observing that is the case, without either arguing the matter or demanding that it be otherwise, so does the self-actualizing person look upon human nature in himself and in others.

Without exception, Maslow found self-actualizing people to be dedicated to some work, task, duty or vocation which they considered important. Because they were interested in this work, they worked hard and yet the usual distinction between work and play became blurred. For them, work is exciting and pleasurable.

Maslow found creativity to be a universal characteristic of all the self-actualizing people he studied. Creativeness was almost synonymous with the terms healthy, self-actualizing and fully human.

Here again, the creativity of these people is similar to that of little children before they have learned to fear the ridicule of others. Maslow believes this to be a characteristic which is too frequently lost as we grow older. Self-actualizing people either do not lose this fresh naive approach, or if they lose it, they recover it later in life.

Spontaneity is typical of this person. Self-actualizing people are less inhibited, therefore, more expressive, natural and simple. And, of course, they have courage, the courage that is needed in the lonely moments of creation. This is a kind of daring, a going out in front all alone, a defiance, a challenge. Thus, while these persons are humble in that they are open to new ideas, they are willing to forego popularity to stand up for a new idea.

The self-actualizing person has a low degree of self-conflict. He is not at war with himself; his personality is integrated. This gives him more energy for productive purposes. As Maslow puts it, "Truth, goodness and beauty are in the average person in our culture only fairly well correlated with each other, and in the neurotic person even less so. It is only in the evolved and mature human being, in the self-actualizing, fully functioning person that they are so highly correlated that for all practical purposes they may be said to fuse into a unity."

Research indicates that the healthy person is most integrated when facing a great creative challenge, some worthwhile goal, or a time of serious threat or emergency.

The psychologically healthy person is both selfish and unselfish and, in fact, these two attitudes merge into one. The healthy person finds happiness in helping others. Thus, for him, unselfishness is selfish. They get selfish pleasures from the pleasures of other people, which is a way of being unselfish. Or, saying it another way, the healthy person is selfish in a healthy way, in a way which is beneficial to him and to society, too.

What are the qualities of a self-actualized person? They possess:
-    The ability to see life clearly
-    A childlike simplicity and lack of arrogance
-    Dedication to some work which they consider important
-    The creativity of children
-    Spontaneity and courage
-    A low degree of self-conflict
-    Both selfishness and unselfishness

Learning to See with the Soul

One of the major tragedies of growing up is that the majority of us lose that wonderful capacity of children to see emotionally. Do you remember how you saw things when you were a small child? Sometimes things—and quite often the simplest—seemed so beautiful to us it was almost unbearable. That's why a small child, still unspoiled by the acquisitiveness of modern society, will keep the box or wrapping paper, and throw away the gift.

I was fortunate to live a part of my childhood on a small farm in Northern California. It was beautiful country, and I can remember how the earth smelled after a rain and how unutterably beautiful everything was: the trees, the grass, the poppies, the sky, the clouds, the birds, the puddles of water in the dirt road. Every walk in the fields or woods was the greatest kind of adventure filled with beauty.

Well, I was reading W. H. Hudson—probably the greatest naturalist of his time—and came across this line: "We may say that impressions are vivid and live vividly in the mind, even to the end of life, in those alone in whom something that is of the child survives in the adult—the measureless delight in all this visible world, experienced every day by the millions of children happily born outside the city's gates; and with the delight, the sense of wonder in all life, which is akin to, if not one with, the mythical faculty, and if experienced in a high degree is a sense of the supernatural in all natural things. We may say, in fact, that unless the soul goes out to meet what we see, we do not see it; nothing do we see, not a beetle, not a blade of grass."

That's why two people can look at the same sight and while one is transformed and struck dumb by the awesome beauty of it, the other person will turn and walk away. And the fact is, the other person didn't see it. He looked, but he didn't see.

I remember coming back from Europe by ship one time, and one morning I came on deck to see the most beautiful and magnificent island I had ever seen—it was Sao Miguel, in the Eastern Azores. I stood at the rail transfixed by its sudden beauty for several minutes, then rushed below to bring my wife and son to see it. They thought it was beautiful too, but I could tell they had not been affected by it as I had. In the case of something else, things could very likely be reversed. But when we see, as Hudson says, somehow with the soul, "... unless the soul goes out to meet what we see, we do not see it."

What makes an artist great (a writer, painter or musician) is that in his work he is able, through some transcendent magic, to make things so real to us we are able to see them in that way—with our souls going out to them. It's very difficult to express, but anyone who's been a child can usually remember the wonderful way things appeared. The trick and the idea is to keep that faculty alive.

The Art of Relationships

The Magic Marble

I was in Fargo, North Dakota not long ago and ran across my old friend, Fred Smith from Cincinnati. He told an interesting story about a friend of his who always holds a marble in his hand whenever he talks with someone. Fred had noticed that whenever he had talked to this man, he would reach into his pocket and out would come the marble which he would hold all during the conversation. Fred asked him about it and told him it reminded him of Captain Queeg's ball bearings in Herman Wouk's The Caine Mutiny.

His friend laughed and said, "This is my magic marble, Fred. Years ago, I had a hard time getting along with people. I knew a great many people, but actually had very few friends. One day, I was talking with one of these friends when I noticed his attention wander. I was talking, but he was looking out of the window, his thoughts a million miles away. Later, I got to thinking about it and made a very embarrassing discovery. I realized that I had been talking about myself. I realized at the same time that I always talked about myself. Conversations with others were really nothing more than opportunities to talk about what I was doing, what I thought about a subject. When others were talking, I wasn't thinking much about what they were saying. I was reloading, getting ready to tell them all about myself. And it dawned on me why I had so few friends. I wasn't being a friend. I wasn't interested in what was happening to others and what they thought at all.

"So, I made up my mind to change. I made up my mind to become interested in others, to let them do the talking, to steer the conversation back to them and their ideas. But it's difficult to break a habit of years, so I dropped into a five and dime, and bought this marble. I call the marble 'Importance', and I make sure it's always on the side of the other person. Whenever someone talks to me, I hold the marble in my hand and make sure it's on the side of the other person. I've never had a problem with people since. That little marble has made hundreds of friends for me. It's also taught me to quit thinking about myself all the time," he went on to say. "And I've found myself becoming genuinely interested in others. When that happens...you make friends in a hurry."

Well, that's the story of the Magic Marble. When I heard it, it made me think, long and soberly, about my own conduct in conversations. I asked myself if I'd been tossing the ball to the other person or trying to hog the conversation with regard to my own interests. I wasn't sure, so I started making sure.

The thing to remember here is that other people are far more interested in themselves than they are in you. You accomplish nothing talking about yourself; but you accomplish a great deal by showing interest in what the other person is saying and doing. You make him feel that he or she is important in your eyes and whenever you do this well, you might call it "instant friendships." It works like a charm every time.

So, ask yourself the same question. How are you in the Magic Marble department? When others are talking, do you find interest in what they're saying, or are you just waiting for your chance to jump in and dominate the conversation?

We'd all do well, I suppose, if we'd buy ourselves a little Magic Marble and hold it in our hands each time we enter into a conversation with someone. The Marble's name, remember, is Importance, and the idea is to make certain it's with the other person.

On Caring

I was reading Studs Terkel's book, Working, and one of the interviews is with a young steel worker.

He hates his work, he's tired and bruised and burned all the time, but he's willing to put up with it because of his kids. He sees his kids getting good educations, even though they're still quite small, and not having to work and live the way he does. As the steel worker says, "This is why I work. Every time I see a young guy walk by with a shirt and tie and dressed up real sharp, I'm lookin' at my kid, you know? That's it." The young steel worker will put up with a job he hates, for all those tedious years, because he thinks he can help his kids do better, not make the mistakes he's made, not find themselves in the trap he's in.

I received a letter from a listener recommending the book On Caring, by Milton Mayeroff. Mayeroff writes, "Man finds himself by finding his place, and he finds his place by finding appropriate others that need his care and that he needs to care for. Through caring and being cared for, we experience ourselves as a part of nature; we are closest to a person or an idea when we help it grow." That's beautiful.

And he says, "In the sense in which a man can ever be said to be at home in the world, he is at home not through dominating or explaining or appreciating, but through caring and being cared for."

And I suspect that that's what keeps millions at work they don't particularly like, putting in year after year, with not much light at the end of the tunnel. It's because there's someone else, someone to care for—someone to hope and plan and dream for. "... [We find our] place by finding appropriate others that need [our] care and that [we need] to care for. Through caring and being cared for, we experience ourselves as a part of nature; we are closest to a person or an idea when we help it grow."

People and/or ideas can give meaning to our lives. If we happen to lack one, we can make do with the other. If we have both, we're most fortunate. It's when both are absent from our lives that we become alienated and depressed and feel there's no reason for living.

Parents by the thousands have spent most of their years in the most menial, backbreaking, discouraging kind of work to make certain their kids are properly fed and clothed and sent to school. Like the steel worker in our example, the well-being of their children fills their minds and their daily lives, and they'll put up with anything and go to work so sick that they can hardly drag themselves out of bed.

And when we see people hurrying home in the evening, we can understand that they're heading for what gives meaning to their lives—someone to care for, and someone who cares for them. They may not put it into words or even fully understand it. But that's what coming home is all about, and that's what keeps them going week after week, year after year—others who need their care and whom they need to care for.

Friendships and Selflessness

As Robert Louis Stevenson wrote, "There is no duty we so much underrate as the duty of being happy." Did you ever think much about that? There is much truth in this—how much, we can barely guess from the many people we all know who live by cursing their jobs, their wives, their husbands, their kids, the weather, and the politicians and the government. How many people drink too much only to forget lives that could make them happy—should make them happy—or lives they should change if they don't! Most of us are luckier than we know, and have much to celebrate.

But happiness and joyful celebration are inconceivable without friends, and it is awful to imagine the loneliness of otherwise fortunate people who have no friends anywhere. Their plight should give us pause, because most of us find that, through neglect, the number of our own friends has declined with the years. So when a person reaches age 50, the condition of his friendships may need more attention than it did long ago.

Aristotle discovered three kinds of friendships worthy of the name. The first is based on utility; an example would be a friendship between people who do business together. The second has its roots in a quest for pleasure; it can be seen in the case of friendship between amusing or quick-witted persons. The third is the best; in it each friend seeks nothing beyond the company and the happiness of the other. Most poets who write about friendships mean only Aristotle's third and best kind, while in everyday speech, we commonly refer to all three types as if they were the same.

Selflessness is the rule in the best of friendships. What benefits my friend benefits me; what benefits me benefits him. This is so not because we share our worldly goods with each other (we don't) but because, being true friends, we take pleasure in each other's good fortune.

It's true that people who are friends in the deepest sense do favors for each other; but these favors, whether large or small, are an incidental part of the friendship and are not essential to its prosperity. A friend is an extension of oneself. It is pleasant to visit with a friend; it is even pleasant simply to know that he exists. Somehow that knowledge improves the world immensely, making it at once a warmer and more secure place in which to live.

Perhaps Walt Whitman put it best in two lines. He wrote, "Stranger, if you're passing, meet me and desire to speak to me, why should you not speak to me? And why should I not speak to you?"

Friendships and Change

"Our best and most lasting friends are those who think along the same lines, believe in the same things and who constantly challenge us to move ahead with them into increasing mental and emotional maturity."

Herbert Bayard Swope once said, in replying to the tributes paid to him
at a testimonial dinner, "I cannot give you the formula for success, but I can give you the formula for failure—try to please everybody."

One of the mistakes frequently made by most people is to believe you should keep all of your friends —all of your life. It not only cannot be done...it shouldn't be done!

H. L. Mencken once said, "One of the most mawkish of human delusions is the notion that friendship should be lifelong. The fact is that a man of resilient mind outwears his friendships just as certainly as he outwears his love affairs and his politics. They become threadbare, and every act and attitude that they involve becomes an act of hypocrisy."

As usual, Mencken put it as bluntly as the English language will possibly allow—but, again as usual, he was right.

If you believe otherwise, you believe that a girl or boy should marry the first person they like, or have a crush on. Or that we should still be going around with the same group we went to school with.

Mencken went on to say, "A prudent man, remembering that life is short, examines his friendships critically now and then. A few he retains, but the majority he tries to forget."

And on the same subject, George Bernard Shaw once said, "The only man who behaves sensibly is my tailor; he takes my measure anew each time he sees me, while all the rest go on with their old measurements, and expect them to fit me."

Living means changing, and changing means, or at least should mean, forming new friendships and discarding some of those we outwear. No two people mature at the same rate; some move ahead faster than others, and it is just ridiculous to try to retain all of our old friendships.

Yet, often people will feel guilty about outgrowing a friendship; they'll think they're becoming snobbish, or too fussy about their friends, when actually it's perfectly natural.

I do think that when we get older, we form stronger and more lasting friendships than when we were young, changing and moving around a lot. Our best and most lasting friends are those who think along the same lines, believe in the same things and who constantly challenge us to move ahead with them into increasing mental and emotional maturity. They are the friends we enjoy spending an evening with, with a lot of good conversation over dinner and, maybe, far into the night.

Again regarding friendship, Mencken said, "A prudent man, remembering that life is short, examines his friendships critically now and then. A few he retains, but the majority he tries to forget."

Have I Told You Lately?

I received a paperback book from some friends of mine. The book is titled A Touch of Wonder, by Arthur Gordon. I opened the book at random to a chapter on "The Gift of Caring." In it, Gordon tells about going through the attic of an old house in Georgia in which the family had lived for a century and a half. The attic was filled with the junk of generations, but he found something of value all the same. Arthur Gordon found it in the letters, a whole trunkful of them. He says most of them were written in faded ink and were grimy with the dust of decades. He wrote, "We'd stand there in the shuttered gloom, ankle-deep in mismated spurs and andirons, in tarnished epaulets, and scraps of torn lace or faded brocade, and read a paragraph or two. And it was like listening to voices, faint and far away, echoing down the corridor of time."

What struck him most about the letters was the frankness of the writers writing in an age when cynicism didn't demand that we withhold our tenderest sentiments; a time when people said what was in their hearts. To quote him, "In a hundred different ways, they spoke of their love and admiration for one another, and you could feel their sincerity warm on the brittle paper:

"You don't know how much your visit meant to each of us! When you left, I felt as if the sun had stopped shining."

"The courage with which you are facing your difficulties is an inspiration to all of us. We haven't the slightest doubt that in the end you will triumph over all of them."

But this is the one that impressed me most and which is no doubt spoken all too seldom in far too many families:

"Have I told you lately what a wonderful person you are? Never forget how much your friends and family love and admire you."

"How wonderful you are!" And then Arthur Gordon writes, "That was the steady refrain, and it made me stop and think. In each of these people, no doubt, there had been much that could have been criticized. But when you remembered the times they had lived through—the way that ended for them in poverty and bitterness and defeat, the terrifying epidemics of yellow fever—it was impossible to escape the conclusion that the writers of these letters were stronger than we are—that they faced greater tests with greater fortitude. And where did they get their strength? The answer lay in my dusty hands. They got it from one another."

They got it from the same place our kids need it—from us, and from their friends; the same place from which we need to hear it and feel it.

When was the last time you said those words to the people who needed it? "Have I told you lately what a wonderful person you are?" Never forget how much your friends and family love and admire you.

Home Is Like a Lifeboat

Here's a little exercise in imagination for you: Let's say you were shipwrecked and found yourself in a small boat, or on a small island, with a handful of other survivors. How long do you think you would all get along well together? How long would it be before different personalities would begin to chafe and wear thin?

A family is, in many ways, like a small group marooned. The members of the family are stuck with each other; every morning, every night, and on weekends the little group must get together and live together. No two of the members are alike; each has a completely different personality—different likes and dislikes. Each has problems which he or she considers to be important; each sees the world and life from his own unique viewpoint and interests.

Yet they must live close together, in the most intimate of relationship for year after year, after year. This can give you an idea why the happy, loving family is about as rare as 25carat diamonds. It's also why, in even the best-managed and usually happy homes, there are times when visiting these homes is like jumping into a river full of piranhas. Someone reaches the breaking point when someone else goes a little too far and suddenly war is declared.

It is believed that much of the discord in the average household could be avoided if more people realized that they're in this lifeboat, or small island predicament; that is, if they understood a little better that human beings—any and all human beings—have trouble getting along when they're jammed into close quarters for an extended period of time.

The man and his wife and the kids who are old enough to be reached with this idea need to understand that the problem does not necessarily lie with Charlie, or Joan, or little Willie...or whatever their names are. They need to understand that the same problem would exist no matter who on earth they happened to live with. Everyone has faults. Changing husbands or wives and raising new kids is nothing more than changing one set of problems for another.

I think the lifeboat analogy is particularly apt because a home is, in many respects, like a lifeboat; it's the way to life and survival. But the problems are built in and should be discussed so that every member of the family makes a constant, conscious effort to contribute to the well-being and success of so precarious a journey. Understanding the problem could keep someone from being pitched overboard.

When all the people in a boat are pulling together, each one giving of himself for the good of all, the odds are good they'll have a safe journey.

When was the last time you got angry at your spouse?

At your children?

At your parents?

Have you ever tried to consciously accept a family member for who they are? Try acknowledging others' faults as a unique part of their total personality, and forgive them for being human.

How's Your Marriage Today?

Well, how's married life these days? You know, during the terrible purges in Russia, a woman would discover one evening that her husband wasn't coming home. Instead, he was being sent to a slave-labor camp in Siberia for 10 or 20 years—probably forever, because of the conditions at the camps. One morning he went off to work as usual, and that was the last time she saw him—unless she joined the crowds at the railway station and happened to catch a glimpse of him as he was loaded into the cattle cars with the other prisoners.

It's a terrible thought, isn't it? And what were his thoughts of her as he began his lonely pilgrimage? Probably both of them thought only of the fine qualities of the other one, and no doubt they were filled with a sudden, poignant love for each other.

They very probably tortured themselves by thinking of all the things they might have said or done but failed to do. (Dostoyevsky has given us some unforgettable glimpses into this sort of thing.)

Well, how's your marriage today? Has it quietly fashioned itself into a smooth, well-worn rut? Do you take your marriage and each other for granted? Or do you, like the few wise ones, keep finding new and interesting ways of renewing your awareness of, and affection for, each other? Ways that keep the marriage young and interesting?

I'll stick my neck out and generalize that the great majority of marriages are about as interesting as the great majority of people. A person will give to his marriage the same attitude that he habitually gives to his life. If his life is filled with interest, so is his marriage. If his life is not interesting, he is a fool. And fools don't build interesting marriages.

Now, let me modify all this by saying that a daily routine can easily form a trap into which just about anyone can fall. The way to keep from falling into the rut of routine and boredom is to remember the principle that anything can be improved upon, and it is the role of the human being to improve upon his life and his world.

Think of the great and sudden leap forward our national industry would experience if, on some morning, every working person went to work with the idea of finding some way to improve his job and his attitude toward those with whom he works. And, at the same time, took the same attitude toward his marriage. Just as the sudden influx of new ideas would bring freshness and new power to his job, the same thing would happen at home. The dullness, the ennui, the routine would vanish. The marriage would be renewed, revitalized.

The thing to watch is your attitude toward your daily life. If you are the kind of person who makes his daily life interesting, who is constantly on the alert for new ways of enhancing and putting new challenges into things, the chances are you have an interesting and enjoyable marriage. If not, you might give some thought to it. And remember the Siberia story, and do and say the things you should now, so that you will never be filled with remorse if anything should happen.

And perhaps I should end this with a comment by Balzac. He wrote, "Love, according to our contemporary poets, is a privilege which two beings confer upon one another, whereby they may mutually cause one another much sorrow over absolutely nothing."

Growing Up Demands Courtesy

"If there's a key word to successful child-raising, I rather imagine it's the same word found as the cornerstone to successful marriage—and the word is courtesy. It's showing those we love, and for whom we are entirely responsible, the common courtesy and respect we show to total strangers and our neighbors."

I remember hearing an angry father shout at his 12-year-old son, "Why don't you grow up?"

There was a sudden silence in the room, and then the boy, his face working to control his tears, quietly said, "That's what I'm trying to do."

That's what all young people are trying to do, and it's not an easy job. As adults, we tend to be impatient with others who cannot do well and quickly something that took us perhaps years to learn, if indeed, we've completely learned it ourselves.

To the skillful in anything, the fumbling, awkward attempts of the novice often seem ludicrous or exasperating, if not totally incomprehensible. "No, no," we say, "that's not the way to do it!" And we charge in to take over. In doing so, we add humiliation and self-consciousness to the beginner's feelings of inadequacy.

And as a person will do when he is humiliated, when he is shown himself as an inept, bungling fool, he will begin to dislike us. And it can change to hate. There will begin building within him a burning, inarticulate lump of pure, raw, primitive, dangerous hate. And each time we tell him how inadequate he is, with loving phrases such as, "Won't you ever learn?" or "You're impossible" or "You can't do anything right" or "Why don't you grow up," we feed a little additional fuel to the furnace.

If someone talked to us that way, we'd punch him in the nose. But a youngster can't punch his parent in the nose, as much as he'd love to at times, so that fire just builds within him. He reacts to the parent who treats him in this manner just exactly as you or I would—he doesn't like him, and eventually he hates him.

He doesn't want to. He's terribly disappointed in the parent as well as in himself. He's torn by the wish to love, the need to love and the hate he feels—this ambivalence.

This is the kind of tumultuous inner battle that an adult finds most difficult to handle and resolve. In a child, or a very young person, when everything in life looms so much bigger, so much more final, more terrible, it takes on catastrophic proportions.

Later, when the young person has grown into adulthood and, hopefully, some degree of maturity, he and his parent, or parents, may become friends again. He may even make exactly the same dumb mistakes with his kids.

But it's a costly shame that we look upon our children, so often, differently from the way we look at other people. And not all parents do. Some parents treat their youngsters with courtesy, respect and love, and, at the same time, lay down firm guidelines and rules of conduct.

Being a good parent must surely be one of the world's most difficult jobs, exceeded in difficulty only by the process of growing up itself. It's a job for which most of us had no training, with little more than the resolution to try to do a better job than our parents did with us.

But if there's a key word to successful child-raising, I rather imagine it's the same word found as the cornerstone to successful marriage—and the word is courtesy. It's showing those we love, and for whom we are entirely responsible, the common courtesy and respect we show to total strangers and our neighbors.

Living in such close and constant proximity makes this difficult, perhaps, but no less necessary.

Strengthening Your Interpersonal Skills

Earning the Right to Be Wrong

The most important subject a person can learn, I suppose, is how to get along well with others. And one of the most important rules in mastering this most difficult subject is knowing when to be wrong, even if you're right.

There is no more exasperating human being on earth than the one who insists upon being right all the time. This is the person who feels that to be wrong, or not know the answer to something, means, at least for the moment, the end of the world.

I was spending some time with friends in Arizona some time back. One night we were going someplace in the car and my friend's father was driving. We came to the road where we should turn, and seeing that our driver was going to go blithely by the turnoff, both of us suddenly told him that this was where we should turn. It caught him by surprise; he suddenly braked the car and managed to make the turn, not easily, and as he did so, he said, "I know...I know this is where we turn."

Now the fact of the matter was that he had not known. It was apparent to everyone in the car, but he was just one of those people who simply cannot admit there's something they don't know. My friend winked at me. But later he said, "I wish Dad would admit once in a while that there are things in the world he doesn't know; I wish he would admit he can be wrong like the rest of us."

How much better it would have been, how much more human a person he would have been if he simply smiled and said, "Thanks for telling me, I'd have gone right on by." This would not have diminished him one whit in our eyes; it's perfectly human to make mistakes, or not know something. But his actual response, his obvious cover-up and attempt to make us think he had known about the turnoff did diminish him in our eyes. It caused us to feel sorry for him, and it pushed him a little ways out of our circle of companionship.

The worker who insists upon always being right is disliked by his associates, his subordinates, and his boss. He'd be much better off to make it a point to be wrong once in a while, and say so.

The smart manager and executive know the value of being wrong occasionally, even when he's right. There will come times when he's going to have to insist upon being right, so he can afford to graciously give in when it comes to small and unimportant matters.

In Nation's Business, it is suggested that before you tell a subordinate that you're right and he's wrong, ask yourself: Exactly what's to be gained—and what is to be lost—by deflating him? It might be a small matter to you; it could mean a complete loss of face to him.

Giving in is also better for your health. Dr. George Stevenson of the National Association for Mental Health, says, "Even if you're dead right, it's easier on your system to give in once in a while." And, he added, "If you yield, you'll usually find that others will, too."

Try it with the members of your family, too. You'll be amazed at how it cuts down on the number of arguments, and amazed, too, at the way you'll find other people suddenly saying to you, "No, I'm wrong and you're right."

It's a whole lot better to say you're wrong, even when you know you're right, and get along well with others, than it is to insist you're right at the expense of being disliked.

The Miserable Moth-Eaten Grudge

"In my opinion, there are two main points here to keep in mind: The first is that disagreements with those we love are inevitable. They will, they must, happen from time to time. The second is that when they do happen, limit what you say to a minimum...and then shut up and wait."

There are thousands of families in the country which are host to running feuds of various kinds. All because they're too dumb to realize that occasional fights are as much a part of being related as consanguinity—as descending from the same ancestors. But you'd be surprised at the number of people who don't understand about disagreements with people we're supposed to like and get along with. Just as occasional hot disagreements are normal, so is the passing of the disagreement, if you'll let it pass.

I know of a case where a young woman will not speak or communicate in any way with her parents or her sister, because of a disagreement and the resulting verbal battle. And this is a common kind of thing. Somebody does something wrong, or says the wrong thing and people act as though it's the end of the world. Let a day or two go by, or maybe a few hours, and with willingness to become friends again; it will all blow over and you'll be laughing about it.

But people will cling to their miserable, moth-eaten little grudge for dear life, feeding it, keeping it alive despite all its attempts to die, whipping it back into life and maintaining their misery and the misery of others at all costs. These people have the depth and breadth of a teaspoonful of tepid canal water, and the sense of humor of a hungry shrew; the lines of bitterness become etched about their mouths. They are people who are filled with themselves—whose horizons are so close that their hair hangs over them. And you'll find a sprinkling of them on every block I suppose. There is little or no light and sunshine in their lives.

In my opinion, there are two main points here to keep in mind: The first is that disagreements with those we love are inevitable. They will, they must, happen from time to time. The second is that when they do happen, limit what you say to a minimum...then shut up and wait. That is, state your case as clearly as you can and then wait for a little time to blow the disagreement away, as it will every time. No matter how serious the disagreement may have seemed at the time—a day or so later it will have softened, blurred, and perhaps disappeared entirely. Quite often people feuding with each other have long forgotten the cause of the original dispute.

The mature, serene person has outgrown petty feuds and realizes that his position is as vulnerable to being wrong as the other person's. And sometimes a difference of opinion can have both disputants in the right but with different ideas. Let the other person have the right to his opinion.

There are times in most of our lives when, at that moment, we would be delighted to agree never to see that particular person again as long as we live. An hour or two, or a day or so later, we'll feel differently about it. The trick is not to go too far—not to commit yourself to a course of action that makes reconciliation difficult, embarrassing or awkward. And the answer is usually silence. You won't make many mistakes with your mouth shut.

The Qualities of a Leader

"A person in authority is not necessarliy a saint, an artist, a philosopher or a hero, but he respects truth, appreciates what is beautiful, knows how to behave himself, and is courageous in meeting his obligations."

"He will have intellectual curiosity and will be always learning. He is tolerant, liberal and unshockable. If he is not always affable and urbane, he at least is never truculent or overbearing. He will be a cultured, broad-minded scholar who lives according to the spirit of reasonableness."

That's a definition of a leader. How did you qualify? A leader is a person in authority, such as a parent, or boss of any sort. A Hindu proverb says, "There is nothing noble in feeling superior to some other person. The true nobility is in being superior to your previous self." Those who have shown that they can lead their own lives effectively are best fitted to accept responsibility and authority. The true function of leadership is to bring out the best efforts of others, and people most willingly pay heed to those whom they consider most able to direct.

The best leaders are almost always those who do not seek leadership, but who have demonstrated in their own lives, in their work and attitude, that they should lead. The desire for power was to the Greeks and the early Christian church a reason for not giving it. Plato's rulers were to be given absolute power only upon the condition that they did not want it, and a man appointed to the episcopacy in the church was required to say, "I do not want to be a bishop."

The problem is that social and industrial progress are impossible where there is no one in authority. There must be someone in control of an operation if anything useful or distinguished is to get done.

"Authority" means having the power to judge and act, to issue instructions and enforce obedience. These are qualities that are not found in committees, but in strong personalities. Yet, you want a person who does not deliberately seek power.

The animal kingdom is studded with evidence of creatures in authority, from the pecking order of the birds to the stamping ground of the buffalo. Every mass human activity needs and has an elite group of qualified persons exercising the major share of authority. The excuse for an elite is that it takes the lead and accepts accountability.

For its very existence, human society demands order. No way had been found in modern civilization of producing order without allocating a degree of authority. This is clearly evident in the armed forces, in education, in law enforcement, in business, in government and in sports. An umpire is a person in authority, and many a player has been thrown out of a game because he failed to recognize that—managers, too.

The leader is the person who acts when the situation requires action. The masses do not accomplish much in history; they follow the lead of people of purpose, able to plan, fit to administer. They make the difference. And we never have enough of the right kind.

Do you have the qualities of leadership?

Can you bring out the best qualities in others?

Have you demonstrated that you can lead your life effectively?

Do you have the power to judge and act, issue instructions and enforce obedience?

Do you act when a situation requires action?

Finding Hidden Reservoir of Potential

The great people of the world, whether they're teachers, parents, business executives or leaders in any field know that where human beings are concerned, there is always much more there than meets the eye. An excellent example of this can be found in a story told by George Marek, formerly Vice President of RCA Victor Records. The story was printed some years back in the Reader's Digest.

It seems that when the NBC Symphony was about to be formed, David Sarnoff, Chairman of the Board of NBC, gave one directive: "Do not hire away any players from existing orchestras because that would only weaken other orchestras." The people in charge, headed by Artur Rodzinski, himself a fine conductor, managed to get together a superb orchestra—all except the first clarinetist.

When the great Maestro, Toscanini, was about to arrive from Italy to take over the orchestra, Sarnoff was asked how the problem should be handled. Should Toscanini be left to find out for himself, or should they tell him frankly? Sarnoff said, "Let's tell him." His associates said, "You tell him." Accordingly, a delegation went down to meet the boat.

In his stateroom, Toscanini greeted Sarnoff and said, "That's a fine orchestra you got together—very fine, all except the first clarinetist." Sarnoff was taken aback. And he asked, "Maestro, how did you find out?" Toscanini said, "I have been listening on a little shortwave radio I had in Milan and I could tell." Yes, he could hear it on a little radio in Milan.

Toscanini then said, "Take me to the studios." There the orchestra was rehearsing, and a special dressing room was waiting for him. He sent for the clarinetist, who arrived in such a state of mind as you can easily imagine. Toscanini said to him, "You are a good clarinet player, but there are certain things that you do wrong." Then he began to work with him. The upshot was that the clarinetist stayed with the orchestra for seventeen years and became one of the world's best.

All too often we're prone to look upon people as they are, instead of in the light of what they might be—what they can be. Instead of firing, or giving up on a person, maybe a little patience, encouragement and lots of training can help him evolve into the person you're looking for.

I remember hearing a story concerning Dr. Robert Hutchins when he was president of the University of Chicago. They were having a discussion of adult education, I think it was, and someone made the comment that you can't teach old dogs new tricks. To which Dr. Hutchins responded, "Human beings are not dogs and education is not a bag of tricks."

Frequently we expect too much, too soon of a person, or overlook problems which may be standing in the way. Parents are quite often amazed to discover their children emerging into intelligent, responsible adults quite capable of living successfully in the world. It just took some time on everyone's part.

As the experts have pointed out, there exists in each of us deep reservoirs of ability, even genius, which we habitually fail to use. It often takes knowledge, care and time to bring ability to the surface.

Learning to Cultivate Your Creativity

Using Imagination to Fuel Your Life

Imagination is everything. I can't remember who wrote those three words in that order, but it seems to sum it up. Imagination is everything. Our lives will reflect the way we use our imagination. The child imagines himself walking like the adults he sees above him. As soon as he can walk, he wants to run. As we reach successive plateaus in life, we begin to imagine ourselves reaching the next one. And that's our imagination. It leads us on from one idea to another through every day and every year of our lives.

But if we're not careful, our imaginations can lead us into mazes of confused complications from which we may find it difficult to extricate ourselves. So it's a good idea, as we use our imagination, to always strive for simplicity, to avoid the complicated.

Are we living the lives we want to live? Or are we living stereotyped lives based on phony values? Usually they're a combination of both—a kind of compromise which says surely other people must have some idea of what constitutes the good life. After all, there are so many of them. But when we look closer we see that they're living shadow lives, as Lewis Mumford calls them. In competition ice-skating, you've seen a couple match each other's movements almost perfectly. It's called "shadow skating," I believe, meaning each might be the other's shadow. In any sort of neighborhood, you will tend to find people living much the same way. Their homes, landscaping, furnishings and lives are typified, if by anything at all, by an almost total lack of imagination.

Imagination, like anything else, needs fuel for production. You can't have something from nothing. Thomas Edison said, "I'm a sponge. I want to know the answer to everything." With his great lifetime inventory of information, he could assemble an incredible array of new combinations and permutations.

Electric light is a combination of elements, and so is any good idea, or any bad idea for that matter. Most of us make the mistake of not asking 'why'. Why do I live here in this house rather than in some other house? Why this life instead of another life? Why this work instead of other work? Why these rewards instead of others? Now this doesn't mean we'll change anything necessarily, but at least we'll be living lives that have been examined and found to be to our personal liking. We'll know that we're not living the lives we're living simply because they reflect and they're pretty much composite copies of the lives we see about us.

They should be, to my way of thinking, deep main currents in our lives: our family lives, our work, our leisure and our rewards in the form of income. Our family lives should be good and richly satisfying. What is our input here? How are we using our imaginations to bring meaning, charm and love to our family relationships? It's an ongoing process that should become richer and more meaningful with the passing of time.

How about your home? Is it what you want? H. L. Mencken once commented that the average home is a house of horrors and doesn't reflect poor taste so much as it reflects no taste at all. People tend to order their steaks medium and their homes and lives the same way. Medium rhymes with tedium.

The family is the most important part of the life of most of us. What good is accomplishment if there's no one with whom to share it? What good is anything if there's no one with whom to share it? And since the family is first in importance, it represents a fertile field for the imagination. Not just for the woman in the family, but for the man and hopefully for the kids as well. Family creative thinking sessions are a lot of fun and a never-ending source of good ideas. Check every idea for basic simplicity. Avoid complication whenever possible.

No matter what it is we want, if it's within the realm of reality, we can get it through imagination applied to our work. Nothing now being done by man is being done the way it can and will be. Everything will be done much better. Not can be—will be, whether it's the result of our applied imagination or not. People who resist change in their work are impediments to progress, yet the first words the new person on the job usually hears are, "Now this is the way it's done around here."

A business leader made the comment that, if we're doing anything this year the way it was done last year, we're obsolete. Now that's an extreme generalization, but deserves careful attention and in most cases, it's true.

Following the Follower

"Habit patterns and ways of thinking become deeply established, and it seems easier and more comforting to follow them than to cope with change, even when change may represent freedom and achievement."

Processionary caterpillars travel in long, undulating lines, one creature behind the other. Jean Henri Fabre, the French entomologist, once led a group of these caterpillars onto the rim of a large flowerpot, so that the leader of the procession found himself nose-to-tail with the last caterpillar in the procession, forming a circle without end or beginning.

Through sheer force of habit and, of course, instinct, the ring of caterpillars circled the flowerpot for seven days and seven nights, until they died from exhaustion and starvation. An ample supply of food was close at hand and plainly visible, but it was outside the range of the circle, so the caterpillars continued along the beaten path.

People often behave in a similar way. Habit patterns and ways of thinking become deeply established, and it seems easier and more comforting to follow them than to cope with change, even when change may represent freedom and achievement.

If someone shouts, "Fire!" it is automatic to blindly follow the crowd, and many thousands have needlessly died because of it. How many stop to ask themselves: Is this really the best way out of here?

So many people miss the boat because it's easier and more comforting to follow—to follow without questioning the qualifications of the people just ahead—than to do some independent thinking and checking.

A hard thing for most people to fully understand is that people in such numbers can be so wrong, like the caterpillars going around and around the edge of the flowerpot, with life and food just a short distance away. If most people are living that way, it must be right, they think. But a little checking will reveal that throughout all recorded history the majority of mankind has an unbroken record of being wrong about most things, especially the important things.

It's difficult for people to come to the understanding that only a small minority of the people ever really get the word about life, about living abundantly and successfully. Success in the important departments of life seldom comes naturally, no more naturally than success at anything—a musical instrument, sports, fly-fishing, tennis, golf, business, marriage, parenthood, landscape gardening.

But somehow people wait passively for success to come to them—like the caterpillars going around in circles, waiting for sustenance, following nose-to-tail—living as other people are living in the unspoken, tacit assumption that other people know how to live successfully.

It's a good idea to step out of the line every once in a while and look up ahead to see if the line is going where we want it to go. If it is, it could be the first time.

A profile of the Creative Person

We've found that creative people, though they may be dissimilar in many respects, have certain attitudes and employ certain techniques, to their own benefit and to the benefit of us all.

I'd like now to use these techniques and attitudes as the basis for a descriptive sketch of a creative person.

As we go through this sketch, I'd like you to think about this person. Where and when have you seen him or her? Is this a person you know at work—or in your neighborhood—or right at home?

It will be helpful to read this message frequently and be reminded of these techniques and attitudes which, if practiced regularly, will result in your living an even more creative, rewarding life. Another good idea is to project the image of the creative person on your own actions—then judge for yourself what areas could stand some improvement.

First of all, the creative person realizes that his mind is an inexhaustible storehouse. It can provide anything he earnestly wants in life. But in order to draw from this storehouse, he must constantly augment its stock of information, thoughts and wisdom. His mind gives him ideas and ideas solve problems.

The person we're talking about has a carefully thought-out and clearly defined set of goals toward which he's working. By knowing where he's going—and determining to get there—he gives meaning and purpose to his daily work—to everything he does. He never wastes time "just drifting." He's always in control of his life.

The creative person knows his brain thrives on exercise, so he uses a part of each day for thinking imaginatively about three things: Himself . . . His Work . . . and His Fellow Man. By asking himself questions involving these three areas, he's prospecting in the richest gold mine ever known. And the answers to his questions are often ideas that he can put into immediate action.

He reaches out for ideas. He respects the minds of others—gives credit to their mental abilities. Everyone has ideas—they're free—and many of them are excellent. By first listening to ideas and then thinking them through before judging them, the creative person avoids prejudice and closed-mindedness. This is the way he maintains a creative "climate" around himself.

You know, ideas are like slippery fish. They seem to have a peculiar knack of getting away from us. Because of this, the creative person always has a pad and pencil handy. When he gets an idea, he writes it down. He knows that many people have found their whole lives changed by a single great thought. By capturing ideas immediately, he doesn't risk forgetting them.

And these "captured" ideas are deposited in "idea banks," eight and a half by eleven-inch envelopes which are labeled with topics of interest. A friend of mine, a very successful writer, writes his books this way. He labels each envelope with the name of a chapter. Then, whenever he gets an idea or finds new material, he sees that it gets into the proper envelope. Before long, his book has practically written itself.

Having a sincere interest in people, our creative person listens carefully when someone else is talking. He's intensely observant, absorbing everything he sees and hears. He behaves as if everyone he meets wears a sign that reads, "I am the most important person on earth." Thus, he makes it a point always to talk with other people's interests in mind. And it pays off in a flood of new ideas and information which would otherwise be lost to him forever.

Widening his circle of friends and broadening his base of knowledge are two more very effective techniques of the creative person.

If he's staying at a hotel where there's a convention not allied to his own work, he'll drop in on it, make new friends, and listen for ideas that might help him. He's always looking for better ways to do his work, and live his life.

The creative person anticipates achievement. He expects to win. And the above-average production engendered by this kind of attitude affects those around him in a positive way. He's a plus-factor for all who know him.

You know, problems are challenges to creative minds. Without problems, there would be little reason to think at all. Welcoming them as normal and predictable parts of living singles him out as an above-average person. He knows it's a waste of time merely to worry about problems—so he wisely invests the same time and energy in solving problems.

He can even avoid problems by anticipating potentially troublesome areas and doing something about them before they turn sour on him. The research and development departments of many leading companies are constantly involved in exactly this sort of advance planning.

The creative person knows the value of giving himself and his ideas away. He's a "go-giver" as well as a "go-getter." The hand that gives always gathers—and doing things for other people is a vital part of his way of life.

When the creative person gets an idea, he puts it through a series of steps designed to improve it. He thinks in new directions. He builds big ideas from little ones; new ideas from old ones; associating ideas; combining them; adapting, substituting, magnifying, minifying, rearranging and reversing ideas.

He steers clear of mind-weakeners: noise, fatigue, needless worry, unbalanced diets, over-indulgence in food or drink and people with negative attitudes.

He asks polite, probing questions that bolster the ego and expand the mind. Questions are the creative acts of the intelligence, and he uses them often and to everyone's advantage.

And the creative person uses his spare time wisely. He knows that many great ideas, books, and inventions were conceived during the creator's spare time. We all have the same number of minutes in a day—and the creative person values each one of them.

A creative person has:

-A clearly defined set of goals towards which she's working;
-A pad and pencil handy for ideas which are deposited in "idea banks;"
-Good listening skills when someone else is talking;
-A widening circle of friends and abroad knowledge base;
-An expectation of winning;
-An understanding of the value of giving himself and his ideas away;
-An ability to put ideas through a series of steps to improve them;
-An ability to make wise of his or her time.

What Drives the Creative Person

Creative and productive people are not creative and productive for the benefit of others. It's because they're driven by the need to be creative and productive. They'd be creative and productive if they each lived on a deserted island and simply had to stack what each produced in a big pile with no one benefiting or even aware of what he was doing. You'll hear people say that we're happiest when we're serving others and that's true, but it's not true because of any great altruism on our part. It's true because we experience the joy of producing something. That others benefit from it is fine, but only secondary.

It's good to know that others benefit from and enjoy what we produce. There's satisfaction in that, ego satisfaction and the desire to produce more. If everyone continually rejected our creative or productive efforts we might become sullen and resentful.

We might even stop all efforts for a while. But eventually we'd begin to produce again in a hope that eventually someone would see the sense of what we're doing.

This is the story of the painters who were before their time. Renoir, who was laughed at and rejected not only by the public, but by his own fellow artists. We look at a painting by Renoir today and marvel that anything so fine and beautiful could ever be an object of scorn. And he painted thousands of paintings. He went right on producing them. When he brought one of his canvases to one of the most eminent Parisian teachers, the expert glanced at the work and said, "You are, I presume, dabbling in paint to amuse yourself." And Renoir replied, "Of course. When it ceases to amuse me, I'll stop painting." Everything he painted delighted him and he painted everything.

Even Manet said to Monet, "Renoir has no talent at all. You who are his friend should tell him kindly to give up painting." A group of artists who were rejected by the establishment of their time formed their own association in self-defense. Do you know who were in that group? They were Degas, Pissarro, Monet, Cezanne and Renoir. Five of the greatest artists of all time, all doing what they believed in, in the face of total rejection.

Since we're on the subject of Renoir, in his later life he suffered terribly from rheumatism, especially in his hands. He lived in constant pain. And when Matisse visited the aging painter he saw that every stroke was causing renewed pain and he asked, "Why do you still have to work? Why continue to torture yourself?" And then Renoir answered, "The pain passes but the pleasure, the creation of beauty, remains." One day when he was 78 and quite famous and successful finally, he said, "I'm still making progress."

And the next day he was dead. This is the mark of the creative, productive person. Still making progress, still learning, still producing as long as he lives, despite pain or problems of all kinds. Not producing for the joy or satisfaction of others, but because he must; because it gave him pleasure and satisfaction.

The Most Valuable Tools of Creative People

Inside the mind of each person we meet there is some knowledge that could benefit us if only we could learn what it is. Open-ended questions let people know we want to hear their ideas, opinions and thoughts. Creative people are invariably intelligent people. And they're curious— about themselves, those around them, and the world in which they live. This is the kind of curiosity that has been called "one of the permanent and certain characteristics of a vigorous intellect."

Questions are the creative acts of the intelligence—and the questions that work hardest for us, and bring us the greatest amount of useful information are the open-ended questions. Now, these are questions that can't be answered with a simple "yes" or "no." They're asked by using the "Six W's, H & I Technique": Who, What, When, Where, Why, Which, How and If.

Rudyard Kipling put it this way, "I had six honest serving men—they taught me all I know: Their names were Where and What and When and Why and How and Who." All we're doing is adding two more: Which and If.

Now, this isn't entirely new to you. You employed the Six Ws, H and I all the time when you were a child. Have you ever tried to count the number of times each day a 4 or 5-year-old uses the word "why"? You see, each question a child asks is an attempt to add to his limited knowledge. When adults lose patience with this constant barrage of questions, a child either finds some other way of getting the information, or just forgets the whole thing, thereby neglecting a valuable tool he'll want later in life—the open-ended question.

Now as adults we know that inside the mind of each person we meet there is some knowledge that could benefit us if only we could learn what it is. The open-ended question technique really opens people up. By asking open-ended questions, we get people to remove the barriers that normally keep this information out of our grasp.

Human beings like to talk about things that interest them. Open-ended questions let people know we want to hear their ideas, opinions and thoughts. Each of us has two ears and one mouth. And it seems to be a good idea to do at least twice as much listening as talking. An old Texas friend of mine used to say, "You ain't learnin' nothin' while you're talkin.'"

But the object of asking open-ended questions isn't merely to get other people to talk. We could spend days standing around gabbing with people who have very little to say that would benefit us. Instead, the object of our Who-What-When-Where-Why-Which-How-If questions is to gather, absorb and utilize that information which will be useful to us—move us ahead in the fields of our own interests and endeavors. But in so doing, we're also employing the best technique known for making friends, for success in human relations, and for selling our own ideas. Oddly enough, the more we listen, the better conversationalist we seem to the person doing the talking.

One of this country's top newsmen set a good example of this kind of purposeful questioning. He knew how to ask open-ended questions so provocatively that he could almost always get world leaders to give him exclusive interviews. His wise questions earned him the highest position in his field—that of chief executive for one of the great news services.

And the open-ended question is equally useful to the businessman. Suppose, for instance, that you've just met a Mr. Smith who is an official of a company operating in an area different from your own. Instead of talking about the weather, you might ask him, "Mr. Smith, how did you get into your line of work?" Now, here's a man who obviously has some degree of success in business—so you stand an excellent chance of learning something that will be useful to you.

One of the best salesmen I know uses open-ended questions to great advantage when he's talking with a prospect. Instead of saying, "We make the best thing-um-a-bob in the world," he asks, "Ms. Prospect, when you buy thing-um-a-bobs, what features are most important to you?" Here's an effective method for taking people off the offensive—for getting them to talk to your advantage. This technique works well for anyone who'll give some thought to what he's going to say, rather than just blurting out the first thing that pops into his mind.

So, ask skillfully probing, open-ended questions. And ask them in a sincere, courteous manner. Anyone who uses the Six W's, H and I Technique wisely, courteously and with those people who can contribute something to his understanding will quickly find this to be one of his most useful creative techniques.

The best way I know to practice asking open-ended questions is to try out a few on myself. If this sounds like a good idea, you might want to try it, too. Ask yourself:

"Who has greater knowledge of my job than I?"

"What can I do to learn some of the things he knows but I don't?"

"Why must my job be done this way?"

And "If there is a better way to do my job, what would it be?"

Take time to ponder these questions. Their answers—the facts and information you will gain—can make your life infinitely more interesting and rewarding.

Whenever you talk with others, use lots of open-ended questions. They're your most valuable creative tools.

Thinking Techniques to Increase Creativity

What are some of the best techniques for using our creative faculties more effectively to solve problems, make decisions, achieve goals and better fulfill our ultimate human responsibility, which is to think? Here are a few I have learned.

First, think association. An example of "thinking association" would be to associate names with familiar objects or words in order to remember them better. Two more examples of "thinking association" are the "Key Word" and the "Association List" techniques. The "Key Word" technique is used by people who want to remember a series of ideas. They join the initial letters of the idea words together to form a simple "Key Word." By remembering the "Key Word," they can recall the whole series of ideas. An "Association List" is used by memory experts to recall prodigious lists of articles by associating each one with another article in a previously memorized list. The creative person is forever associating ideas and continually searching for associative relationships.

Next, think combination. Almost everything in nature is a combination of elements. You're quite a combination yourself. Scientists calculate that if the energy in the hydrogen atoms of your body could be utilized, you could supply all the electrical needs of the entire country for nearly a week. A DuPont scientist says that the atoms of your body contain a potential energy of more than eleven million kilowatt hours per pound.

A simple pencil is a combination of wood, carbon, rubber, paint, and metal. A few more examples might include: pie à la mode, the radio-TV-and-film combination, and orbiting satellites combined with microwave telephone relay stations. Somebody dreamed up the idea of combining comedy and music, and musical comedy was born.

You can come up with some really great ideas by finding new combinations yourself. Everything you see, hear, touch, taste and smell during the day offers opportunity to consider new combinations. When you brush your teeth, you might think of a toothbrush that contains the toothpaste in the handle. You might combine your mirror with a motto reminding you to start the day right. It might read, "How can I increase my service today?" or "Today is the only time I've got. I'll use it well." So...let's "think combination."

Next, think adaptation. Burlap fabric originally used for making gunny sacks has been adapted for drapes, wall covering and stylish dresses. (Some salesmen were thinking adaptation.) Airplane seat belts have been adapted for use in automobiles to bring new safety to highway driving. The tape recorder and motion picture, originally developed for entertainment, are today adapted for instruction and education. Rocket motors, which were developed to propel atomic missiles, have been adapted to lift peaceful space vehicles into orbital and interplanetary flight.

During the next year you are going to see the result of people thinking adaptation and coming up with ideas worth thousands of dollars. Why couldn't one of these people be you? The only limit to what you can achieve by adapting old products to new uses—old methods to new applications—is the limit of your own creativity.

Next, think substitution. When you "think substitution," you ask yourself how you might substitute a different material or thing for the one now used. For example, plastic is used as a substitute for wood and metal. Aluminum is a substitute for other metals; stainless steel is often substituted for chrome; the transistor often replaces the vacuum tube. Old, weathered planking can be used as a substitute for a conventional wall in a family room or study with dramatic and interesting effect. In short, don't assume that because a particular thing has always been used in the past, that you have to use it now. Perhaps there's a substitute that will work better, or last longer, or cost less, or be light, or more colorful and so forth. Let's "think substitution."

Next...think magnification. Think big! Examples: skyscrapers, the Pentagon, king size soft drinks, giant economy size packages. What do you work with that might be made larger?

Or...think minification. Think small! Examples: the solar battery, the transistor, the compact car, tiny radios that fit into your pocket, small portable TV sets, smaller-sized food products. How about the bikini? That's certainly thinking small!

And now, to keep your mind moving...think rearrangement. That is—turn things around, backward, upside down or inside out. An interesting example of this was when someone came up with the idea of putting the mink on the inside of a woman's coat—all the warmth, luxury and status of full length mink, in a casual coat! And it's nothing more than a mink coat turned inside out.

Another good example of this is the building with its skeletal framework outside; the building is suspended inside. Insects have their skeletons outside; we have ours inside. They both work fine.

What do you work with that can benefit from this kind of thinking? What can you turn around, revolutionize?

Rearrange things, change pace, alter sequence, think of modifying— changing color, motion, timing, sound, odor, taste, form and shape. This type of thinking works for everyone. Salesmen use these creative techniques to discover new applications for products or services, new ways to emphasizing customer benefits, new ideas to solve customer problems, better ways to organize their time and effort.

Summing up: If you want to spur your mind to new action, think combination, association, adaptation, substitution, magnification, minification and rearrangement.

If at first you force—literally force—your mind to think in all these seven ways, you'd probably be amazed with the ideas you develop. And before long, you'll find yourself thinking in each of these ways as a matter of course. This kind of thinking increases the scope of your mind power and enables you to achieve fuller use of your brain. Your mind has an infinite variety of things it can do and an infinite capacity for work. Let it work for you. Take nothing for granted; everything can and will be changed, improved. The only thing you can count on for certain is change. Don't wait for it—be in the forefront—help bring it about.

How to Apply Creativity to Problem Solving

Creative Problem Solving Using Lateral Thinking

Here's a little story to test how good a thinker you are.

Many years ago, a merchant in London had the misfortune to owe a huge sum to a mean moneylender. The moneylender, who was old and ugly, fancied the merchant's beautiful, young daughter. He proposed a bargain. He said he would cancel the merchant's debt if he could have the girl instead.

Both the merchant and his daughter were horrified at the suggestion. So the cunning moneylender proposed that they let Providence decide the matter. He told them that he would put a black pebble and a white pebble into an empty moneybag, and then the girl would have to pick out one of the pebbles. If she chose the black pebble, she would become his wife, and her father's debt would be canceled. If she chose the white pebble, she would stay with her father, and the debt would still be canceled. But if she refused to pick a pebble, her father would be thrown into jail, and she would starve.

Reluctantly, the merchant agreed. They were standing on a pebble-strewn path in the merchant's garden as they talked, and the moneylender stooped down to pick up the two pebbles. As he did, the girl, sharp-eyed with fright, noticed that he picked up two black pebbles and put them into the moneybag. (He wasn't taking any chances.) He then asked the girl to pick out the pebble that was to decide her fate and that of her father.

Imagine that you are standing on that path in the merchant's garden. What would you have done if you had been the girl? If you had to advise her, what would you have advised her to do?

What type of thinking would you use to solve the problem? You may think that careful logical analysis must solve the problem if there is a solution. This type of thinking is straightforward vertical thinking. The other type of thinking is lateral thinking.

Vertical thinkers are usually not much help to a girl in this situation. If you were to examine the way they would analyze it, there are three possibilities:

(1) The girl should refuse to take a pebble. (2) The girl should show that there are two black pebbles in the bag and expose the moneylender as a cheat. (3) The girl should take a black pebble and sacrifice herself in order to save her father from prison.

None of these suggestions is very helpful, for if the girl does take a pebble, then she has to marry the moneylender. If not, her father goes to prison.

The girl in the story put her hand into the moneybag and drew out a pebble. Without looking at it, she fumbled and let it fall to the path where it was immediately lost among all the others. "Oh, how clumsy of me," she said. "But never mind. If you look into the bag, you will be able to tell which pebble I took by the color of the one that is remaining."

Since the remaining pebble is, of course, black, it must be assumed that she has taken the white pebble, since the moneylender dare not admit his dishonesty.

That's what's called lateral thinking. It not only solves problems, but it also improves the situation.

It is a well-established, yet always surprising, bit of knowledge that the answer to even our most pressing problem (provided, of course, that it lies within the realm of human solution) is usually at hand. It requires, however, a different kind of insight to see it.

It's like the old story of the big truck that was stuck in an underpass. They didn't know what to do until a youngster, observing their perplexity, suggested that they let some of the air out of the tires. It was a perfectly simple and obvious solution to a tough problem. But it takes a different kind of thinking—it takes lateral thinking, thinking in new directions. Someone once said that thinking in new directions is the definition of genius.

This kind of thinking characteristically produces simple answers; they're the kind that usually trigger the response, "Why didn't I think of that?" or "The answer was so obvious." It's obvious only after someone else comes up with it.

A friend of mine loves to lie on the beach and soak up the sun with a good book. She likes to listen to the radio at the same time, and on receiving a very good little portable for Christmas one year, she was worried about getting sand in it and its being ruined. Her 11-year-old son suggested that she put it in a plastic bag and fasten the top. It would be sand-proof. Yet it could still be dialed, tuned and heard through the thin plastic.

These are small, relatively unimportant things; but big, vital and very critical problems can be solved the same way. It's been said that the solution to every problem is so close, you can reach out and touch it. But you can't touch it with your hand until you touch it with a bit of lateral creative thinking.

Children seem to be better at lateral thinking than grown-ups, unless grown-ups work at it, practice it. And then they can learn the knack or, perhaps, relearn it would be more appropriate. We all were highly creative children at one time, before we had it worn off or knocked out of us by unimaginative, dull adults.

The management of a large electronics firm had struggled for months with a production problem that resisted all their efforts to solve. There were nine women working on that particular assembly line, and finally, in desperation, the management people asked their help in solving the problem. They solved it in a week and, in so doing, greatly reduced the cost of producing the product. They had been producing it the old way because that's what they had been told to do. They hadn't been asked to do it the best way they could think of.

Go to work on your problems in the same way, if you're in a problem-solving kind of work. (If you're not in a problem-solving kind of work, you're unemployed.)

I understand that it's particularly difficult for professional people to think creatively and laterally. It's because they have been so thoroughly conditioned by their education. They've always been told what to do, and they've been told how it's always been done. And they were never asked how to do it better.

How to Brainstorm

What are the similarities in problem solving, decision-making, and goal achievement? Actually, they're alike in many ways. A decision that must be made is little more than a problem awaiting a solution. We might even call it a simple problem. When we're faced with a decision, we rarely have to choose between more than two or three alternatives, whereas, in solving a problem, we sometimes face what seems to be an endless list of possibilities. And what about goal achievement? Isn't a goal a point we wish to reach? The problem is to move from where we are now, to where we want to be. So, you see, problem solving, decision -making and goal achievement are all closely related functions of creative thinking. It's important that we keep this in mind.

The first step in solving any problem is to define it. We should always be sure we understand a problem before we go to work on its solution.

Next, you should write down everything you know about the problem. This information might come from your own experience, or from books which contain background and statistical data, or from friends and business associates who know something about the area in which the problem lies.

Third, decide who to see. List the names of people and organizations that are recognized authorities on the problem. This is your opportunity to go "all out" for facts. After determining who can help you, contact them, talk with them, and pick their brains for all the information they possess that can help you solve the problem.

After doing this, be sure to make a note of each thing that's germane to the problem. Don't risk forgetting anything that could help you find the best solution.

The fifth step in solving a problem creatively is called "Individual Ideation." This is personal "brainstorming," or thinking with the brakes of judgment off! Don't try to decide whether an idea is good or bad—just write it down the moment it comes to you. You can pick and choose—rate these ideas—later. Right now, all you're after is a lot of ideas.

Remember the four rules for brainstorming: (1) No negative thinking; (2) The wilder the ideas, the better; (3) A large number of ideas is essential; and, (4) Combination and improvement of ideas is what you're after.

One idea often leads to another, better idea. Don't worry if some of your ideas seem far-fetched or impractical. You're looking for all the ideas you can possibly find. Don't reject any—write them all down!

Then, "Group Brainstorm". This is your opportunity to put the minds of others to work on the problem. Handle this session the same way you did your "Individual Ideation." No negative thinking, no criticism at this stage; the wilder the ideas the better; get as many ideas as possible; and, try for idea combination and improvement. Write down all the ideas the group comes up with.

When you have all your ideas written down, rate them for effectiveness and facility. The effectiveness scale ranges from "very effective" to "probably effective" to "doubtful." And the facility scale ranges from "easy" to "not so easy" to "difficult." This rating of ideas will clearly indicate the likely success of any possible solution. Of course, it's best to consider first the idea or ideas that are rated both "very effective" and "easy."

Suppose you're a manufacturer. And suppose your sales and marketing team brainstorm comes up with some ideas to increase sales. Let's say one of the ideas is to revamp completely one of the products that your company is offering to the public. Let's rate this idea in terms of effectiveness. You know the present product meets a need and is acceptable to the buying public. What about an entirely changed product? Without a lot of marketing tests and then a period of actual manufacturing for sale, it would be hard to say just how effective this idea would be in increasing sales. Better rate it "doubtful."

And how does this idea of completely revamping one of the products check out in the facility area —"easy," "not so easy" or "difficult"? It would be "difficult," wouldn't it? It would require new engineering, new tools, new manufacturing plans, new packaging, new marketing methods.

Suppose, however, that one of the salesmen's ideas is to feature the company's product on a network television program. This would be "probably effective." It would be "not so easy," but it could be done.

Let's say another idea is to set up a new motivational or sales incentive program, a program directed to those people who are at the front of the problem, the salesmen. If it were a well-designed and implemented motivational or incentive program, it would stand a good chance of being "very effective." It would be "easy" to do. It should increase the company's sales.

There are many other evaluation yardsticks you might use. Two more are time and money. Try rating your ideas against these measurements. For example, in the case of a manufacturer who wants to increase his sales, certainly to change the product would take a great deal of time and money. And to advertise it on a popular network television program would cost a great deal of money. On the other hand, to introduce a new motivational or sales incentive program might be neither too costly nor too time consuming.

Remember, when you evaluate your ideas, measure them against these four rating yardsticks: effectiveness, facility, time, and cost. Every idea you have may not be worth creative action, and that's why you must skillfully evaluate each of them. But once you've carefully judged your ideas, it's time to take action.

When you've written an idea into your "Action Plan," decide who might do it, when it might be done, where to start, and how to do it. These are important considerations.

Be certain to give yourself a deadline for putting your plan into action. We work hardest and most efficiently when we know there's a definite time element involved. So, make a note of the date when you must put your solution to work. It's good to remember that timing is often critical when a new idea is introduced. Carefully calculate the deadline in the light of the general situation. You also might like to write down a second date—the one by which you intend to have the action completed and the problem solved.

Remember what was said earlier about problem solving, decision- making, and goal achievement? They have a great deal in common. They can all be attacked in much the same way.

You know, for any problem, no matter how big or complex it may be, there is a solution. All you have to do is find it!

Remember these steps for brainstorming:

-Define the problem
-Write down everything you know about the problem
-Decide who to see
-Make note of everything that's germane to the problem
-Conduct a personal brainstorming or Individual Ideation
-Consider Group Brainstorming
-Rate your ideas for effectiveness and faculty
-Try rating your ideas for time and money
 -Evaluate your ideas and take action on them
-Create an "Action Plan"

-Give yourself a deadline for putting your plan into action

The Power of Our Intuitive Force

When we think long and hard on a problem, with an open and receptive consciousness, we put to work energies and forces about which we can only speculate. Most of us have stewed over a difficult problem for weeks when suddenly, during a period of relaxation, the answer to the problem appears — complete, simple and beautiful before us.

Dr. Willis Harman gave a talk about a friend of his, the president of a high-tech company who, together with his scientific staff, had been trying to solve an especially knotty problem for weeks. One Sunday afternoon, while he was sitting in his living room, as Dr. Harman recalled, "He was once again puzzling over the fact that he didn't have anybody in the organization who could solve this technical problem, when he heard a voice say, 'Well, what about this?' And there drifted into the living room a three-dimensional model that just sat there...which embodied the technological advance that he needed.

"He got his pad and pencil and started to sketch it, and when he'd finished the sketch of the front view, it turned around so he could sketch the side view. After he finished that, it flipped over so he could get a top view.

"He took his completed sketch into his office and showed it to his top design engineer, who asked him where the idea came from.

"He very reluctantly told him about the episode in his living room. The engineer broke into a broad grin and said, 'That's where I get all of my ideas.'"

Earlier, in the same talk, Dr. Harman had told of an architect who used the same mysterious source for his best building designs. He'd feed all the necessary information into his mind, stew about the project for a few days, and then, at some odd time, the finished sketches would appear so clearly in every detail, he had only to copy them. One time the idea he was waiting for appeared in front of him on the windshield while he was driving his car.

Dr. Harman calls this strange source of answers the 'creative, intuitive deep mind'. Those who don't believe in it, can't use it. By not believing in it, they've shut off the means of reaching it. Those who believe in it a little, tend to use it a little. Those who believe in it a great deal, use it all the time.

In science, we know that just about all the great advances were made by these kinds of intuitive leaps in the creative process—by some sort of remarkable solving of problems behind the scenes.

Most people find the system working when they try to remember someone's name. The more they try to force the forgotten name into their consciousness, the more it remains hidden. So they drop it and turn to other things, and after a while, when they're relaxed and doing something else, the name they were looking for floats into their consciousness.

Most people don't realize that the same system that will dredge up a forgotten name will dredge up practically anything else they happen to want or need.

I've used this creative-intuitive source for answers all my life. Call it collective intuition, call it the subconscious—call it anything at all. But call it. Use it. Believe in it.

How to Build Your Imagination

People historically have stood in the way of virtually every good idea, and especially if it isn't theirs. While getting new ideas in business is usually the best way to guarantee unpopularity, it's still the only way to renewal and growth. People resist new ideas, from the top to the bottom of an organization, especially if it's an older organization. Championing a new idea is a lonely business. But if you believe it's a good idea, if your research causes you to believe it will be a significant benefit, and the costs and disruption necessary to test the idea are not completely out of line with its ultimate benefits, then fight it through. Do it as diplomatically as you can, make as few enemies as possible, but fight it through if you believe in it.

Your good ideas can lead to your dismissal from an organization. But ideas are more important than a job. With good ideas you have independence. There's always a way to succeed. A friend of mine found he couldn't get his ideas through the Board of Directors. He resigned, and beginning at about the age of 60, he built a $300 million a year business on his rejected ideas. Walt Disney used to ask 10 people what they thought of a new idea. If they were unanimous in their rejection of it, he would begin working on it immediately.

Our world today consists of thousands of things people once thought were impossible. How many good ideas have you followed through to completion in your work during the past year? A business's very beginning and success were based on innovative imagination and will become a model of stodgy convention with a few years of good profits. You know Arnold Palmer's success as a truly great golfer was based on his ability to never try to play it too safely, too cozy.

He was never foolhardy, but he would try the more testing shot when others would have played it safe. He lost some tournaments as a result, but he won a great many and achieved world fame and respect, too. There's much to be said for the conservation of assets. But it should be remembered that they tend to slow you down and put more emphasis on saving what you've got than on building for the future. And, of course, there's a happy balance between conservation and innovation that should never be lost sight of.

When it comes to input, we should never stop building our store of information. We can never get an idea without raw material, which is information and application. If there's real talent there too, so much the better. But talent has a way of developing with hard application, daily application, perspiration, long hours of study and deep thought. Become a sponge for information that applies to what you do. Read everything you can find on the subject. Build a fine library of books that are filled with the ideas of others on your specialty—whatever it may be.

You know each of us has a gold mine between his ears. If he fails to mine the gold, well, that's his business. But it's there—all that we can want and much more.

Learn to Create, Not Compete

Some time ago, I made a speech to the members of a large national organization. These people were executives at or near the top of the companies they represented. I told them that in my opinion, none of us thinks enough; as a rule, we let our minds lie dormant—sort of in neutral, until we're confronted with a situation that requires mental effort.

I mentioned that even corporation presidents of my acquaintance seldom indulge in serious, concentrated thinking between problems. They think in times of crises. The fact that they can solve problems and steer their companies safely through crises qualifies them as executives and justifies their large incomes. But what about all that time they have between problems? Why not have some sort of systematic daily plan of creative thinking?

An intelligent person works out some program of physical exercise for the proper maintenance of his body. Why not a daily program of mental exercise?

I know of a lumber dealer in New York who became an outstanding success in a surprisingly short time. He made millions in the lumber business while his so-called competitors were scrambling around, trying to keep up with him.

When reporters asked him the secret of his success, he told them that every night, he sat quietly all by himself in a darkened room. During this time, he simply meditated, trying to imagine how the lumber business would be conducted ten years from then. He would jot down the ideas that came to him and tried to put them into effect in his business at once, instead of waiting for the ten years to pass. In this way, while his contemporaries were competing with each other, he was always creating.

His secret? Never compete; create. Makes sense, doesn't it?

A psychiatrist who was addressing a group of his distinguished colleagues got a big laugh from the audience with this description of the modern executive: "There are four types of executives. First, there's the ulceroidal type, who worries about the problem. Second, there's the thyroidal type, who runs around the problem. Third, there's the adenoidal type, who screams and yells about it. And fourth, there's the hemorrhoidal type, who sits on it and waits for everything to clear up."

Every adult is an executive, if not of the company he works for, at least of his own life and his family. What kind of an executive are you? Are you creating, or are you competing?

Why not try each day to do some concentrated, independent thinking about yourself, your life and the people you serve? I think you will agree with me that anything, however good, can be improved.

Henry Ford said, "Thinking is the hardest work there is, which is the probable reason why so few engage in it."

Make a deal with yourself to set aside one hour each night for creative thought.

Instead of worrying about the competition, try forecasting new paths for growth in your life. Be sure to examine:

-your job
-your company
-your personal relationships
-your health
What new ideas can you think of?

Developing Your Creative Mind

You might want to think about this trenchant statement, "Thus the materials for the creative product lie all about us, equally accessible to everyone. What keeps us from being more creative is a frame of mind that persists in seeing only the commonplace in the familiar. We become frozen in the ice of our own conservatism, and the world congeals about us."

Care to think about that for a year or two? A tremendous, devastating, magnificent indictment. I've said before that every day of our lives every one of us walks by more creative opportunity than he could probably effectively develop in a lifetime. There is no situation that is not charged with possibilities.

There are possibilities for creativity in the things by which we're surrounded in our daily work: in the home, in all the rooms of the home, in the yard or garden, on the drive or commute to and from work, in the daily newspaper, the radio and television (not necessarily in that order, by any means). In the clothes we wear, the houses we pass, and the empty lots. In everything we do with every waking moment of every day, 365 days a year, we are face-to-face with an abundant supply of the materials of creativity. But it takes that "state of mind," that sense of ambient opportunity, of the nearness of and the excitement of a possibility-charged existence. Otherwise, we persist in seeing only the commonplace in the familiar. We become frozen in the ice of our own conservatism, and the world congeals about us.

There is no security in life; why do we try to play it so safe? We eat and wear and are sheltered by what we have produced. If, through the great lever of our imagination and latent creative ability, we can make a more significant contribution from the spot on which we stand, there is perhaps much to gain and very little to lose. Besides, we certainly don't have to stop with one attempt!

I remember the comment of the well-known motion-picture producer, Mike Todd: "Being broke is a temporary situation; being poor is a state of mind."

We can say that creativity is a state of mind as well. It's a state of mind that typifies the very young because of the newness of the world. In time, through social pressures to conform and the repetition of experience, most children lose this sense of wonder and become less and less creative, trapped in a concrete mold not of their own making.

It's been said that the creative person is essentially a perpetual child. The tragedy seems to be that most of us grow up.

How to Gain the Most from Creative Thinking

"When you ask yourself why the steering wheel on your car is round, it's not necessarily because you want to invent a square one—it's because you're practicing your art—the art of creative thinking."

Most people today agree that the once fervently-spoken line, "What was good enough for my father is good enough for me," was a fatuous, absurd remark. What was good enough for Dad is not good enough for us today, and what's good enough for us, won't be good enough for our youngsters. That's the way this old world improves itself, and that's the way it should be.

A leading businessman has said, "If you're doing anything this year the same way you did it last year

—you're in serious trouble." The trouble might not come from the way you're doing things, but it very likely will come unless you maintain a constant awareness of the necessity, the inevitability of change.

Creative thinking is a learnable skill, and a practical art. But creative thinking, by its very nature, resists perfect definition and rigid rules of conduct, as does music or painting, or any other art.

Becoming accomplished at any art takes practice and more practice—years of it. You can start practicing it right now; you can make it one of your most valuable assets now and from here on out. And, if you'll continue to practice every day of your life, you'll become a master at it, and win a master's rewards.

Maybe it doesn't make any difference if you still lace your shoes the way you have always laced them. But it does make a difference if you don't challenge the way you lace them, or why you lace them. Just such a challenge changed the shoe industry, and today a good many men's shoes are made with no laces at all.

So, form the habit of really thinking about, of questioning, everything you do, everything you see. Some people can walk by an empty lot for years without giving it a second thought, without really seeing it at all. But one man will see it, not as a vacant lot, but as a beautifully landscaped property sporting a handsome new office building. He'll do something worthwhile for his community and probably make himself a fine profit in real estate.

When you ask yourself why the steering wheel on your car is round, it's not necessarily because you want to invent a square one—it's because you're practicing your art—the art of creative thinking. You're sharpening your mind, and encouraging it to perform the highest function a human being is capable of—deliberate, creative thought!

Then, when you apply your art to your work, to your home and family and friends—your mind flashes out of its scabbard like a finely tempered steel blade—probing, seeking, penetrating through the old to the new that lies just under the surface.

Creative thinking is an exciting pursuit: it's exhilarating, and it makes for wonderful conversation at the dinner table, while riding in the car, at any time. In the evening, your creative awareness might result in your asking yourself, "Why am I sitting here like a mesmerized chicken watching people kill each other from the backs of horses on my television screen? Isn't there something more interesting, more rewarding I could be doing with a part of this time? Isn't there a subject I would like to know more about? What about that book I've been meaning to read?"

You know, one hour a night adds up quickly to a really enormous amount of time. Time is one of the few things man can't buy more of and it's a good idea to use all of it as wisely as we know how.

When you get an idea you think is good, hang it up on an imaginary hook and walk all the way around it. Look at it from every angle; poke it, pull it, twist it. Stretch it in new directions. Try to improve it. If it's an idea you can't use, give it away and get another you can work with. Ideas are free, yet they're the most valuable commodities known to man. And great ideas enable the minds that conceive them.

Make creative thinking a normal part of your life and attitude, and you'll find your world being filled to the brim with wonderful new interest. And one of these days, you're going to get the idea that will make a really substantial contribution, one that will revolutionize your life! For it will be an idea that will make the world a better place because you happened to live here for a while.

In the meantime, just looking for that idea can be a challenge, an inspiration and a lot of fun!

Good hunting and good creative thinking!

Building Effective Communications

Sharpening Your Listening Skill

The experts estimate that most of us spend about 70% of our waking hours in some form of verbal communications. It breaks down this way: 9% of our time is spent writing; 16% is spent reading; 30% is devoted to talking; and—45%—almost half the time we're awake is spent listening. So you see, it really is a good idea to know how to listen—how to get better out of what we hear.

The first suggestion is to recognize the importance of skillful listening. If we don't realize it's worthwhile to hear more of what people say to us, there's no reason to bother improving this creative power.

Second, we should pay attention. Now, while this may seem too obvious even to mention, it's surprising how many people try to fake their attention. And it's awfully embarrassing when they get caught at it. While listening to someone, we should look at them—squarely in the eye is always best —and give them the attention and respect we appreciate so much when we're speaking. If, instead of listening to a person, we're trying to figure out what we're going to say next, we can't possibly keep up with what that person is telling us.

Third, we should keep alert to the speaker's gestures and facial expressions. Empathy is one of the outstanding marks of a good listener. None of us likes to talk with someone who persists in wearing a deadpan expression—so try smiling occasionally and nodding agreement. This tactic is just as positive as a yawn is negative.

Fourth, we ought never to rule out any topic of discussion as totally uninteresting. Creative people are always on the lookout for new and different information. While we may rightly classify some topics as "drivel"—gossip being one candidate for this list—it's wise to be sure the subject is not worthwhile before tuning it out. Keep your mind open to new ideas. They're all around you—and many of them will come by way of the spoken word.

Fifth, avoid prejudging the speaker—pay attention to what he's saying rather than the way he says it. Closed-mindedness and jumping to conclusions might well come under this heading. An excellent example of prejudging and missing the point entirely occurred about a hundred years ago when a brilliant speech by Edward Everett which lasted some two hours was followed by another delivered by a gangling giant of a man who spoke only ten sentences. When he finished, there was a smattering of polite applause. But what that battlefield crowd had just listened to and not heard—had dismissed completely because of the second speaker's brevity and awkward manner—was the Gettysburg Address delivered by Abraham Lincoln.

Here's the sixth suggestion for increasing your listening power: take brief notes while listening. When these are reviewed later, they jog the memory and bring back to mind the speaker's main points. Here again you can see the value of keeping a pencil handy.

Seventh, look for the speaker's purpose—what he's trying to get across. Search for his main ideas, and distinguish facts from fiction.

Eighth, we should beware of our "emotional deaf spots" that have a tendency to turn off our hearing. These are often words or ideas that strike us the wrong way. If we know of such "deaf spots," we can begin removing them by defining the word or idea that's bothering us, analyzing the matter completely, and discussing it with a good friend or a member of the family. Once we realize that a situation like this exists, it's relatively simple to cure it.

Ninth, be observant—listen for areas of mutual interest—and resist distractions. You know, while our minds can think at a speed of 500 words per minute, we normally talk at about 125 words a minute. There are three things we can do to keep our rapid thinking concentrated on what's being said: First—weigh and evaluate the material as we listen, think more about it; second—think ahead, anticipate the next area to be covered; and third— think back, recapitulate. A quick recap helps our memory. It greatly increases our retention of what we've been told.

Tenth, and finally, discuss the skill of listening with your business associates, your friends and your family. By talking about things that are important to us, we reinforce and amplify our own understanding. Good listening pays high dividends—in business, socially and in our personal lives.

The Art of Listening

"Listening really is the key to good conversation. You can't learn much with your own mouth open."

The late Bennett Cerf told of a college professor, much admired in his field, who would often invite his more promising students to his home for informal get-togethers. On one occasion, an eager sophomore asked, "Professor, what's the secret of the art of good conversation?"

The professor held up an admonishing finger and said, "Listen."

After a long minute had passed, the sophomore said, "Well, I'm listening."

And the professor said, "That is the secret."

It is also something that we would do well to check ourselves on from time to time. What brought this story to mind was a luncheon I recently suffered through in the company of a person who obviously had never taken the time to learn the secret of the art of conversation. I am sure you know the type. He can be recognized by his rapidly moving mouth, from which issues little or nothing of value. He seems to feel there is something wrong with silence and reflection.

Someone else has said that good conversation is like a tennis match in which the subject of conversation is lobbed back and forth, with everyone participating. But with those who have not learned this valuable art, you are more like a spectator at a golf match, simply standing by while someone keeps hitting his own ball.

These are times when you would like to have a tape recorder and a hidden microphone so you could send the conversation-dominator a recording of his one-way diatribe. Then he could hear himself riding roughshod over others, curtly dismissing their comments, and churning back into his own stream of sound like a hippopotamus in a millpond.

Listening really is the key to good conversation. You can't learn much with your own mouth open. Whatever you say has to be something you already know—unless you are guessing or, worse still, faking, in which case you are riding for an embarrassing fall.

The most embarrassing moments I can recall have been times when I was talking when I should have been listening. So every once in a while, I remind myself to be a good listener. Then, when it is my turn to add something to the general conversation, perhaps I can add something of value or interest.

It's not an easy thing to do, especially when the conversation turns to a subject on which you have a strong opinion. There is a great temptation to jump in with both feet, flailing arms and working jaw, submerging the entire room in one's great wisdom. But if one will summon the self-control and resist the urge, one can then parcel out his familiarity with the subject in small amounts. This permits others to share the topic. A person just might, through this method, manage to sound relatively intelligent all evening—or even learn something.

And if you run across a conversation hog, don't try to compete. If he runs down, which isn't likely, toss him another subject. You will find he is an expert on everything under the sun, and while he is talking, you can be thinking constructively of something else—and enjoying your lunch.

On Conversation

Once upon a time there was an old man who was given to talking to himself. One sunny morning, he was engaged in this practice and an old friend of his said, "Charlie, you're talking to yourself again!" "I know it," Charlie replied. "Well, why do you do it?" his friend asked. "For two very good reasons," the old man answered. "The first reason is because I enjoy talking to an intelligent man. And the second is that I enjoy hearing an intelligent man talk."

This is a story you might want to remember the next time someone catches you talking to yourself. The fact is, every normal person enjoys good conversation. And in a pinch, if he runs out of people to talk to, he'll talk to himself.

But it's believed that few people ever learn the art of successful conversation. Those who do are very popular wherever they go. Being a good conversationalist is a little like walking a tightrope; it must be done in perfect balance. A good conversationalist is not only a good speaker, with a wide range of interests and knowledge, he is also an excellent, interested listener and very comfortable to be around.

He refuses to be swept up into arguments and respects the opinions of others even if they are at sharp variance with his own. He seems to know that conversation—good conversation—is not an exercise in debating a subject but, rather, in discussing it. He never jumps up and waves his arms or tries to shout down another person or make another person appear stupid or ridiculous.

The good conversationalist never loses his sense of humor or flexibility. He will bend gracefully when the discussion is going against his point of view. And he'll wait, with attentive good humor until others have completed what they want to say. He will then come back with an opening comment, such as "I can certainly see the validity of your point of view." Then with the opposition disarmed for the moment, he will try to present his case in a gentle, more telling way.

And if he sees the conversation is headed for trouble, he will try to head it off into more agreeable areas. If he fails in this, he will simply stay out of it.

And invariably the best conversationalist is the best listener. Albert Einstein was once asked to define success and he said, "If A equals success, then the formula is A equals X plus Y plus Z. X is work, Y is play. Z is keep your mouth shut."

As T. S. Eliot wrote in his play, The Cocktail Party, "Most of the trouble in the world is caused by people wanting to be important."

The good conversationalist does not want to be important. He wants the person or persons he's talking to, to have a good time, and to enjoy thinking about and discussing an interesting subject. He puts others and the subject matter ahead of himself. And his conversation is such that it camouflages him, and highlights the subject and the others present.

As a result, he emerges from it all, as a person people are naturally attracted to, perhaps without knowing why. He's always high on the invitation list.

Good conversation is an art, and, like any art, must be learned. As in learning anything, listening is the best way to go about it. We not only make friends this way, we might even learn something.

Are you comfortable listening to others?

Do you always try to steer the conversation back to the other person?

Practice seeing how much you can learn through the fine art of listening.

I Might Be Wrong, But...

Author Leroy Ramsey said, "Speaking with passion but without the facts is like making a beautiful dive into an empty pool." To convince or persuade others to come closer to your point of view, you have to base your opinion on incontestable facts that are honestly come by and readily grasped. As someone else put it, "Make sure your mind is in gear before you set your mouth in motion."

Unless you can back up your argument with unassailable logic, or know where you can get the facts, it is best to remain quiet, or simply say, "In my opinion," and so on. Ben Franklin was a great one for that. He said that one of the greatest lessons he ever learned in winning others over to his side of a question was to begin everything he said with the words, "I may be wrong about this...but it seems to me..." and the combination of humbleness of attitude, linked with overwhelming logic, quickly had people assuring him that he was absolutely right.

To take the stand that you're right, even before you've made your point, is to make sure others will oppose you. It's also a sign of immaturity. Speaking with passion, but without the facts, is like making a beautiful dive into an empty pool and it has brought many otherwise intelligent people into positions of embarrassment, even disaster. In fact, it killed William Jennings Bryan, I believe.

We've all been guilty of it. "It seems to me..." are magic words. They soften and clear the way; they open others' minds and dispositions toward us. And then, if we're proven wrong, we're not so far out on the limb that we can't get back with good grace. But more important even than the escape route that it holds in readiness for us, it does not offend others and it helps bring them around to our way of thinking.

Avoiding an Argument

"I have found that an argument, like a potential highway accident, can generally be spotted from some distance away and it can be avoided the same way. Slow down and approach with caution."

Here's a wonderful way to avoid an argument—simply ask questions. Instead of jumping in and disagreeing before you know any more about the subject under discussion and the other party, ask the person to state his case, specifically, and to define his terms. People who like to argue, and will at the drop of a word on any subject, are people who enjoy ruffling the feelings of others. Willard Sloan once wrote an article entitled: "Arguments Don't Win Friends" in which he points out that arguments are useless and largely ridiculous. They're more a matter of temper than temperate conversation and discussion.

Subjects such as politics and religion can almost always provoke an argument. Racial prejudices can bring forth the most ridiculous statements in the form of arguments for or against certain practices. But if you'll apply this rule, to make your opponent be specific about some point you know backward and forward, you may avoid a foolish and endless fight, the kind of argument where nobody wins.

I have found that an argument, like a potential highway accident, can generally be spotted from some distance away and it can be avoided the same way. Slow down and approach with caution. In conversation, as in your car, the worst danger is speed. It's pretty hard to get seriously hurt going 10 miles per hour. And you can avoid a serious argument that could lead to a lot of heartache by just being extremely careful when you come upon a situation that's likely to erupt into a serious argument.

If someone makes a statement that you feel is wrong or ridiculous, you should not remain silent. As you feel the adrenaline pumping into your system, instead of jumping on the other person with both feet, just ask, "Why do you say that?" If you get another absurd generalization ask, "Would you mind being specific about that?" Ask questions such as "Why?" and "How do you know?" Instead of trying to prove your opponent wrong, make him prove himself right or discredit himself, which he will probably do if he's skating on thin ice. Put the burden of proof squarely where it belongs—on the shoulders of the person who started it.

Then you can sit back calmly and enjoy yourself while he gets in over his head, flounders in the swamp for a while and finally tries to change the subject. No argument. And he won't be so quick to start another one the next time.

Robert McNamara, one of the nation's top executives asks, "Why?" when something is proposed, even if he is immediately against the proposal; he wants all the facts. Perhaps he's been wrong about it and if he's right, he forces the person making the proposal to prove its merits.

Now, no one can even guess at the number of families living between arguments in a state of unnecessary and uneasy truce. Since it takes two to argue, let's make sure we're not one of them. All we need to say is, "Why do you say that?" or "Exactly what do you mean by what you just said? What is your proof?" Keep the ball and the pressure on the person who is driving recklessly. It works like a charm and you come out of it looking professional, wise and levelheaded.

The Most Accessible of Pleasures

The great Robert Louis Stevenson once wrote, "Talk is by far the most accessible of pleasures. It costs nothing in money, it is all profit, it completes our education, founds and fosters our friendships, and can be enjoyed at any age and in almost any state of health."

In Carl Sagan's marvelous book, Broca's Brain, we learn that it was a French physician, Doctor Broca, who first discovered that portion of the human brain responsible for human speech. It came late in our development and is given complete responsibility for our having invented civilization.

Without articulate speech, we would be simply howling and grunting like the beasts in the jungle. Writing could not have been invented nor information passed along from one generation to another. We would have nothing at all that we have today, other than our bodies, had it not been for the development of intelligible speech. It's an astounding, miraculous kind of thing.

And, it's why our speech to one another plays such an important part in our lives. I once had a long talk with a young man, age 16, who was planning to become an architect. He was a very good student and quite serious about his education. He told me he found math easy, but he was having a hard time with English. It's been my experience that that is often the case and works much the same in the reverse. Students with a facility for English often find math difficult.

I explained to him why giving his English studies a lot of attention was so important. I told him that as an architect, he would still be dealing orally with the people necessary for his success. Additionally, he would be expected to write letters, prepare written presentations, and so on. He would find that his ability to use his language would be called upon far more than his skills as an architect. None of us can work in a vacuum, nor want to. We interface with hundreds of other people. And it is our mastery of our language that determines their consideration and evaluation of us.

It is not done consciously. I doubt if few people even think about it once during their lives. But it is a fact nonetheless, that our use of our language determines, to an enormous extent, our place in human society. As an architect, I told him, he would be dealing with other university people on a daily basis. His business clients would evaluate him on the basis of their contact with him.

He didn't have to become an expert in the use of English. That was for English teachers. But he must have a large and flexible vocabulary, and an unconscious ease with his language. He must not have to think about it too much as he spoke. His ideas and responses must flow from him with facility. That's all. And I believe we parted with his having a new respect for that hated subject in school. I wish more English teachers would give students the whole story on why our speech is so vitally important to our lives.

Improving Your Writing Skills

On Persuading the Multitude

In the Dialogues, Plato says, "Georgias, what is there greater than the word that persuades the judges in the courts, or the senators in the council, or the citizens in the assembly, or at any other political meeting? If you have the power of uttering this word, you will have the physician your slave, and the trainer your slave, and the money-maker of whom you talk will be found to gather treasures, not for himself, but for you who are able to speak and to persuade the multitude."

As so much that we read in Plato, it's as true today as it was then: the person who has an excellent command of the language has tremendous advantages over those who do not, especially in getting jobs, and moving quickly up the ranks. In politics, it is of particular advantage; in getting elected, surely, and getting what you want done after you get there—and in getting re-elected.

I've seen it happen hundreds of times in meetings—business meetings, executive meetings, all kinds of meetings: the person who can stand on his feet and make an excellent and articulate presentation wins the admiration of everyone, and he is marked for advance by his superiors. On the other hand, a person who misuses, or fumbles and mumbles the language—even though that person is bright and competent—is at a distinct disadvantage. He's at a disadvantage because a prime prerequisite of management is the ability to communicate clearly and effectively and to motivate those in one's charge.

In difficult situations, the person with a first-class command of his language can usually extricate himself without too much damage and difficulty. Now perhaps it should not be this way; but there is no doubt that it is, whether we like it or not.

Looks, too, make a tremendous difference. They shouldn't but they clearly do. It's been found that good-looking people have a much better chance in court—especially with juries—and it applies to men as well as women. Juries tend to think good-looking people are less apt to be guilty, or, if they are guilty, less apt to be at fault or to go on committing other crimes. It's a fact that everyone looks with more favor on good-looking people. They tend to advance more quickly in business, all other things being equal.

We can't do a great deal about our looks, that being our ancestral plight—for good or bad—or somewhere in between. But we can certainly, any of us, obtain an excellent command of the language. That's simply a matter of study. It can be learned in the same way one learns any other subject: by reading books on the subject, by assiduously looking up words one does not understand, and by reading aloud until one develops a well-modulated, clearly enunciated way of speaking.

More than anything else, it depends simply on understanding how important our speech is and giving it the attention it deserves. We don't have to become professors of English to have excellent speaking habits, to speak clearly and to use actual words for what we mean instead of dumb comments such as "you know" or "you know what I mean." The facts seem to be that people don't know what you mean unless you state it clearly and effectively.

How to Sell Your Ideas

Elmer Wheeler, the famous "Sell the sizzle, not the steak" man, had some good advice about how to sell your ideas. Have you ever approached your boss with a red-hot idea for increasing efficiency, only to have him become resentful instead of enthusiastic? Have you ever offered your wife or husband or the neighbors so-called good advice? If you have, you know what I mean when I say that people resent having other people's ideas forced on them.

When someone approaches us with a new idea, our instinctive reaction is to put up a defense against it. We feel that we must protect our individuality and the status quo; and most of us are egotistical enough to think that our ideas are better than someone else's.

There are three tested rules for putting your ideas across to other people so as to arouse their enthusiasm. Here they are:

Rule 1: Use a fly rod, not a feeding tube. Others won't accept your idea until they can accept it as their idea. When you want to sell someone an idea, take a lesson from the fisherman who casts his fly temptingly near the trout. He could never ram the hook into the trout's mouth. But he can entice the trout to come to the hook.

Don't appear too anxious to have your ideas accepted. Just bring them out where they can be seen. You might say, "Have you considered this?" instead of "This is the way." "Do you think this idea would work?" is better than, "Here's what we should do." Let the other person sell himself on your idea. Then he'll stay sold.

Rule 2: Let the other person argue your case for you. He instinctively feels called upon to raise some objection to save face. Give him a chance to disagree with you—by presenting your own objections!

"The way to convince another," said Ben Franklin, "is to state your case moderately and accurately. Then say that, of course, you may be mistaken about it, which causes your listener to receive what you have to say and, like as not, turn about and convince you of it, since you are in doubt. But if you go at him in a tone of positiveness and arrogance, you only make an opponent of him."

Abraham Lincoln used the same technique in selling his ideas to a jury. He argued both sides of the case—but there was always the subtle suggestion that his side was the logical one. An opposing lawyer said of him, "He made a better statement of my case to the jury than I could have made myself."

Rule 3: Ask; don't tell. Patrick Henry, another famous idea salesman, knew how to do this. In his famous "liberty or death" speech, he asked, "Our brethren are already in the field—why stand we here idle? Shall we lie supinely on our backs? What is it that gentlemen wish? What would they have? Is life so dear or peace so sweet as to be purchased at the price of chains and slavery?" Try saying the same thing in positive statements, and see how much antagonism it would invoke.

Three rules for selling your ideas: (1) Use a fly rod, not a feeding tube. (2) Let the other person argue your case for you by not being too sure. And (3) Ask; don't tell. It's very good advice, I think. Don't you?

Are They Buying What You're Offering?

"Our main purpose is to get the people to buy what we have to say. We're not trying to win prizes as orators, arm swingers or podium thumpers. We're there to sell the people on an idea, to transfer our enthusiasm for our subject to our listeners."

We all remember funny and far-out advertising campaigns that had the whole country laughing, but tests after the campaigns showed no appreciable gain in sales. The test of all communication is, "Does it sell the product?" Now, this kind of rule can, of course, be abused. Tedious, ridiculous and hateful ad campaigns have been excused by the advertising people who say, "Well, it sells the product." Selling the product is the idea, but not at all costs. Not at the cost of good taste, good manners or good morals. But still we must sell the product and that's where burning the midnight oil comes into play.

That's where study, experience, trial and error, deep knowledge, and education all count in our favor. We want to sell our ideas, but we don't want to get so cute or clever in doing so that the people concentrate on the smokescreen and fail to get the point of it all, fail to see and/or buy what we're trying to sell, the reason for all the sound and fury.

Originality and creativity are of tremendous importance here. Now that applies to the preacher and his sermon, the father or mother talking to the kids, selling them on the good life, better way to live, pitfalls to avoid. It applies to selling ourselves to our superiors and our fellow workers and subordinates and it applies to the actual selling of our organization's product or service. Now, when we accept an invitation to make a speech, we accept the challenge to sell our ideas to others.

Our main purpose is to get the people to buy what we have to say. We're not trying to win prizes as orators, arm swingers or podium thumpers. We're there to sell the people on an idea, to transfer our enthusiasm for our subject to our listeners.

That's why I think it's a good idea to go easy on the jokes. In all speeches, except those of a very serious nature, there are perfectly natural places for a funny line or two. Adding that line and getting the audience to laugh and relax is good. But it should remain subsidiary to your theme and purpose. If there is the slightest doubt in your mind as to whether or not to use a funny line or a joke, by all means leave it out. When it's right you'll know it. It will fit like a glove. It will be perfect.

After giving a speech, it would be great if we could poll the members of the audience and ask them a few questions like, "In one sentence, what was the theme of my talk?" And then the big question, "Did you buy what I talked about here today?"

I had a man come up to me at a social gathering not long ago. He introduced himself and said, "I've heard you speak, Mr. Nightingale, and you make a very interesting talk. I don't buy what you're selling, but it's an interesting talk." I immediately put him down as a crackpot or a total moron, but I smiled and shook his hand and said something such as, "Well, you can't sell everybody." But I felt a stab of failure all the same, and I knew he wasn't a moron. A crackpot, maybe.

It's hard for us to imagine that any rational person on the face of the globe could find disagreement with our devastating logic, supported as it is with indisputable facts and buttressed with overwhelming reason. But they do. Some of them do. I wanted to say to my criticizer, "You could have easily come up with a friendlier comment than that." But he was right. He obviously had not bought what I had to say that morning. The applause after my talk had convinced me that I'd made a sale. Obviously, I had not sold everyone and it helps us to realize it.

And you won't either. People who drive a certain make of car can't understand why everyone doesn't drive that make. Republicans are amazed that rational, intelligent human beings can belong to the Democratic Party and vice versa.

People drive dozens of makes of cars, believe in many different ways, and are devoutly loyal to hundreds of various religions and sects. And you and I can jump up and down on the stage until we drop over from exhaustion trying to change their beliefs and very probably to no avail. But when we have something to say, we can do our very best to persuade them to buy what we're trying to sell. If we persuade some of them, we're doing fine. If we persuade most of them, we're true spellbinders and can top the best salespeople. But we're not going to sell all of them, I don't think, all of the time. But it's good to remember that that's the name of the communications game: to sell an idea, to get the good people to actually buy what we're selling.

On Writing

If you've ever had the urge to write, but felt you couldn't because you didn't know enough about the English language, forget it, and start writing. The trick, and it isn't easy, is to write the same way you talk. The reason I say it isn't easy is because it's difficult to learn to read and sound as though you're not reading, but talking in a normal, conversational manner.

Have you ever heard an inexperienced person being interviewed for a so-called spontaneous commercial? Sure you have, and you know darn well he's reading from a cue card, a script, or has memorized his speech.

It's the same with writing letters, or for those of us who are neurotic enough to want to write for a living. Don't worry about splitting infinitives, dangling participles or using prepositions to end a sentence with. All that stuff has long gone out the window. Today, conversational English is the secret to, if not good, at least enjoyable, and possibly salable writing. Personally, I think enjoyable, interesting writing is good writing.

For a long time now, people have been putting forth an effort to take the formality and stiffness from their business letters. And it's really not difficult if they'll just dictate their letters the same way they normally talk. If they received a letter from a customer, and called him on the phone, they would never think of saying, "Thank you for your letter of the 15th. After due consideration we have reached the conclusion..." and so on. Instead, they'd say something like, "I got your letter and after thinking it over, I've decided to go ahead."

The next time you write a letter, try putting down the words just as you'd say them if the person to whom you're writing is sitting across the table. Use lots of contractions and apostrophes—just as you would in conversation. Don't write "cannot" if you would naturally say "can't"; don't write "do not" when you'd normally say "don't," nor "let us" when you'd more naturally say "let's."

And if you've got a story you want to write, sit down and write it as though you were telling it to an old friend, or a youngster. Write as long as the writing comes easy and natural. Stop when it becomes forced and unnatural. Gradually, you can increase the periods of productive writing and probably stretch them in time to three or four hours. Did you know that four double-spaced typewritten pages a day will turn out the equivalent of a full-sized novel in three months?

You might remember what Leo Tolstoy said, "A writer is dear and necessary for us only in the measure in which he reveals to us the inner working of his soul."

Simplicity Is the Key

I used to know a man who was one of the principals of a large and very successful advertising agency, who had a hard and fast rule against clichés. A cliché, as you know, is a trite phrase which has lost its meaning through constant use, but which often becomes so much of a habit with us, we use it automatically, without thinking about it. I used one, just for fun, in my opening sentence. Did you notice it? I said, "...who had a hard and fast rule against clichés." What is a "hard and fast" rule? It's much better to say, "He had a rule against clichés." The words "hard and fast" are unnecessary. In advertising, they take up valuable space and increase the cost without adding a thing to the message.

Sometime back we went through a two-page letter, just for fun, and by cutting only the superfluous words, reduced it to a one-page letter consisting of just three paragraphs. Not only was about 70% of the letter completely unnecessary, but the new edition was fast, lean and muscular. The original letter was fat, unwieldy and full of clichés—phrases that you put into letters without even realizing you're doing it.

We have a tendency to speak the same way. Have you ever noticed how often you hear people say, "I mean"? If you simply say what you mean, you don't have to tell anyone what you're doing. Other examples are, "stuff like that" or "you know what I mean" or "in other words" or "like I said." And one time I had a cab driver in Philadelphia who, after every sentence would look around and ask, "Am I right or wrong?"

There's nothing wrong about this particularly, but it does add a lot of unnecessary weight and excess baggage to something that can be simple, direct, clean and powerful.

It's been said that the late Ernest Hemingway would sometimes spend most of a complete morning writing a single paragraph. And if you read Hemingway, you'll notice his effectiveness in saying what he wants to say in the fewest possible words.

The next time you write a letter—particularly a business letter—see if you can do a better job by using simple, strong, hard-working words. Cut out all clichés, such as "however" or "with reference to your letter" and all those silly wind-ups. Whenever you write a letter, read it over and ask yourself if you talk like that. If not, don't write like that. And join the crusade against clichés, bromides and old sayings that have no meaning or value. Some of them, like fine old bridges, we want to keep. Especially one such as "Heaven helps those who help themselves."

How to Get Started Writing

Success as a writer is the same as in any other field—it's a matter of forming the right habits. And the best way to form the right habits is to do something you know you should be doing, every day.

You know, the person who writes a daily column for the newspapers, the cartoonist with a daily syndicated feature, or, perhaps, the Hollywood scriptwriter on a definite assignment, sooner or later finds himself drawing a blank. That is, with a deadline approaching, a deadline that must be met, he finds himself without a single idea. The same thing happens to me. It happens very rarely—but it happens. You put a piece of paper in the typewriter and then stare at it. You let your mind wander— you concentrate—you glance around your library—you read something. Then you begin to think of all the things you'd rather be doing...fishing maybe, or playing golf, or traveling to some distant place. You forcibly bring your mind back to the job at hand, and start the whole thing all over again.

There's the typewriter with the blank sheet in it and there's the approaching deadline. Do you know what you do? You begin to write. You just begin!

This is why the professional writer laughs when he hears someone say, "I have to wait for the mood. I must court the muse and wait for inspiration." The men and women who earn their living writing against deadlines would starve, or find some other business, if they waited for inspiration.

One time, some years ago, I spoke before a university journalism class. One of the comments I made was later to come back and haunt me. I told them that if they were really serious about writing, writing for a living, they should write something every day. Even if it was nothing more than making a few notes on the back of an envelope—write something every day. And if they found they couldn't think of anything to write, to write anyway.

I still believe I was right but there have been many times when I've sat and stared at a blank sheet of paper for 4 or 5 hours before I could write a single word. Success as a writer is the same as in any other field—it's a matter of forming the right habits. And the best way to form the right habits is to do something you know you should be doing, every day. The more you do it, the easier it becomes— the more competent and confident you become—and the work becomes steadily better. Also, the more you do, the more ideas you get for future work.

I guess we all know that the longer you put off what you know very well you should be doing, the more you dread doing it. Finally, because of our procrastination, the job looms far larger than it did in the beginning until we finally, in a kind of desperation, pitch into it and discover that it really wasn't nearly as bad as we thought it was going to be. We should have done it at once, in the beginning, without wasting all that time—storing up all that apprehension and being miserable sidestepping our responsibilities.

I'm willing to make a guess right now that you've got something you should have done days, or maybe even weeks ago, but you've been putting it off, hoping it will go away. If you don't mind taking some advice from a person who makes it a practice to do the same thing—do it now! Just pitch in and start. Before you know it, it'll be finished—you'll feel really proud of yourself—until the next time.

You know, if every day each of us would just do the things we know very well we really should be doing, we'd always be ahead of the game, instead of lagging forever behind and then having to run like mad to catch up.

How to Be a Master at Public Speaking

They Laughed When I Stood Up to Talk

Are you nervous or just plain scared when it comes to standing up on your feet and talking to a group of people? It seems that millions are. It used to terrify me, as a matter of fact. I remember years ago in Los Angeles I was to make a talk before six thousand people in the Shrine auditorium. I hadn't done a great deal of public speaking before then, and I remember walking up and down the street outside the stage door in a sweat verging on pure panic for an hour before the time arrived. When I finally walked out on the stage before so many thousands of people I was in a kind of walking coma. Once I got started, it was all right. But the anticipation was pure torture. It doesn't bother me like that any more, although I still get the ubiquitous butterflies in the stomach.

My friend Norm Guess, formerly of the Dartnell Company in Chicago, sent me a little piece on some of the causes of our fear of groups.

1. The fear of self. Just plain self-consciousness, a feeling that expresses itself in the mental question, "What in blazes am I doing this for? How in the world did I get into this situation?"

2. Reflections from the past. The remembrance, even subliminally, of old classroom failures, being laughed at or ridiculed.

3. Over-concern about what others think. The questioning of our authority to be talking before such a group.

4. Poor preparation. The panicky feeling that the speech needs work, or complete overhauling or throwing away.

5. Lack of courage to try new things. The fear of doing the unusual.

6. Lack of encouragement from others. I know it always helps me tremendously to hear a comment such as, "The group is looking forward to hearing what you have to say."

7. The place, itself. The room can be arranged wrong. Too few people in too large a room.

And the worst thing of all, as far as I'm concerned, is a five-and-dime public address system that sounds bad, or one of those little microphones you have to practically swallow, or a stand mike in front of the podium, so that you have to reach around it with both arms to work with your notes. One night the equipment was so bad, I just quit talking and told the chairman of the meeting that his organization should invest in some good equipment before they invited people to speak to them.

Well, what do you do about these problems?

1. Recognize that others have the same fears.

2. Try to analyze what and why you fear.

3. Find a compulsion to speak, realize that you have important things to say and that you want to say them.

4. Be prepared.

5. Try to practice participation when in small groups.

6. Take notes. Writing ideas down helps so much.

7. If it's absolutely crucial, practice beforehand.

8. Learn to counter fear before a meeting begins. That takes time and practice.

9. You can take a course; join Toastmasters, it's a great organization full of people you'd like to know anyway.

10. There's nothing like actually doing it. Do it.

And my personal admonition is to talk only on a subject you know very well, something you're an expert on, and feel comfortable with.

Someone has said, "The human mind is a wonderful thing. It begins at birth and never stops until you get the chance to say something before a group of people." Turn the situation around; realize that if you were in the audience, you'd be interested in what you have to say.

The Most Important Element in a Speech

"That's the secret: be interesting. If you can't be interesting, shut up. There's nothing wrong with silence."

"What is the single most important element necessary to make an effective speech?" I don't think that's a difficult question at all.

The most important element necessary to make an effective speech is to be interesting. If you cannot make what you have to say interesting, you shouldn't be making a speech in the first place. Some say the one vital ingredient is enthusiasm. I don't agree. I've heard many speakers who were extremely enthusiastic about their subjects and left me completely bored. I agree that it's good to be enthusiastic about your subject and if it's interesting you should be, and so will the audience.

The one ingredient vital to selling anything—education, religion, hope, marriage, a product or service—is to be interesting. Unless you have the person's interest you're simply not going to really reach him or move him to make some kind of commitment.

I remember the story about the little boy who came crying to his father with the news that his turtle had died. His father looked at the recumbent creature in his son's hand and thought fast. "I know," he said, "we'll invite some of your friends over and we'll have a big funeral. We'll dig a little grave in the backyard and make a little coffin, and we'll have a parade. I'll speak some words over dead Herkimer there and..." And at about that time, the father noticed that the turtle was moving. "Hey, son, look! Your turtle isn't dead after all!" The boy looked at the now animated creature then looked at his dad with a sly grin and said, "Let's kill him!"

The father had been such a great salesman in selling his son the benefits of a funeral with all the trappings...it now loomed larger and more interesting to the boy than the survival of his pet turtle. And that's the secret: be interesting. If you can't be interesting, shut up. There's nothing wrong with silence.

The secret to being interesting, if you don't have the natural talent of the little boy's father in our story, is to plan what you have to say. Even in conversation you can take a moment or two to arrange your words and the way you say something so as to make it more interesting. But that's the key—it's the most important factor in selling anything. And we're all selling something all the time.

Our responsibility in attempting to get others to do things we want them to do is to be interesting. A little thought, a little planning, will usually do the trick.

How to Make a Speech

Have you ever been asked to make a speech? There are two kinds of public speakers: There are those who are asked to talk to a group; and there are those who, because of their position, are forced to talk before groups—people such as ministers, teachers, executives and sales managers.

In the first instance—that is, if you're asked to make a speech—it means you know something others want to hear. It usually means you're an expert on some subject. If you're not an expert on the subject, don't accept the invitation to make the speech. If you do accept and have before you the prospect of standing alone in front of a crowd of people, you have quite a responsibility.

The person whose job demands that he talk before groups has an even greater responsibility. In the first case, people come because they want to; in the second case, they have to listen to you whether they like it or not.

But in either case, you can make a good speech with a little preparation. Here are some guidelines:

The first thing to understand is that if it's your first speech you're going to be scared. You'll find a dull, leaden dread begin to build up within you as the fateful day approaches. Finally, as you're being introduced, you'll come close to panic. This is perfectly normal and happens to just about everyone —and it doesn't stop after the first speech, either. You'll find yourself trembling (particularly at the knees), your hands will perspire, your mouth will become dry, and you'll feel like you're in the terminal stages of some kind of tropical fever. Don't worry about it—just stand up, smile, and begin!

Now, about the preparation of your speech: Write it out completely—this is the way I suggest that you do it. This is a particularly good idea if you've never made one before. Start with an interesting statement that will capture your audience's attention; state your case; give them enough corroborative facts to prove your case; summarize what you've said; bring it to a close; and then sit down. One of the dangers of making a speech is that our voice sounds so good to us after a while that we start believing it sounds just as good to everyone else. This is not necessarily true. It's a thousand times better to quit too soon than to talk for five minutes longer than you should. Besides, you should finish with your audience still interested and wanting more. Don't talk until they're bored.

Don't ever tell jokes. This is one of the worst mistakes most public speakers make. Unless you're a real comedian—unless you're a genuinely funny person—don't enter one of the most difficult fields in the world, the field of the comedian. If you can tell a humorous incident that ties in with what you're talking about, fine. But don't ever—as long as you live—say, "This reminds me of a story," and so on. The only person worse than the one who tells jokes is the fool who tells off-color jokes.

I make it a principle to always arrive for a speech early so that I can talk to the officials of the group. I find out what the people do, and their general educational background, to make sure they're square with what I had believed when I had prepared my talk. What's the average age? The idea is to know your audience as well as possible so that you can speak to the people in it in their language.

You will remember that when Bob Hope made his hundreds of appearances before service men and women all over the world, he would go to some pains to pick up some of their vocabulary and the names of some of their officers. In that way, he could personalize his performance to that particular unit. Well, we should do the same without becoming too cute or personal. We just want them to know that we've gone to the trouble to do some research and that we know to whom we're talking, that we're not delivering a canned speech without consideration for the people who must sit through it.

Almost anyone can make a good speech. Just be sure you're talking on a subject you know thoroughly and in which you're deeply interested. Say what you want to say as best you can. Avoid clichés. Never say, "As you know..." If they already know it, you don't have to say it. Tell them what you know in a heartfelt and interesting manner. Become so interested in what you're talking about that you can forget yourself; in this way, you'll lose your self-consciousness. And then sit down. That's all there is to it.

Remember these steps for a good speech:
- Accept that you'll be nervous;
- Write out a speech that's concise, interesting and that proceeds in a logical order;
- Don't tell jokes; avoid clichés;
- Arrive early to learn about your audience;
- Become so interested in your subject that you forget yourself.

The Single-Theme Formula

Professional sales people, marketing experts and leaders in the advertising profession know the importance of selling one thing at a time. Only catalogs can successfully handle a multitude of items. In a five-minute speech or even a long speech, I think it's important to have a single theme and, like a good salesperson, you pose the problem and then give your solution. At the end, the problem is restated and the solution quickly summarized.

Your opening statement should be an attention getter. For example, you might say, "Scientists all over the world are agreed that the world's oceans are dying." A sobering thought indeed. It captures immediate interest and everyone is thinking, "Why, that would presage the end of the world. What are we doing about it?"

Using an internationally recognized authority as your reference, someone such as Jacques Cousteau, you provide the supporting evidence that your opening remark is indeed true and then you proceed to outline the possible ways that the disaster might be averted. At the end, you might say, "Yes, the oceans of the world are dying today, but if we can marshal the combined efforts of the world's peoples, if we can influence every maritime country to pass laws governing the pollution of the seas by oil tankers..." So you end on a note of hope and at the same time enlist the sympathy of every one of your listeners in your cause.

Not all talks are about social problems, of course. You might be talking about a recent fishing trip, in which case you find something of special interest in the story and open with that. You might say "Ounce for ounce, the rainbow trout is one of the gamest fish on earth." It's a much better attention getter and interest stimulator than saying, "I want to tell you about my recent fishing trip." A few words about the fish you were after and then you can work in the rest. "Two weeks ago, John Cooper and I decided to try our luck on the White River near Carter, Arkansas. It's one of the most naturally beautiful spots in the country" and so on. Stay with the trip and that rainbow trout, the hero of your story, and how good it tasted cooked over an open fire on the bank of the river. Then at the close, to more closely link your listeners to the subject, you might say, "If you've never been trout fishing let me recommend it as one of the world's best ways to forget your problems, clear your brains and gain a new perspective. And when you hook a rainbow trout, you're in for one of the greatest thrills of a lifetime."

Watch your personal pronouns. Keep yourself out of your conversation as much as possible. As with the case of the fishing story, talk about the fish, the beautiful scenery and your companions, other people you met, a humorous incident or two perhaps, but don't keep saying, "I did this and I did that." The purpose of the speech is not to talk about you but rather the subject matter. There's an old saying that small minds talk about things, average minds talk about people and great minds talk about ideas. What you're selling is almost always an idea, even if it's painting the house. The idea is the good appearance or the protection of the house. The fishing trip story is about the idea of getting away and going after exciting game fish. One idea, well developed, is the key.

If you're talking about a long trip you've made, the idea is the trip itself, even though your talk may include many interesting and unusual events and sites along the way. It's still one theme, just as a beautiful painting is put together by a thousand brush strokes. Each stroke makes a contribution to the main theme, the overall picture. And it's the same with a good speech.

The difference, I think, between a memorable speech and an ordinary one is usually the degree of involvement on the part of the speaker. If he's wrapped up in his subject, and he knows what he's talking about, and he's personally involved in it, that comes through. It's not in the words he uses; it's in the feeling that's transmitted. If you want to test this out, listen to news broadcasts on your radio or watch them on television. The performer who's only reading the news from a script or teleprompter, who has no real knowledge or personal interest in it, tends to be superficial or generally dull.

The reporter who's been there, who's lived the news, who's made the collection and dissemination his life work, brings conviction and interest, involvement you and I are caught up in. We simply know that he knows what he's talking about, while the other person is only reading. It's the same when giving a speech. If the person telling the story about the fishing trip is an avid fisherman and loves it, it comes through. So try to talk about things in which you're very interested. And use the single-theme formula. It makes preparing a talk much easier and the delivering of it much more effective.

On Writing a Speech

"The ideas are the important thing. If you're successful in getting the ideas across from your mind to the minds of your audience, you're as successful as a speaker is supposed to be. Audiences have a way of knowing when you're more interested in what you're saying than in how you appear."

The person who does a lot of speaking will usually have a fine library and be a good reader and have a good working knowledge of his language. If you're writing a speech and you're not sure of your grammar, especially syntax, have a person who's more knowledgeable on the language edit it for you. You might brush up a little bit too. If you're at all unsure of a word's pronunciation, by all means, look it up and check it carefully. Mispronounced words drop like bombs into an audience.

Sloppy speech habits must go if we're to stand up and speak to an audience. We owe it to them. It's offensive otherwise. It's very difficult to write and speak flawless English, of course, but we can do the best we are capable of and pursue the subject on a regular basis. I think I own about a hundred and fifty books on the English language, on writing and so on. I think a speaker has a responsibility to set a good example when he speaks. If he can't do that, he should remain in the audience. The exception would be the entertainer who depends on homespun colloquialisms for a part of his humor. When I was with CBS many years ago, I once interviewed a well-known newspaper columnist. I was amazed to hear him mispronouncing words I'd read in his columns. Then it dawned on me that he was print-oriented. He knew the words well and their meanings and used them regularly in his writing, but they weren't in his speech vocabulary. I remember that he mispronounced the word "indisputable." He said "indisputeable" and there were a sprinkling of other mispronunciations.

It's a good idea not to use words in your speech that you're not accustomed to in your ordinary speech, unless you're sure of their pronunciation.

Now we come to the critical part. No more critical than the writing, of course, but certainly of equal import. Read what you've written. Unless you're an expert at it, and few are, I suggest you read it over numerous times. Now this, of course, is for the speech that must be letter perfect. As you do, you'll always find ways of smoothing it out, adding a bit here, deleting something there. When the time comes to present your speech, you'll be intimately acquainted with its every word and nuance. Remember to keep your sentences very short. When you look at a sentence or even a short paragraph, you'll quickly grasp its meaning and intent.

Don't be too concerned about how great you look. The ideas are the important thing. If you're successful in getting the ideas across from your mind to the minds of your audience, you're as successful as a speaker is supposed to be. Audiences have a way of knowing when you're more interested in what you're saying than in how you appear. No phony gestures or posturing. When the gestures come, they're genuine and everybody knows it. The good speaker is like the good salesman who's more interested in how great his product is and in helping the customer than in his commission check.

Or the fine actor who so loses himself in his part that the character he's playing takes the stage and the actor actually disappears. You've heard it said of some actors, that no matter what part they're playing they're still themselves. Well, it's the same with speakers. Few of them have the interest in what they're saying and in the audience enough to forget themselves.

For practice in writing your own speeches, I recommend that you simply start writing them. Write two or three speeches and see how they come out. Remember to keep your sentences very short so you can breathe in the right places. And keep your copy lean and muscular. Cut out superfluous words and clichés. Get to the point. Stay with the point. And do a wrap up. Find something interesting for the close and sit down. We learn to write well by writing, by sitting down and making little black marks on paper. The more we do it, the better we get at it, as it is with anything else.

A Good Speech Is Like Good Conversation

A good conversationalist will make a good speaker. He's sensitive to the presence of others. His antennae are forever alert, picking up signals from his audience and involving them in his talk.

Good conversation is one of the great joys of human commerce. Good conversation should be like the game of tennis, in which the ball is struck back and forth with each player participating equally. Bores are like golfers who just keep hitting their own ball, over and over and over again.

A good conversationalist is one who, after he's held the floor for a minute or so, or has completed saying something he wanted to say, will end with a well-phrased and directed question, involving another player in the game. He will see to it that the conversation shifts from him to someone else. That is a good conversationalist. And they are so rare they could hold their annual convention in the back seat of a compact car. We love such people. They're a joy to be around.

All right. What does that have to do with making a speech? Well, it has a good deal to do with it.

The good speaker is able to achieve a marvelous give-and-take with his audience, just as a good conversationalist does with the person he's with.

He talks with the audience without their having to say a word. He will actually ask his audience questions such as, "Do you agree with that?" Then he'll pause and watch for clues, for evidence that they either do or do not agree with what he's said. Now that's a form of conversation.

Well, the audience can talk to us, too, by their silence, by their attention, by their nods and their poking of the person sitting next to them; also, by their laughter and by their seriousness at the right places.

We've mentioned that people in our society desire recognition more than any other factor. Pausing for a response of the kind I've mentioned here is a form of recognition. It's looking at your audience. It's really seeing them. It's asking them questions and waiting a moment for a response of some kind. If they're bored, they'll find ways of showing it, despite their best efforts. If they're interested, they'll show that too.

And when we ask a question, they'll respond. That's why the seminar approach is so interesting and often welcomed by the participants. It involves the audience in a very literal and vocal way. A seminar involves a smaller number of people, usually, and asks for their actual participation in the subject under discussion.

I rather imagine that a good conversationalist will make a good speaker. He's sensitive to the presence of others. His antennae are forever alert, picking up signals from his audience and involving them in his talk. The bore will also bore an audience. He'll keep hammering away at the same ball over and over again, totally oblivious to the feelings or negative feedback of his audience. Then he's outraged when people begin falling asleep, or talking to each other in the back of the room or sneaking out.

We're free to handle our subject as we will, but freedom does not mean license to impinge on the rights and feelings of others. We have a duty to be interesting or we shouldn't get up in the first place.

Now, that's the task of the speaker, whether he's the manager of the sales force, in a car dealership, an insurance agency, real estate office, or a large international organization. When interest leaves, the sell goes out of his message. Watching and listening for the response of the people we're talking to is a good way to find out how we're doing. It's also the mark of a good conversationalist.

Our responsibility is not only to create a speech that will lead an audience to a believable conclusion;

we must also make the very building blocks of that conclusion as fascinating as we can. It is in this way that we can hold the attention of our audience until we get to that all-important, final point. In addition, if we can develop techniques that make our audience feel that we are conversing with them, we will convey that we care what they are thinking—and that will create the emotional climate for them to accept us as favorably as possible.

Using Humor

Humor isn't something that can be forced, nor should it be reached for. It's something that almost comes naturally to those with the ability, or at least it seems to.

First, it should be fairly quick. I think it was Will Rogers who said, "Never make the porch too big for the meeting house." By that he meant don't ever make the mistake of spending more time building up a story than the punch line can support. They both should be in a beautiful kind of balance, the kind for which every good humorist has an intuitive feel.

But you know if you're a funny person or not. The knack for humor, I imagine, starts early, as does the reputation for it. I once looked at my autograph book from high school graduation after thirty years and was amazed to find my friends had written such things as "good luck to our storyteller." It seems that I was getting ready for my years in the broadcast business while still in my teens. Such things appear early. And I'm sure humor does also. If you have it—congratulations. Use it wisely. If you don't have it, use it sparingly and make certain it's really funny before you use it at all.

Does it really tie in with what you say or are you reaching out into left field to drag it in by the heels? I've heard so many tedious speakers say, following the introduction, "That reminds me of a story..." and then proceed to tell a story that hasn't the faintest resemblance to anything said in the introduction at all. It didn't remind him. He just wanted to tell a joke and everybody in the audience knows it and begins to move their feet and cough and look around for the exit.

Why tell it? Jokes aren't necessary to the opening of a speech; why do a speech at all? Neither are funny comments, unless they have a clever tie-in of some sort that the audience will genuinely appreciate and enjoy.

Here's a good rule to follow that I've found works. If there is any doubt in your mind whatever, if there is the faintest feeling of uneasiness about a story, never tell it. That feeling of uneasiness is your more intelligent subconscious trying to tell you to forget it. Save it for the locker room at the club if you must tell it. Even then, you may see a man you admire turn and walk away.

I don't think we should ever use a so-called joke that in any way insults a member of any minority.

If you want a foolproof system, use the enormously successful Jack Benny system: make yourself the joke. Benny has produced the most prolonged, helpless laughter in the history of show business. It happened on his old radio program when he was approached by a robber who said, "Your money or your life." What followed was simply silence, the deadly, convulsively funny silence that only Jack Benny could manage. The silence lasted only a few seconds when the laughter began; then mounted and mounted and continued for a record-breaking period of time, I think something like fifteen minutes. Finally, when it did subside, the robber repeated, "I said, your money or your life," And Jack Benny replied, "I'm thinking. I'm thinking."

Again the laughter took hold and the program nearly ran out of time before it could even attempt to finish. A simple silence did it as Jack tried desperately to decide which was more important to him, his money or his life. He was always the loser in his elaborate plans, as is the coyote in his attempts to trap the roadrunner. People love us when we're foiled by our own weaknesses.

The most pitiful person to ever stand before the microphone is the totally tactless person who isn't aware that he's offending his audience and, despite the total lack of laughter at his stories, persists. Fortunately for all of us, he tends to disappear in a short time and is never heard from again.

If humor is your forte, then you don't need any advice or help from me. If it isn't, use it sparingly and in good taste. It's wonderful when it's right. It's so awful when it isn't.

Speaking with Style

I was a speaker at a hospital benefit and as I waited in the wings of a large theater where the benefit was being staged, one of the officials for the evening was on stage in front of the lectern reading the names of the various high school graduates from the community who had won scholarships in nursing. He never looked up at the audience. He spoke in such low monotones that he was difficult to hear, even with an excellent public address system, and his performance was as lackluster as any I've ever seen. When he was through, he walked back to where I was standing in the wings. As he disappeared from view to the audience, his face broke with a beautiful broad smile and he said in a strong voice, "Man, am I glad that's over." I stopped him and I said, "You should have flashed that wonderful smile to the audience and used your normal voice. It's excellent." "Oh, that," he shuddered. "I'm scared to death out there."

Now, the audience got a picture of a very lackluster man with no personality and no style whatsoever, a total cipher. Yet, here was a good-looking man with a beautiful smile, an excellent style of his own that his friends and acquaintances no doubt greatly admired. I wanted to go on stage and say to that great audience, "I wish you could see so and so as he really is. He's quite a guy."

Everyone has his or her own special style. It seems to come with the genes and the upbringing and the education, all of thousands of experiences that coalesce to form a person's own unique style. You have only to study prominent people on television to quickly see that each of them has a style all his own of which he or she is completely unconscious. Just as we should never doubt our hunches or our own unique powers, we should never doubt that we have a natural style. If—and it's a big if—if we can be natural.

It's what made Arthur Godfrey one of the highest paid radio and television salesmen in the business. People loved him because he was just Arthur; the same with Johnny Carson, Perry Como or the late Bing Crosby and just about every truly successful star in the business. They play themselves when they're on. And you and I should, too.

However, and I think this is also of extreme importance—we need to understand what we might call the star factor. We need to understand the importance of losing ourselves in our subjects. We don't lose control. We know where we are and what we are doing.

Our minds reach for the proper words and phrases, the pauses come in the right places and we've got good eye contact with our audience. You might say we're conscious of putting on a performance, but at the same time we're so interested in what we're talking about and we know our subject so thoroughly, we can immerse ourselves in it.

I was chatting with a salesman on an airplane one time. It turned out we were both going to the same convention. I had to speak. He had to receive his company's highest honor as national sales leader. As our conversation grew more animated, I asked him the secret of being number one in sales with his company. And he gave me the most interesting answer. He said, "I was in this business for several years, and I tried hard and I worked hard, but I was a long way from the top. Then one day, a wonderful thing happened. All of a sudden things were turned around. Instead of my being in this business, the business got into me."

He looked at me and his eyes were shining and he asked, "Do you know what I mean?" I told him I knew exactly what he meant and he could number himself among the most fortunate human beings on earth, the people who actually enjoy what they're doing—the real stars. It reminded me of John Stuart Mills' theory of happiness in his book Utilitarianism. He said that those only are happy who do not seek happiness directly, but who spend their time helping others, who are engaged in some art or pursuit followed not as a means but as itself an ideal end. Doing something else, they find happiness along the way. The important part is that those are happiest who are daily engaged in a pursuit followed not just as a means, but as itself an ideal end. And it's the same in making a fine speech.

Unless the speech is in us to the extent that we can forget ourselves to a degree, it will never carry the impelling, moving effect of a great speech, the kind that brings the audience to its feet at the end of it.

I'll never forget as a youngster hearing Franklin D. Roosevelt say in a campaign speech in that high, stentorian and effective voice, "We must prevent the princes of privilege from dominating this great country." I remember so vividly the beautiful alliteration "prevent the princes of privilege." Alliteration sticks in the mind as does short poetry. At one time earlier in our culture, virtually all oral traditions, passed from one generation to another, were in a kind of poetry because it was easier to remember. How can we ever forget "Mary had a little lamb" or "Thirty days hath September, April, June and November" or "A, B, C, D, E, F, G, H, I, J, K..." Or how about powerful onomatopoeia such as "the stock market hit bottom with an ominous thud?" Well, perhaps I could have thought of a more cheerful example.

But there is poetry in the proper use of words. We hear so many bad speeches, a good one is like a cool green oasis in a burning desert. A good, but unaffected style helps.

On Moderating a Panel

If you're asked or volunteer to handle the job of panel moderator, you're already well acquainted with the topics to be discussed or you have considerable experience in the field about which the meeting has been called. Given your familiarity with the general topics to be discussed and questions which may come from the audience, I would say your second most important job is to familiarize yourself with the backgrounds of the panel members. By doing so, you're in an excellent position to steer questions to the appropriate panel member and to make comments of interest in background material, which will prime the pump and give your panel members enthusiastic participation.

If the manager of the meeting appoints or asks you to moderate a panel after the general meeting has arrived at the meeting site, try to spend some time with your panel and make notes that will help you get the meeting started and/or keep it moving in the event it stalls, which I've seen happen many times. The interest generated in the liveliness of a panel discussion will depend on the moderator, who also assumes the job of master of ceremonies once the meeting is in progress.

If you know you're to moderate a panel well in advance of the meeting, which should be the case, there are some excellent ways to practice the job. For example, bring up subjects of interest and ask the members of your family to tell you when a comment begins to run dry. Switch to another person or bring up another aspect of the subject and direct a question to a specific person. You can do this at business luncheons, too.

The good moderator is one who asks interesting and germane questions, and/or can take a poorly phrased question and rephrase it to make it clear and more interesting. Another good idea is to watch the good panel shows on television, especially those that are news-oriented such as "Face the Nation" and others which have earned for themselves places of creative permanence and excellence.

When you're asked to handle a panel discussion or to field questions from the audience, never forget that your job is to feature your panel members, not to make a speech yourself or in any way dominate a discussion unless the questioner from the audience asks you the question directly. Panels at conventions tend to draw interested audiences. People are there to learn and get answers to their questions. Quite often, a question is much more critical to the inquirer than members of the audience realize.

The moderator should see to it that the questioner receives more than a superficial answer, if one exists, without dwelling too long on any one question. Moderators should be on their guard against notice-seeking or thoughtless people in the audience who attempt to dominate the question process or use the meeting as a forum for their own long-winded views. Such people should be cut off and the audience reminded of the purpose of the sessions. You may need an extrovert or two out there in the audience to get the meeting rolling, but you want to make sure that those with important questions are heard and their questions properly commented upon.

Keep a good casual perspective. Consult the questions in your notes to make sure the most important have been discussed and keep your sense of humor.

Panel discussions must be unrehearsed and can, therefore, be surprising at times. They're also often terribly dull which is a sign of a poor moderator or one who has not had time to properly prepare. If you're in charge of a meeting, find your panel members and moderator as far in advance of the meeting as practicable. And in appointing or finding them, make them aware of the importance of this meeting and that it should be interesting and informative.

What's the role of a good moderator?

Have you prepared yourself to keep the discussion interesting and germane to the subject at hand?

Are you prepared to keep the discussion moving forward and to maintain a sense of humor?

How to Develop a Winning Attitude

Two Keys to Enthusiasm

Reading Bernard Levin's excellent piece, "In Praise of Exuberance," I became concerned anew, as he has, about the general disappearance of exuberance and enthusiasm in the modem world.

It reminded me again of the powerful cartoon I saw some years back by the European artist, Fernando Krahn. In the first panel, he shows a group of small schoolchildren entering a street-level subway station. As the children head down to the subway they're the picture of exuberant joy. They're laughing, playing and tossing hats in the air, as children do. But in the next panel, we see a group of middle-aged adults coming out of a subway station. They wear the facial expression of zombies. Their faces display dullness, tedium and a complete lack of interest or enthusiasm.

There is no caption on the drawing, nor is one needed. The question screams out, "What happened to these people in the years since childhood that has removed every vestige of their zest for life?" In a world filled with wonder and the opportunity for growth and exploration of options, these adults, so representative of big-city crowds—and small-town people, too—have apparently lost every vestige of interest. They are in neutral—in a kind of modem limbo we might characterize as "survival." What happened?

Is it a matter of responsibility? A factor of competition for survival? There's no easy answer, that's for sure. To tell someone he or she should be more enthusiastic is meaningless unless at the same time stimulating triggers of enthusiasm are brought into the picture.

The saddest days of our lives are those days in which we can find nothing to be enthusiastic about. I think you can say that a person's enthusiasm is in direct proportion to the importance of what it is he's looking forward to. Thus, there are all sorts of degrees of enthusiasm. People tend to be mildly enthusiastic on Friday simply because it's the last day of the week and they've got a free weekend coming up. People tend to be more enthusiastic about going home after work at night than they are about leaving for work in the morning. But the most fortunate people on earth are those who live most of their lives in a state of energizing enthusiasm.

And do you know what the key to enthusiasm is? Well, there are two keys, really. One comes from learning. The other comes from accomplishment. Learning new things tends to keep our enthusiasm high. Perhaps this explains the natural enthusiasm of the children depicted in Krahn's cartoon. They're naturally enthusiastic, and they're naturally happy. The reason adults tend to lose a lot of their enthusiasm for living is that they usually stop learning.

As soon as school's over, they take the position, consciously or unconsciously, that they know enough. Any learning they do from that point on, they do passively through the natural passage of time and experience, or, again, passively through the media, newspapers, radio and television. If new learning comes to them, it does so largely through no efforts or at least minimal efforts on their part.

Learning little that is new or interesting, their lives become repetitious and settle down into well-worn grooves. They see the same people and go through the same motions every day, and gradually or quickly, all or most of their enthusiasm fades from their lives.

The second key usually ties in with the first, the second key being accomplishment. It's really hard to accomplish something new without first learning something new, even if the accomplishment is limited to improving one's golf game or making furniture in the basement. But we're enthusiastic when we're working on a project we want to complete or master. The key word there is 'want'. It has to be something we want very much to do, as opposed to those duties and projects we must do whether we like them or not.

Did you ever get a good look at a dog's face when he's chasing a rabbit? It's the happiest, most alert expression you'll ever see in your life. He's got something wonderfully worthwhile to do. And he's having the time of his life trying to do it.

You'd hardly know it was the same dog you saw snoozing and twitching on the back porch before the rabbit came into the picture; he couldn't even keep his eyes open then. It's the same with people. The rabbit may be different for each of us, but it's our job to flush it out.

Perhaps the difference is a matter of positioning. Enthusiastic people seem to be on top of life—in control of things—and have a multitude of interests. They are people who tend to be committed to something in which they find enjoyment and challenge and the satisfaction of achievement.

If you sit in a café and watch the passing crowd outside, you will see this clear-eyed oasis from time to time. There's a quickness to the step and a brightness in the eyes. If this man or woman were present in that crowd of adults Fernando Krahn depicted, he or she would be instantly recognizable. There's energy in such a person—direction, intentionality and delight.

As for the rest—the dull-eyes, the slack-faced plodders, the survivors, we might say—they seem to be in a defensive mode vis-à-vis this business of living. They react to events; they don't cause them. They're like the fighter who has given up any hope of winning and who simply concentrates on defending himself from more serious injury.

The enthusiastic people are on top of life—regardless of their status; the others are on the bottom. And perhaps those on the bottom don't know about getting on top.

The word "enthusiasm" comes from the Greek word "entheos" which means the God within. And the happiest, most interesting people are those who have found the secret of maintaining their enthusiasm, that God within.

Our Idea of Reality

Let me quote something found in Carl Sandburg's account of the Kansas sodbuster. Who was that early sodbuster in Kansas? He leaned at the gate post and studied the horizon and figured out what corn might do next year and tried to calculate why God ever made the grasshopper, and why two days of hot winds smothered the life out of a stand of wheat, and why there was such a spread between what he got for grain and the price quoted in Chicago and New York. As he was contemplating these notions, a newcomer drove up in a covered wagon.

"What kind of folks live around here?" he asked.

"Well, stranger," said the sodbuster, "what kind of folks was there in the country you come from?"

"Well, there was mostly a low-down, lying, thieving, gossiping, backbiting lot of people."

After a few seconds of reflection, the sodbuster replied: "Well, I guess stranger, that's about the kind of folks you'll find around here."

And the stranger had just about blended into the dusty gray cottonwoods becoming a clump on the horizon, when another newcomer drove up.

"What kind of folks live around here?" the stranger asked.

And again the sodbuster replied, "Well, stranger, what kind of folks was there in the country you come from?"

The friendly stranger said with a smile: "Well, there was mostly a decent, hardworking, law-abiding, friendly lot of people."

And again the sodbuster said, "Well, I guess stranger, that's about the kind of folks you'll find around here."

And the second wagon moved off and blended with the dusty gray cottonwoods on the horizon while the early sodbuster leaned at his gatepost and tried to figure out why two days of hot winds smothered the life out of a nice stand of wheat.

Noel McGinnis tells us that what Carl Sandburg means here is that the world cooperates with us by conforming to our expectations of it. The classic example of this is, of course, the paranoid who suspects that everyone's against him and who, therefore, relates to people in such a way that they're bound to be against him.

Psychologists have demonstrated that our idea of reality is determined by our perception of things, the way our senses interpret things, rather than the way things really are. Edward T. Hall has written that the relationship between man and the cultural dimension is one in which both man and his environment participate in molding each other. Man is now in the position of actually creating the total world in which he lives. In creating this world, he is actually determining what kind of an organism he'll be.

Carl Sandburg, Dorothy Lee, Benjamin Lee Warth, Edward Hall and numerous others have told us in essence that we create our own space. Now what does this mean? Well, as with Albert Einstein, it means that space is relative. Unlike Newtonian physicists, Einstein did not conceive of space as an absolute entity in relation to which things were organized. Quite the contrary, he defines space as the relationship that exists among things as a result of their organization.

Well, the tendency for reality to be a self-fulfilling prophecy rather than an absolute given, has been explained by some modern anthropologists. Dorothy Lee does a good job of it in Freedom and Culture. And what all this means for you and me is that our individual worlds will respond to us in the way in which we see them. They will become for us what we expect of them. We are the creators of our own surroundings.

Keeping The Luster In Your Life

"People who allow themselves to get in a rut usually don't realize that a rut is little more than a grave with both ends knocked out."

Have you ever thought much about newness? You know, it's the quality people talk about when they say, "A new broom sweeps clean," or "Turn over a new leaf." Well newness, like most things, has its good side and its bad, depending on how we look at it.

A person in a new job, for instance, may feel he's at a disadvantage. He may be nervous, uncertain of just what he's supposed to do and just how to do it. Sometimes he's bewildered by all that's going on around him. Maybe he's even a little scared. Even so, the person who's new to a business has a unique advantage over some of the other more seasoned women or men in the company. His job has a sparkle about it; there's a luster, a challenge in a new job that isn't always present once that position becomes familiar.

Do you remember your first day at work? I do. I can remember the first time I sat down in front of a microphone as though it were yesterday, instead of a good many years ago. Even though it was a radio station so small they used an old walk-in refrigerator for a studio, to me it was one of the most exciting days of my life. I was scared and nervous, and I sounded like a man with his neck caught in a car door, but I was thrilled, too.

How about your job? Does it still hold the excitement it did that first day? It should and it can, but does it? One of the most common mistakes we make is to let the luster fade from our lives. As it does, we gradually lose our enthusiasm, and if we're not careful we'll settle down into a worn, tired groove of boring habits. We become like oxen yoked to a mill, going around in circles with our eyes fixed only on the worn path of our feet.

People who allow themselves to get in a rut usually don't realize that a rut is little more than a grave with both ends knocked out. Now how can we stay out of this deadly rut? How can we keep our enthusiasm and maintain the luster in our lives instead of allowing it to fade with time and familiarity? The answer lies in reminding ourselves of things we already know but sometimes tend to forget.

A Chicago executive once told me how he maintained the luster in his job, how he charged his batteries during the early days of his career. Whenever over-familiarity with his product and service, or the negativism of some of his prospects or associates began to undermine his enthusiasm for what he was selling, he'd simply make a service call on one of his best customers. There he could reassure himself of the excellent results being realized through the use of his company's products. Then my friend would head out again with renewed confidence in himself, in his ability to be of service, and in the benefits he could deliver to every new prospect.

You see, even though the everyday details of our work may seem old hat to us, we should remember that those we serve look forward eagerly to the product or service. A person may be indifferent about many things, but the things he spends his money on aren't among them.

We shouldn't be indifferent either, and we won't be if we look at our product or service through the eyes of a happy customer.

People are on stage every day. Like the actors in a Broadway play, they're sometimes required to say the same words and go through the same basic actions day after day and week after week. The professional actor learns his lines and movements, and then performs the part every day, often twice a day, for as long as the play will run. He can never allow himself to become bored with the role, any more than we can afford to become bored with our work. The actor knows his audience is a new one for every performance. What he is doing isn't boring to them.

What does the actor do to maintain enthusiasm, to keep excitement in his acting? He studies and works. He continues to improve his role. He lives his part, constantly refining his timing and movements, forever finding ways to put even greater meaning into the words he must say.

All of us are in the people business. Each day we have the opportunity to learn first hand one of life's most valuable lessons: how to get along well with people, how to make friends of those with whom we work, and how to persuade them to decisions that will benefit both them and ourselves. Our success in most any type of activity will always be in exact ratio to our ability to influence people.

And the best way I know to influence people is to care enough, to know enough, to serve them well. Sometimes we lose sight of the value of our work and when we do, we lose the luster, not just from our work but from our lives. So here are some more luster-restoring ideas you can use right now, and every day from now on.

One: Understand that anything, no matter how exciting in the beginning, will grow, not may grow, but will grow stale in time if we're not careful.

Two: Keep in mind that fighting off staleness in our lives is a daily job. There's something you can, something you must do every day in order to keep vitality in your performance. It is simply the actor's technique: live the part.

Three: Realize that there's no such thing as a job without a future. Every job has a future just as every person has. Whether or not that future is great or small depends entirely upon the person holding it.

Four: See the big picture. See your work in relation to the whole scheme of things. Your work is important to those you serve. Your success will depend on how well you provide that service.

Five: Finally, keep developing your ability to see yourself, and your work, through the eyes of that most important person, the recipient. And remember: don't ever lose the luster.

Turning Problems into Projects

When we use a euphemism, we use a word that is perhaps less expressive or direct, but often less distasteful or less offensive than another. When we say a person has passed away instead of saying he has died, we are speaking euphemistically. In that particular case it's less than ideal, but euphemisms, properly used, can change one's entire outlook on a situation.

My old friend, Parky Parkinson, reminded me that by changing the word "problem" to "project," we can change our attitude toward the situation.

The great Arctic explorer, Roald Amundsen, said that he and his men could never have gotten through the situations they faced if they had not given them euphemistic names—the light touch. These euphemisms took some of the strangeness, the hazard, the challenge—even the terror—out of their experiences.

A problem might seem ominous or threatening, but if we call it "a project" instead, our approach to it changes; we view it as something that has a solution—a solution we are engaged in finding. In the same way, we can remind ourselves that our opportunities are often in exact proportion to our problems. Polio was a problem worldwide, but to Dr. Jonas Salk and his fellow researchers it was a project on which they were working and which they were successful in solving. Cancer is a problem to millions worldwide, but it's a project to thousands of hardworking people in the sciences, and it will be overcome.

When we have a pressing problem—and who is without one for long—I think we need to take this intelligent attitude toward it. This is not a Pollyanna attitude, unless you want to call all the people who have been solving human problems for centuries Pollyannas. It is, rather, a very human, intelligent attitude.

Following an operation one time, I had to go back to my surgeon for checkups, which involved a very painful re-examination of the work he'd done. At first, I would holler and curse and tell him it hurt like you-know-what. But he would just smile benignly and say, "No, that's stimulating!" It still hurt, but thinking of it as stimulating did something to make the situation a bit less serious and painful, and we could laugh about it.

What might seem like a forthcoming problem might be termed an adventure instead. Thinking of the move to a strange community and a new job as an adventure could change one's attitude toward it. And it's our attitude toward something that, more than anything else, will determine its successful outcome.

So try changing the words you use for situations normally thought of as bad or threatening, or painful, to euphemisms, which can give you a more positive outlook. Think of them as projects or adventures, and go tearing into them, looking for solutions. It's all a matter of semantics and attitude.

Problems are a necessary and unending part of living. Our job is to solve them for as long as we can. And solve them we do.

How do you react to the problems in your life?

Have you ever looked for opportunities that might stem from the problems you face?

Can you think of a way to reframe your problem so that it becomes an adventure?

The Lasting Benefits of Good Service

Why Are We Here?

"It's been said, 'If the universe is an accident, we are accidents. But if there is meaning in the universe, there is meaning in us, also.'"

How would you answer the question, "Why are you here?" Go ahead; ask the question. Ask, "Why am I here?" Do you know? Dr. Albert Einstein was asked to answer that question, and he did. Do you know what he said? I'll get to that in a moment.

It's been said, "If the universe is an accident, we are accidents. But if there is meaning in the universe, there is meaning in us also." And since it is believed that Dr. Einstein understood more about the laws governing the universe than any person who ever lived up until his time, let's go to him for some answers. He believed there was some sort of meaning in the way things are. He was sure of it. He said, "The more I study physics, the more I am drawn toward metaphysics." The word metaphysics simply means "beyond physics," the study of what is beyond measure, the invisible forces at work.

If you haven't done so, you would enjoy reading Einstein: The Life and Times by Ronald W. Clark. Albert Einstein was so remarkable a man that it was as if he had arrived on this planet through some mistake in celestial navigation and, as a result, devoted his life to solving the problems of time and space so that the mistake would not be repeated.

Dr. Einstein belonged to no formal religion or sect, yet he was a deeply religious man in the cosmic sense. He believed that such magnificence and colossal order—the great "cyclotron of the universe," as Ronald Clark puts it—could not have been an accident.

And he addressed himself to the purpose of life. He answered the question, "Why am I here?" as well as it has been answered, when he said, "Man is here for the sake of other men only." He used the word man in its classical sense, the idiomatic "man" meaning human beings of both sexes, of course.

So he said that we are here for the sake of others only. Is that the way you would have answered it? Do you believe that you are here solely to serve others and, through serving others, are being served and enjoying life as a result?

We are here for the sake of serving others only! And to the extent that we serve others will we know the joy of living. To many, that would sound silly and "square." But that's what it comes down to nevertheless. And sometimes it takes a long time to learn the truth of it. Millions never learn it and grow old in querulous discontent, wondering what went wrong with their lives.

Our Rewards Equal Our Contribution

"Our rewards in life will always be in direct proportion to our contribution." This is the law that stands as the supporting structure of all economics and of our personal well-being.

Unfortunately, most people either don't know about this wonderful rule or think that somehow it applies only to the other guy. Most people believe that we should have speed-limit signs, too, but that they're for other people who don't know how to drive as well as they do.

Let's get back to the law of rewards equaling contributions. The law is in operation all the time, whether or not we know about it and go along with it. It's like an apothecary's scale—you know the kind, with a cross-arm on top, from which hang two bowls on chains; a delicate and honest mechanism. Let's label one of the bowls "Rewards" and the other one "Contributions."

Most people concentrate on the bowl marked "Rewards." That is, they want things—more money, a better home, education for the kids, travel, retirement and so on—all rewards. They're hungering for the rewards, but the rewards aren't materializing because they're forgetting the bowl marked "Contributions." In other words, they're concentrating on the wrong bowl. They're like the man who sat in front of the stove and said, "Give me heat, and then I'll give you wood." He could sit there until he froze to death. Stoves don't work that way, and neither does life or economics.

We can actually forget about the bowl marked "Rewards." All we have to do is concentrate on the bowl marked "Contributions." Life and basic economics will automatically take care of the rewards. It's a fact that most people have this backward.

What do we mean by contribution—and to whom do we contribute? You can define contribution as the time you devote to whatever it is you do and the degree of excellence you put into it. And your contribution is to mankind, and mankind can be defined as the people you serve.

So you can break it all down to a simple equation: Your rewards will be determined by the way you do your job, multiplied by the number of people you serve.

If a person isn't happy with his rewards, he should take a good, long look at his contributions. This may seem like a hard, cruel way of looking at things, but laws are good or bad only in the way we look at them.

If you feel you're being held back in life, or that you're not getting enough of the things you should, to paraphrase the late John F. Kennedy, ask not what you can get but what you can do—what you can contribute to the causes and people it is given you to serve. Your rewards, believe me, will always take care of themselves.

Back in the year 1690, over three centuries ago, a wise gentleman by the name of John Locke wrote an essay on human understanding. In that essay, he said something I think all of us should remember: "There seems to be a constant decay of all our ideas; even of those which are struck deepest, and in minds the most retentive, so that if they be not sometimes renewed by repeated exercises of the senses, or reflection on those kinds of objects which at first occasioned them, the print wears out, and at last there remains nothing to be seen."

He was saying that we need reminding, from time to time, of our personal philosophies, of the things in which we believe and which mean so much to us in living successfully. If we're not reminded, we tend to forget, and gradually these truths, on which a successful life can be built, fade out until finally they disappear completely.

You can compare a human life to a plot of land—the yard in front of your home. Anyone can tell by looking at the front yard how much attention it's being given. There is no such thing as a poor-looking yard that's getting a lot of care and attention. Similarly, there is not, in all of the world, a bad-looking plot of ground that's getting a lot of care and attention. If we take an average, sort of lackadaisical attitude toward our grounds, they'll reflect exactly that—and never get a second glance from anyone passing by.

It's the same exact thing with life. We'll get back—we must get back— exactly what we put into it; no more, no less. If we don't like the rewards we're receiving, we should examine our service, our contribution.

Now, I'm sure everyone will agree with this paraphrasing of the Golden Rule—when you remind them of it! But how about in-between times? Isn't it a fact that even after we're forcibly brought to see this wonderful opportunity to get just about anything we want from life—it gradually begins to fade from our consciousness?

I think it's a very good idea for every human being to ask himself, "What am I contributing to those with whom I come in contact? Am I giving all that I can—am I doing as much as I can—and in a cheerful, helpful spirit? Or am I going at my daily life in an average, or even below average, manner?"

If you're tremendously pleased with the results you're getting from life—you're giving a lot. If you're not too pleased, well, you might think about it.

Every great law of life, like a coin, has two sides. If we work with these laws, we'll reap the benefits and rewards; if we try to work contrary to them, it will be to our cost—we cannot win.

Examine the rewards you are receiving in life. Are you giving as much as you could?

When was the last time you felt like you were stalled?

Do you know why?

Did you stop contributing?

Give to Get Rich

Here are a few thoughts that you can make your own thoughts—if you do make them your own—that will guarantee your success all the years of your life. Now, that's quite a statement, but it's true.

To begin, let us understand that growth and increase are a part of mankind and all of nature. It is inherent in each of us to desire more. This is not wrong; it's perfectly natural, and the way it should be. This is true of all of us—the members of our families, our friends and associates, our customers. You should want to get rich in every area of your life. But what do I mean by "rich"?

Getting rich, for you, is getting what you want very much. It may mean obtaining more love, greater peace of mind, owning the home of your dreams or accomplishing something else you've set your heart upon. For some, it means a bigger income or a large sum of capital. That's fine. You can get it without hurting, or even competing with, any other person. In fact, you can thereby increase the general well being of everyone with whom you come in contact.

Unfortunately, the uninformed believe that you can get ahead in the world only at the expense of someone else. This is not true. No one can become rich in any way without serving others. Anyone who adds to prosperity must prosper in turn.

The first step is to understand completely that it's right for you to want what you want. All human activities are based on the desire for increase—people seeking more food, more clothes, more knowledge, more pleasure, more life.

The next step is to understand that you need not compete with or deprive anyone. Don't compete—create! In this way, you add to the general well being without taking anything away from anyone.

Remember to give to every person more than you take from him. Now, at first, this may sound absurd, so let's dig into it a little. In order for a business or a person to expand—and remember, expansion is the natural desire of mankind—we must give more in "use value" than we charge. A building nail doesn't cost much; yet its use is great and goes on for years. This book didn't cost much; yet if you can get ideas from it that can bring you more than you now have, its use value will greatly exceed its cost.

How much does it cost to give love, respect and consideration to those near you? Very little—just a little extra effort. Yet love, respect and consideration are priceless to the person receiving them. This is the key: give more than you receive in everything you do. In this way, you are building a great credit for yourself that must come to you in some form, sooner or later. You are taking out less than you are putting in, and by so doing you are building a tidal wave of future prosperity. This is the law of increase. It is understood and followed undeviatingly by every successful businessperson, artist, professional and worker, by every successful mother and father and friend. It is the most striking attribute of all successful people, companies and institutions.

Now, let's go back to the idea of creating instead of competing. You are the point from which all increase must stem—not your company, your spouse, your parents or your friends. You are the creative center of your universe. Increase must come from you personally. Find ways to do the things you do that reflect you and your own unique talents and abilities. If you do this, no other person in the world can operate exactly as you do. You will not be competing with anyone; you will be creating from within yourself.

As you find new and better ways of giving more in use value than you are receiving in money, more and more people will turn to you. You will find your circle of friends increasing. If you are in business, you will find it continually growing, expanding. Do this in a quiet and unobtrusive manner. You don't have to shout about how much you are doing for others; they will recognize it and be drawn to you.

One of the most interesting things about such increase is that totally unexpected and wonderful things will begin to occur in your life. People you don't know, who have exactly what you need, will make their appearance at the right time and in the right place. Everything will begin to dovetail, and your life will take on new meaning and direction and bring you far greater rewards. Let the impression of growth, of increase, mark everything you do.

As you do these things, keep constantly before you the vision of what it is you intend to accomplish. Don't worry about it; don't fret about it. Just know you are going to accomplish it. And following these rules, you can't fail.

The Importance of Remaining Grateful

"More than any other factor, gratitude projects the kind of picture that is irresistible. It attracts men, women, dogs and cats. It also attracts a condition mistakenly called 'good luck.'"

Have you ever noticed that when someone calls you on the telephone you immediately form a mental picture of the person? You get not only a mental picture of his face and figure but also a feeling with regard to his personality. And that feeling you get is either good or bad. That is, the person affects you either pleasantly or unpleasantly. Your feelings are hardly ever neutral. They are either favorable or unfavorable.

And, to carry it a step further, you project a picture in the minds of the people with whom you come in contact. And again, whether it's on the telephone or in person, that picture is either favorable or unfavorable.

You're projecting these pictures all day long to your children, your marriage partner, the people who serve you, your associates, your boss—everyone—all day, every day. So how's your picture?

How do you appear to people passing by on the street? Do you appear happy? Unhappy? Bored? Disinterested? Worried? Successful? Or unsuccessful?

The picture you project, the way in which you communicate to every person you come in contact with during the day is a reflection of your total personality; the picture you project is determined by how you feel inside.

The people who project the best pictures are those who know how to be grateful. Their gratitude for what they have, for what they are, radiates about them. They don't worry about what's missing but are grateful for what's there. They don't concentrate on the shortcomings of their marriage partner or their children; they're grateful just to have them. They look upon problems as things to be solved and are grateful for the capacity and wisdom to overcome them. These are the people who run deep.

More than any other factor, gratitude projects the kind of picture that is irresistible. It attracts men, women, dogs and cats. It also attracts a condition mistakenly called "good luck."

These people are easy to recognize. There's a calm, level look to their eyes, and smiling comes as naturally to them as breathing does. They don't complain about what's to be done; they simply do it and do it well and then start looking around for something else to do. They radiate ability and good cheer like an old fashioned stove radiates heat on a cold morning. They project a great picture, and the world projects it back to them.

Every minute of every waking hour of every day of your life, you're projecting a picture of yourself and your personality. You can tell how it looks to the world by looking at what you're getting back.

A personal Creation of Value

One of the truly great things that accrued to the old time craftsman, and to the few still remaining, was the joy that came from the meaning of doing. The feeling of value that pervades a person's whole being when she does something of which she's proud. This feeling is found in the person who knits or does needlepoint, the painter, the writer, the cabinetmaker, the really good cook, the workman or woman who creates something of value. And I think that's where it comes from—the personal creation of value.

Do you know what I mean? If you do, you know that it's a large part of a person's income, his psychic income, so important to living and good healthy adjustment. The distinguished social critic, Louis Mumford, has written that: "The fact is that with all of our super-abundance, abundance of energy, food, materials, products, there's been no commensurate improvement in the quality of our daily existence."

He said, "The great mass of comfortable, well-fed people in our civilization live lives of emotional apathy and mental torpor, of dull passivity and enviable desire, lives that belie the real potentialities of modern culture." He's also pointed out that the fault lies in forcing something that is capable of producing goods in great numbers, to provide more and more, more on top of more, more every month, every year, until quality and beauty must be destroyed in the process. Until there's so much that we no longer appreciate it.

Mumford's concern, and I think every thinking person will agree with his concern, is with balance and self-discipline, with the sort of person who will do intelligently and well whatever he turns his hand to because he understands the meaning of doing, the meaning of value—not only in that to which he turns his hand, but in his life as well.

There's meaning in doing something well, anything really. You know there are no so-called "good jobs" and "bad jobs." Every job holds within it the road to greatness if it's done well. And it can give us the meaning and satisfaction that come from doing a job as well as we can learn to do it. It's wonderful these days when we find a person who does an unusually good job—a waitress, a service station attendant, a mechanic, a salesperson, a carpenter, plumber or other craftsman, an attorney, doctor, whomever. We run into them from time to time, and we never fail to notice and be aware of them, to be grateful to them. Such people always seem happier, more cheerful and have a much better self-image. They seem to find joy and delight in their work, in their days. And they seem to understand that there is meaning in doing, in doing what they do as well as they can. They take a few extra pains that converts what would otherwise be an ordinary job, into something special. They stand out like a fresh oasis in a dismal desert of uninteresting sameness and they realize that the meaning they find in doing brings meaning into their lives. They're happier people because of it. You know them. Perhaps you're one of them. If so, congratulations! You're the member of an exclusive club.

Do you find meaning in the job you do?

Are you happy during your work day?

How does this reflect how you feel about the work you do?

Is it time to make a change?

The Art of Excellence

James B. Conant, when he was president of Harvard University, commented, "Each honest calling, each walk of life, has its own elite, its own aristocracy, based upon excellence of performance." Beautiful. People in every field of human endeavor will agree with that remark.

Aristotle said, "Excellence is an art won by training and habituation. We do not act rightly because we have virtue or excellence, but we rather have those because we have acted rightly. We are what we repeatedly do. Excellence, then, is not an act but a habit."

By judging the excellence—or the lack of it—of our work, we can tell if we're in the right calling. If it's of paramount importance to us to strive for excellence in what we do, chances are we're in the kind of work for which we're best fitted—or, at least, one of the fields for which we're qualified.

One of the problems of the businessperson is that after developing and profiting from a few good ideas, he will tend to stay with it in unchanging form for too long. For some things, that will work; but for most things, it won't—they need updating on a regular, annual basis. We need to ask ourselves at regular intervals a number of times each year, "How can we make it better, more efficient? How can we bring it up to the best of present—even future—standards?

People will cling to an idea as though it's the best—if not the only—idea they'll ever get. And when we're creating or building something, are we anticipating the future? A good example of foresight is found in the main streets of towns and cities built by the Mormons when they moved west. They were riding horses and driving wagons then, but they built broad, beautiful streets that easily accommodate the heavy automobile traffic of today.

We tend to cling too long to past successes, systems and methods. If it's working well today, look at it with the future in mind. We're seeing an accelerated rate of change unprecedented in history. And because so many businesses are still living in the past, there are yawning opportunities on practically every side.

How many businesses in your town haven't made a single change in twenty years? In some cases, that may work—for example, a fine old restaurant that is perhaps better now than ever because of its age and strict adherence to quality. But the business people of a community owe it to their customers and the community to keep abreast of excellence, to put part of their profits back into the business to accommodate changing times and tastes.

As James B. Conant said, "Each honest calling, each walk of life, has its own elite, its own aristocracy, based upon excellence of performance." That applies to every field of human endeavor.

We can develop habits of excellence in everything we do. We need to think in terms of excellence. We should demand it in what we buy and produce it in what we do.

Don't Do Something New, Do Something Better

"To become successful and outstanding at something, we don't have to come up with something new; we need only find ways of doing it better."

A friend of mine passed along to me an old, out-of-print book entitled The Magic of a Name. It's about the beginnings of the Rolls Royce automobile, written by Harold Nockolds and first published in 1938. It makes interesting reading. But the point that underlies the story is the fact that the originator of the Rolls Royce automobile, Henry Royce, was an indefatigable perfectionist. He didn't invent the automobile; he just wasn't happy with it. He thought it was too noisy, for one thing, and too heavy and inefficient.

And so it happened that in Manchester, England, on April 1, 1904, there came into being a motorcar unlike any other that had been seen or heard before. As Harold Nockolds put it, "Save for a gentle phut-phut, phut-phut from its exhaust pipe, it made no noise at all. There was no clatter from the engine, no grinding from the gears and back axle; and this comparative silence, in the days when the noise of a motorcar had been likened with deadly accuracy to 'an avalanche of tea trays,' was something indeed to marvel at.

"At the wheel of this miraculous machine sat a bearded figure of some 40 years of age, whose piercing eyes were lit with a gleam of triumphant concentration..." It was Henry Royce—later called Sir Henry, the perfectionist.

The trade name Rolls Royce went on to become synonymous with anything excellent or outstanding. The Spitfires of the Battle of Britain in 1940, which had Rolls Royce engines, were a big factor in winning that war. In fact, there's a beautiful stained-glass memorial window at the Rolls Royce aircraft engine plant, commemorating the pilots of the Royal Air Force, and it reads: "...who, in the Battle of Britain, turned the work of our hands into the salvation of our country."

But the point I want to make is that to become successful and outstanding at something, we don't have to come up with something new; we need only find ways of doing it better. If you'll think about it, it's the key element in virtually all success stories: Hilton Hotels, Holiday Inns, Kentucky Fried Chicken—the list is endless. If you want to succeed at something, just do it better.

Henry Royce was so wrapped up in the business of producing a superior automobile, he would forget to eat for days at a time and sleep on a bench in the foundry. A boy was hired to follow him around with a glass of milk and some bread so he wouldn't get sick from malnutrition.

He once heard a mechanic make the statement, "OK, that's good enough!" and they almost had to tie Royce down. Nothing was good enough for him, and his name and the name of his salesman-distributor-partner, C. S. Rolls, is a symbol of quality.

It's the same in every field—advertising to zinnia growing. Give it the kind of study and all-out dedication that Royce gave to his cars, and your name will someday stand like some of those I listed earlier.

I remember reading a few years ago about a Canadian farmer who sold his Stradivarius violin for, I think, somewhere in the neighborhood of $460,000. They're worth much more than that now. He sold it back to the same New York City dealer he'd bought it from many years before, and for the same price. The farmer sold his precious violin by the world's most famous violin craftsman because, as he put it, "I'm getting old, and I have no children to leave it to." By getting it back into the hands of the dealer, he knew that it would get into the hands of someone who would treasure it as he had.

Antonio Stradivari, the Italian violin maker, lived from 1644 to 1737. That's 93 years—a remarkable life span at a time when the average life expectancy was perhaps about 30. He lived for his work, and his work has lived on ever since. He worked alone, although later in life his sons helped him. His tools were rather primitive by our standards, but that was not important. He put himself and his genius into his work, and his instruments sang with a power and poignancy—a purity that, in the hands of fine violinists, delighted all who heard them.

When he was finished with an instrument, and he was sure that it was up to his personal standards, he signed his name to it. And still today, nearly 250 years later, his name is famous the world over, and his fine instruments still are delighting millions.

Throughout history, there have been many with similar standards of excellence in many fields—artists such as William Shakespeare and Leonardo da Vinci, craftsmen such as furniture maker Thomas Chippendale and silversmith Paul Revere. Everything they did was done exceptionally well—not because there was any pressure other than their own insistence on excellence beyond the reach of others of their time.

A good violinist can give you the names of other violin makers who are great and whose instruments are cherished, and it's the same in all fields. There are many thousands of craftsmen and women who will not turn out shoddy or even ordinary work and who would be glad to sign their names to their work.

The respect for excellence never changes. It still commands the highest price; it is still revered wherever we find it. And the people performing the work have gained for themselves two precious assets: (1) They have gained the kind of security that lasts a lifetime, of course. They never need worry about income. There is always a ready market for the best. And (2) their work is a source of satisfaction and joy to them. They derive deep satisfaction from being uncommon people turning out uncommonly fine products or services.

Would you be willing to sign your name to what you do? I think most of us would. Our work, after all, is a kind of mirror of ourselves.

Mastering Your Self-Image

Creating Your Greatest Image

Imagine that you are seated in a theater, looking at the curtain which hides the blank screen, as you wait for the movie to begin. What will this movie do for you? How will it affect you? What impact will it have on your life? Will you feel moved—perhaps even to tears? Will you laugh at a comedy, or feel terrified at the crises faced by the hero or heroine? Will you feel wonderful waves of love and compassion—or surges of resentment? All these feelings will pulse through you—and more. For the movie you will see is about the most fascinating person in the world—yourself.

In this theater, which is in the mind and heart of each of us, you are the producer, director, writer, actor or actress, hero and the villain. You are the film technician up in the booth—and the audience which reacts to this thrilling drama.

The exciting story unfolding upon this inner screen is one which is invented every second of your life —yesterday, tomorrow, but most important, right now.

You watch the image upon that screen and you invent the image upon that screen—right now. Will the story have a happy ending? Is it full of happiness and success or sorrow and failure? The story line is already there and the discerning eye can tell the direction in which the story will go.

But one realization can comfort you. Since you are the dramatist, the director and the actor, you can change the story as it unfolds. Now. This instant. And for your whole lifetime.

You can make this a success story. You can be the hero and conquer the villain. And you can make this a heart-warming story which will enrich the lives of all who know you—rather than a drab mechanical tale, a chronicle of boredom.

It's all inside you. It all depends on what you do with an image you carry inside you, an image which is your most important tool for good or for ill. It all depends on you—and your self-image.

The self-image is your own conception of the sort of person you are. It is a product of past experiences, successes and failures, humiliations and triumphs, and the way other people react to you, especially in early childhood. From these factors, and from others, you build up a picture of yourself which you believe is true. The picture may be false—and in many cases is false—but the important fact here is that you act just as if it were true. For all intents and purposes, it is true.

If it's a good, healthy, successful self-image, fine. But if it can stand some improvement, you can change it for the better and start getting the kind of results such a change will bring about.

The Positive Use of Imagination

"We form a mental picture of ourselves through experience, and we can change that picture the same way, through experience."

Our thoughts, habits, even our abilities must be those of the person we believe ourselves to be. We can set new limits in place of old ones. But we can't surpass the limits of our current self-image.

There's a story about a Wisconsin farmer who was walking through his fields one day when he stumbled over a little glass jug in his pumpkin patch. Out of curiosity he poked the young pumpkin through the neck of the jug, being careful not to break the vine, then he placed his little experiment back on the ground and walked away. When harvest time came, the farmer was working his way down a row of big ripe pumpkins, when he again came upon the glass jug. But this time it looked different. Picking it up he discovered that the young pumpkin he'd poked inside now completely filled its glass prison. Having no more room, it had stopped growing. The farmer broke the jug and held in his hand a runt pumpkin, less than half the size of all the other pumpkins and exactly the shape of the jug.

Well people aren't pumpkins, but our self-image is something like that jug. It determines the size and kind of person we become. The similarity ends with the fact that we can remove our self-imposed limitations by enlarging our self-image. We form a mental picture of ourselves through experience, and we can change that picture the same way, through experience. If the actual experience we need is not available to us, we can, according to self-image psychology, create that experience synthetically. Now scientists agree that the human nervous system is incapable of distinguishing between actual experience and the same experience imagined vividly and in complete detail.

Worry is a good example of this synthetic experience. When a person worries about something he projects himself mentally, emotionally, even physically, into a situation that hasn't even occurred.

The man who worries intensely about failure, finds himself experiencing the same reactions that accompany actual failure—fFeelings of anxiety, inadequacy and humiliation, and eventually headaches and an upset stomach. As far as his mind and body are concerned, he has failed. And if he worries about it long enough, if he concentrates on failure intensely enough, he will upset himself to the extent that he will fail and he'll get sick.

Now everything can be used in either of two ways: positively or negatively, constructively or destructively. Worry is the negative use of creative imagination. It's a negative synthetic experience. But most people apparently never realize that positive results, just as real as the negative results of worry, can be achieved through using our imagination constructively.

The man who worries about failure is unwittingly defeating himself. He is feeding his mind the wrong data. If he spent the same amount of time visualizing success as he spends in thinking about failure, he could reverse the process of synthetic experience. Instead of anxiety, he can develop confidence, self-assurance and poise, and a feeling of well-being would replace apprehension. By concentrating on the success he desires, by synthetically experiencing that success, he can expand his self-image into that of a person for whom success is normal, expected.

Why not practice holding the self-image of the person you most want to become? This is the person you can become. Use your spare moments to concentrate on your goals and the greater success you seek. Analyze your past successes and formulate ways your success can be increased in the future.

Put more into the positive use of your imagination than you ever put into its negative use, worry. You're merely reversing the same creative process. Now it's working for you instead of against you.

Nobody pokes us into the glass prisons beyond which we can't grow. But all too often, almost unknowingly, we set unnecessary limits for ourselves by holding a self-image that's restricted, inadequate for the full realization of our potentialities.

Each of us is at this moment the product of all his thoughts and experiences and environment up to this point. Through thought we can control to an almost unbelievable degree both our experience and our environment from here on. Whether or not we choose to direct our own course through life is entirely up to us. The important thing is to know that it can be done.

Four Steps to a Healthy Self-Image

One time the late Dr. Maxwell Maltz, whom we called Uncle Max, dropped by my office for a chat and lunch. We got to talking on his favorite subject—namely, how a person can come to grips with himself, develop a healthy self-image and find freedom in the world.

He told me he had discovered four important steps a person can take on a regular basis to form the new habits that can build a healthy, new self-image. As he talked at lunch, I made notes on a scrap of paper. Here are his four points in the order in which he gave them to me:

1. Forgive others, with no strings attached. You must clean the slate absolutely, forgive every person against whom you might hold some kind of grudge. You do this for your own sake, your own peace

of mind. We don't hurt others when we hold hatred toward them; we hurt ourselves—seriously. It can lead to serious illness. So, number one, forgive others—all others. If you cannot take this first step, you can forget the rest; you haven't grown up yet.

2. Forgive yourself. See yourself with kind eyes. Try to forget completely all the idiotic things you've done, the pain you've given to others, the embarrassments you've suffered, the mistakes you've made in the past. Again, wipe clean the slate, and forgive yourself. "Look in the mirror," he said, "and forgive yourself." Practice this, and you can actually pull it off. It's not easy to forgive ourselves. We tend to be much tougher on ourselves than we are on others. But the fact is, blame doesn't help; it's a destructive emotion.

3. See yourself at your best. As Dr. Maltz put it, "We can start the day in frustration or confidence; take your pick." The intelligent thing to do is to pick confidence, if it's at all possible. There are bad days, but it's better to begin the day in a confident mood than in a mood of frustration.

4. Keep up with yourself; don't worry about what others are doing or what others have done or have. Keep your pace; it's different from the pace of others. It's faster than some, slower than others. Forget the Joneses, and don't feel guilty about moving ahead of some of your contemporaries. The person who deliberately holds himself down to a slower pace, just to be one of the gang, is a fool. Keep up with yourself. Live the life you want to live; earn what you want to earn; do what you want to do. Live your own life, and don't be too concerned about how others are living theirs.

Four steps to a healthy self-image: (1) forgive others; (2) forgive yourself; (3) see yourself at your best—choose confidence instead of frustration; and (4) keep up with yourself—march to your own drummer, and don't worry about what others are doing.

Are you holding a grudge against someone in your life?
Are you able to look in the mirror and feel good about what you see?
Are you focused squarely on your own achievements instead of how much you achieve in relation to others?

How to Restore Your Self-Esteem

In his book, Psycho-Cybernetics, Dr. Maxwell Maltz wrote:"Of all the traps and pitfalls in life, self-dis-esteem is the deadliest, and the hardest to overcome; for it is a pit designed and dug by our own hands, summed up in the phrase, 'It's no use—I can't do it.'

"The penalty of succumbing to it is heavy—both for the individual in terms of material rewards lost, and for society in gains and progress unachieved.

"...On those days when we are most subject to... 'fearful unbelief' [in ourselves], when we most doubt ourselves and feel inadequate to our task— isn't it precisely then that we are most difficult to get along with?

"We simply must get it through our heads that holding a low opinion of ourselves is not a virtue but a vice. Jealousy, for example, which is the scourge of many a marriage, is nearly always caused by self-doubt. The person with adequate self-esteem doesn't feel hostile toward others, he isn't out to prove anything, he can see facts more clearly and isn't as demanding in his claims on other people.

"The housewife who felt that a facelift might cause her husband and children to appreciate her more really needed to appreciate herself more. Middle age, plus a few wrinkles and a few gray hairs, had caused her to lose her self-esteem. She then became supersensitive to innocent remarks and actions of her family."

And here's Dr. Maxwell Mate's prescription for restoring your self-esteem: "Stop carrying around a mental picture of yourself as a defeated, worthless person. Stop dramatizing yourself as an object of pity and injustice...

"The word esteem literally means to appreciate the worth of. Why do men stand in awe of the stars and the moon, the immensity of the sea, the beauty of a flower or a sunset and at the same time downgrade themselves? Did not the same Creator make man? Is not man himself the most marvelous creation of all? This appreciation of your own worth is not egotism unless you assume that you made yourself and should take the credit. Do not downgrade the product merely because you haven't used it correctly. Don't childishly blame the product for your own errors, like the schoolboy who said, 'This typewriter can't spell.'

"But the biggest secret of self-esteem is this: Begin to appreciate other people more; show respect for any human being merely because he is a child of God and therefore a thing of value. Stop and think when you're dealing with people. You're dealing with a unique, individual creation of the Creator of all. Practice treating other people as if they had some value—and surprisingly enough your own self-esteem will go up. For real self-esteem is not derived from the great things you've done, the things you own or the mark you've made—but an appreciation of yourself for what you are..."

If you're lacking in self-esteem, it's because you don't understand who or what you really are. If you'll take the time to learn more about yourself, you'll be delighted at what you discover.

Be an Actor, Not a Reactor

"Nobody is unhappier than the perpetual reactor. His center of emotional gravity is not rooted within himself, where it belongs, but in the world outside him."

Sydney Harris began his "Strictly Personal" column back in 1943. He had a number of books published—all of which I think I own and enjoy. One of my favorite columns was one in which he told about walking with a friend of his to the newsstand. His friend bought a paper, thanking the vendor politely. The vendor didn't even acknowledge it.

"A sullen fellow, isn't he?" Harris commented.

"Oh, he's that way every night," shrugged his friend.

"Then why do you continue being so polite to him?" Sydney Harris asked.

"Why not?" inquired his friend. "Why should I let him decide how I'm going to act?"

As Harris thought about the incident later, it occurred to him that the operating word was act. His friend acts toward people; many of us react toward them.

He has a sense of inner balance lacking in many of us frail and uncertain creatures; he knows who he is, what he stands for, and how he should behave. No boor is going to disturb the equilibrium of his nature; he simply refuses to return incivility with incivility, because then he would no longer be in command of his own conduct but a mere responder to others.

When we are enjoined in the Bible to return good for evil, we look upon this as a moral injunction, which it is; but it is also a psychological prescription for our emotional health.

Nobody is unhappier than the perpetual reactor. His center of emotional gravity is not rooted within himself, where it belongs, but in the world outside him. His spiritual temperature is always being raised or lowered by the social climate around him, and he is a mere creature at the mercy of these elements. Praise gives him a feeling of euphoria, which is false because it does not last and it does not come from self-approval. Criticism depresses him more than it should, because it confirms his own secretly shaky opinion of himself. Snubs hurt him and the merest suspicion of unpopularity in any quarter rouses him to bitterness or aggressiveness.

Only a saint, of course, never reacts. But a serenity of spirit cannot be achieved until we become the masters of our own actions and attitudes, and not merely reactors of other people's feelings. To let another determine whether we shall be rude or gracious, elated or depressed is to relinquish control over our own personalities, which is ultimately all we possess. The only true possession is self-possession.

Managing Your Inner World

The Advantages of Calmness

Here's something we should read or listen to once a day for the next 45 years. It was written back at the turn of the century by William George Jordan. He was editor of several magazines during his lifetime, including the Ladies Home Journal and The Saturday Evening Post. He wrote, "Calmness is the rarest quality in human life. It is the poise of a great nature, in harmony with itself and its ideals. It is the moral atmosphere of a life self-reliant and self-controlled. Calmness is singleness of purpose, absolute confidence and conscious power ready to be focused in an instant to meet any crisis.

"The sphinx is not a true type of calmness. Petrifaction is not calmness; it's death, the silencing of all the energies. While no one lives his life more fully, more intentionally and more consciously than the person who's calm, the fatalist is not calm.

"He's the coward's slave of his environment, hopelessly surrendering to his present condition, recklessly indifferent to his future. He accepts his life as a rudderless ship drifting on the ocean of time. He has no compass, no chart, no known port to which he is sailing. His self-confessed inferiority to all nature is shown in his existence of constant surrender. It is not calmness.

"The person who is calm has his course in life clearly marked on his chart. His hand is ever on the helm. Storm, fog, night, tempest, danger, hidden reefs—he's prepared and ready for them. He's made calm and serene by the realization that in these crises of his voyage, he needs a clear mind and a cool head. Then he has nothing to do but do each day the best he can by the light he has. That he will never flinch nor falter for a moment. That though he may have to tack and leave his course for a time, he'll never drift. He'll get back into the true channel. He'll keep ever headed toward his harbor. When he will reach it, how he will reach it matters not to him. He rests in calmness knowing he's done his best.

"When the worries and cares of the day fret you and begin to wear upon you and you chafe under the friction, be calm. Stop. Rest for a moment and let calmness and peace assert themselves. If you let these irritating outside influences get the better of you, you're confessing your inferiority to them by permitting them to dominate you. When the tongue of malice and slander, the persecution of inferiority tempt you to retaliate, when for an instant you forget yourself so far as to hunger for revenge, be calm. When the grey heron is pursued by its enemy, the eagle, it does not run to escape. It remains calm, takes a dignified stand and waits quietly facing the enemy unmoved. With a terrific force with which the eagle makes it attack, the boasted king of birds is often impaled and run through on the quiet, lance-like bill of the heron. No person in the world ever attempted to wrong another without being injured in return some way, somehow, sometime. Remain calm."

Now all of that was written at the turn of the century and in language that today might sound a bit affected and archaic. It's a good message. If ever there were a quality needed in the crisis-filled world of today, it's calmness and the kind of clear thinking calmness produces.

I wonder how improved our days would be if we would make it a point to go over that little message every morning.

What to Do When You Feel Inferior

The words "know thyself" are still two of the most important words ever put together. Do you know why people sometimes—quite often, as a matter of fact—have inferiority complexes? It's because their thinking is based on a false premise. The false premise is that they compare themselves to other people when this is actually something they should never do, since no two human beings are alike.

Everybody on earth is inferior to everyone else on earth in certain areas—and superior in other areas. A wise man once wrote, "To be human is to feel inferior." This is why the well-adjusted person, the person who knows himself, isn't bothered because he can't dance as well as so-and-so, or play golf or bridge as well as someone else. It would be completely impossible for any one human being to be as good at everything as every other human being.

The well-adjusted person admires others for their talents and abilities without feeling envious. In fact, he doesn't bring himself into comparison at all. He is happily resigned to the fact that he is not the best-looking, best-built, smartest, most talented, fastest, cleverest, funniest, most engaging person on earth.

Without even thinking about it, he seems to know that every person is a potpourri of strengths and weaknesses inherited from all his ancestors. No two of them were alike, but each one had a slightly different strong point with the standard collection of weaknesses.

In his fine book Psycho-Cybernetics, Dr. Maxwell Maltz wrote, "Inferiority and superiority are reverse sides of the same coin. The cure lies in realizing that the coin itself is spurious... you are not 'inferior' [or] are not 'superior.' You are simply you.

"You as a personality are not in competition with any other personality simply because there is not another person on the face of the earth like you, or in your particular class. You are an individual. You are unique. You are not 'like' any other person. You are not 'supposed' to be like any other person, and no other person is 'supposed' to be like you."

The doctor went on to write, "God did not create a standard person and in some way label that person by saying, 'This is it.' He made every human being individual and unique, just as He made every snowflake individual and unique.

"God created short people and tall people, large people and small people, skinny people and fat people, black, yellow, red and white people. He has never indicated any preference for any one size, shape or color. Abraham Lincoln once said, 'God must have loved the common people, for He made so many of them.' He was wrong. There is no 'common man'—no standardized, common pattern. He would have been nearer the truth had he said, 'God must have loved uncommon people, for He made so many of them.'"

Anybody could make himself feel inferior if he didn't realize that he is unlike any other human being who ever lived on earth. If he understands—fully and completely, intellectually and emotionally—that he is a unique and different individual, he cannot have an inferiority complex. How could he, since there's no standard against which to judge if every person is different? And every person is different.

Nothing on earth happens purely by accident. A person is living because he was meant to live, and he has talents and abilities that are totally his own—unique with him. His job, then, as a person, is to learn to know himself. If he does, he will like himself, for he will discover he's quite a person after all. He will recognize and accept the things he cannot do as well as some other people, but he will also understand and appreciate those things it has been given him to do well. He will accept himself for what he really is—one of a kind, as different from every other person on earth as his fingerprints or his signature.

A human being is the finest, the noblest, the most godlike creature ever produced on earth. Not to be thankful for such a gift is the worst kind of ignorance, and an inferiority complex is a phantom—a ghost with no real substance. In the light of knowledge, it disappears.

The Wonders of Praise

"We should try to find some way to commend those we love every day. Praise to a human being represents what sun light, water and soil are to a plant—the climate in which he grows best."

One day a few years back, I stopped my car for gas at a service station in Hollywood, California. While the middle-aged owner of the station cheerfully went about taking care of my car's needs, I noticed the station, although not new, was spotlessly clean. I was particularly surprised at the driveway—it was as clean as if my car was the first to use it.

I asked the owner how in the world he managed to keep the driveway spotless with dozens of cars dropping oil and tracking the dirt of the highways on it. He told me how a common product, sold in every supermarket, was in his estimation the best driveway cleaner in the world. He beamed in response to my comment on the way he kept his place of business. It was a valuable moment for both of us: I learned something of value, and he experienced the pleasure of honest praise.

The need for praise is basic to everyone. With it, a person blooms and grows. Without it, he tends to shrink and withdraw into himself.

We all know children need constant praise and encouragement. When a child brings home a piece of artwork that looks for all of the world like an unfortunate accident, he still expects an encouraging word. But his need for encouragement is no less than his mother's or father's. Far too many parents aren't getting any praise, or at least not nearly enough.

Understanding the importance of self-esteem and seeing the never-ending need for reaffirmation of a person's worth, we should make it our business to watch for honest opportunities to give praise—especially to the members of our families and those with whom we work.

There is a subtle but enormously valuable by-product or backfire to this sort of thing: In order to praise others, we need to look for the good. It forces us to concentrate on what's right with people and the things they do, rather than on what's wrong. It focuses our attention on the positive side of the ledger and, as a result, makes us happier, more productive and more pleasant to be around. Then, too, people like those who praise them and recognize their value. When we give praise, we attract a larger circle of friends. And finally, giving praise is the best known way to receive it. It's hard for anyone to compliment a chronic grouch.

Whenever you hear someone say, "Nobody appreciates me; nobody gives me credit for all I do," the chances are he is so wrapped up in himself and in getting happiness from others, he has completely forgotten how to give.

We should try to find some way to commend those we love every day. Praise to a human being represents what sunlight, water and soil are to a plant—the climate in which he grows best. He does not just want it; he needs it as he needs the air he breathes.

Moliére said, "The most agreeable recompense which we can receive for things which we have done is to see them known, to have them applauded with praises which honor us."

Why You Don't Have to Be a Loner

My father was a regular and avid reader of the old Zane Grey books (that's how I got hold of them) which invariably, or so it seemed, began with a stranger riding into town. He was tall, lean and always covered with alkali dust. Cool, gray eyes peered evenly from under straight brows, and his hand hovered near the six-gun strapped to his thigh.

He had no friends or acquaintances and seemed to like it that way. He was a man of few words and kept his own counsel. His world consisted of little more than himself and his horse and the bad guy he was usually after.

It makes a good story, and everyone seems to be intrigued by this sort of man of mystery. But, in real life, it's a lonely way to live, especially since few of us have horses these days.

You cannot know too many people. And we'd all be better off if we could overcome our natural timidity where strangers are concerned, if we could open up more.

As a friend of mine who has attained an unusually high position in the world says, "Open the doors and windows of your mind and heart to others, and you'll reap a wonderful harvest of friends."

Many of us have a tendency to speak or smile only after another person has spoken or smiled at us first. We tend to be reactive instead of proactive. It reminds me of the person who sat in front of the cold stove and said, "Give me heat, and then I'll add the wood."

The world just doesn't work that way. With a little effort, a person can form the habit of smiling and saying "hello" first. Nineteen times out of 20, you'll get a favorable response.

I know a man who was the foreign representative for an American electronics firm. He was something of an introvert, and on his frequent flights all over the world, he'd bury himself in a book to keep from having to talk to the passenger next to him.

On one trip, a friendly Englishmen managed to get a conversation started with him. It turned out the Englishman was on an electronics- buying trip to the States, and a large order resulted. Then and there he decided to change his attitude toward strangers. While it may not result in another business deal, he's meeting all sorts of interesting people and making many new friends.

We should never say, "He's not my kind of person" or "That's not my sort of crowd." Wherever there's a human being, there's a human story, and it's invariably interesting and informative. It stretches our minds, broadens our horizons and adds to our collection of acquaintances and friends.

And all it takes is a smile, the word "hello" and a comment or two to get a conversation going. The chances are that the other person is as anxious to add to his collection of friends as we are. But he or she may be just a little on the timid side, as many people are in the presence of strangers. It's true: You can't know too many people, and as we grow older, we should cultivate all the friends we can.

The person who shuts others out of his life ends up shutting himself in. Try my friend's advice. Throw open the doors and windows of your mind and heart to others, and reap a harvest of friends.

Who wants to live with a horse?

The Strength to Be Happy

"It is in the expectation of happiness that much of happiness itself is found. And it takes courage to expect happiness."

On the occasion of his 75th birthday, Mark Van Doren, the American writer, poet, critic and educator, was interviewed by a reporter for Life magazine, and one of the things he said stuck in my mind. I saved this.

He said, "It takes courage to be happy." Now in those six words he said a great deal. Any person can wallow in misery and self-pity. It's easy to rail against the world and its injustices. Easier still to sit down and do nothing like the famous hound dog with its tail in the crack, but it takes courage to be happy.

When he said it takes courage to be happy, he didn't mean happiness today or tomorrow or a week from next Thursday. He meant to be happy as a general, relatively constant way of living. To be a happy person as opposed to a generally unhappy person. And it does take courage, courage of a high order. The world is full, it seems, of the "it's too good to last" or "it's just my kind of luck" people who expect bad luck and rejection as confidently as they expect the sun to rise the next morning. They are people who were given bleak and disappointing starts in life.

Tolstoy said, "Man is meant for happiness and this happiness is in him, in the satisfaction of the daily needs of his existence." And La Rochefoucauld said, "Happiness is in the taste and not in the things themselves. We're happy from possessing what we like, not from possessing what others like."

In a passage that I think is very revealing, Jane Austin wrote, "No temper could be more cheerful than hers, or possess in a greater degree that sanguine expectation of happiness, which is happiness itself." It is in the expectation of happiness that much of happiness itself is found. And it takes courage to expect happiness.

Balzac wrote, "All happiness depends on courage and work." I've had many periods of wretchedness, but with energy and, above all, with illusions, I've pulled through them all.

My old favorite, George Santayana, said, "Happiness is the only sanction of life. Where happiness fails, existence remains a mad and lamentable experiment."

Bertrand Russell put it well when he said, "Contempt for happiness is usually contempt for other people's happiness and is an elegant disguise for hatred of the human race."

The Chinese philosopher, Lin Yutang, said, "I've always been impressed by the fact that the most studiously avoided subject in Western philosophy is that of happiness."

A French philosopher said much the same as did Mark Van Doren. He said, "To live, we must conquer incessantly. We must have the courage to be happy."

We've all seen people seriously handicapped in one way or another who are wonderfully cheerful and happy people. And we've wondered how they do it. We've said to ourselves, "I don't think I could be happy if I had his or her affliction." These people are happy because they are courageous, and because they don't like the alternative.

Liberate the Power of Your Mind

The Truth ofthe Mind

In John Milton's Paradise Lost, Satan says, "The mind is its own place and in itself can make a heaven of hell, a hell of heaven." When Satan says this, he does not realize its truth or the ironic fact that his hate-filled mind has indeed made for him "a hell of heaven," but cannot make a "heaven of hell." And Satan, in this great work by Milton, has lots of company. Read that line again. "The mind is its own place. And in itself can make a heaven of hell, a hell of heaven."

No one knows or can even guess at the uncounted millions who are living in a virtual heaven of opportunity in every department of their lives, and yet turn it into a living hell. They have every opportunity to love, and yet they hate. They have every opportunity to trust, and yet they mistrust.

They have every opportunity to work and give of themselves. Yet they hold back in the suspicious dread that they're being cheated. They have every opportunity to share in the wealth of the richest society since the beginning of the world, yet they sit and grumble because it's not given to them for being lazy and ignorant. They're ignorant even though they are surrounded on every side, with a free and abundant opportunity to learn to their full capacity. The public libraries in their towns and cities are half empty waiting in vain for them to enter and learn. The schools and their parents begged them to stay in schools, to qualify themselves for a fast changing world, but they drop out.

But it's not just the sum of these that the mind turns a possible heaven into a hell. In every walk of life, in every strata of society, you can see the bitter, desolate expressions, the hollow eyes, and listless hands of those whose minds have condemned them to the tortures of the damned or a life of endless tedium and ennui.

The Roman, Seneca, put it this way, "A great, a good, and a right mind is a kind of divinity lodged in flesh and may be the blessing of a slave as well as of a prince. It came from heaven and to heaven it must return. And it's a kind of heavenly felicity which a pure and virtuous mind enjoys, in some degree even on earth."

And Chaucer said, "My mind to me a kingdom is. Such present joys therein I find that it excels all other bliss that earth affords. Every person's mind is his kingdom. And he as the reigning monarch decides what kind of a kingdom it is to be; bleak or bountiful, rich or poor, interesting or dull, happy or unhappy."

And the most important moment of our lives is when we understand that we can fashion our minds as we will.

What stubbing, plowing, digging and harrowing is to land, that thinking, reflecting, examining is to the mind. We know the soil is rich. The harvest is up to us.

The Remedy for an Anxious Mind

Few people in the history of the world had more responsibility in their hands, or greater crises to face, than Winston Churchill during the years when he was Prime Minister of England. He was able to stand up to the kinds of problems that would have killed a dozen lesser men because of a system he developed early in his life—a systems for relieving worry and tension. It can be invaluable for us today.

He wrote, "Many remedies are suggested for the avoidance of worry and mental over-strain by persons who, over prolonged periods, have to bear exceptional responsibilities and discharge duties upon a very large scale. Some advise exercise, and others, retreat. Some praise solitude, and others, gaiety. No doubt all these may play their part according to the individual temperament. But the element which is constant and common in all of them is change.

"Change is the master key. A man can wear out a particular part of his mind by continually using it and tiring of it, just in the same way as he can wear out the elbows of his coat. There is, however, this difference between the living cells of the brain and inanimate articles: One cannot mend the frayed elbows of a coat by rubbing the sleeves or shoulders; but the tired parts of the mind can be rested and strengthened not merely by rest but by using other parts. It is not enough merely to switch off the lights which play upon the main and ordinary field of interest; a new field of interest must be illuminated.

"It is no use saying to the tired 'mental muscles'—if one may coin such an expression, 'I will give you a good rest,' 'I will go for a long walk,' or, 'I will lie down and think of nothing.' The mind keeps busy just the same. If it has been weighing and measuring, it goes on weighing and measuring. If it has been worrying, it goes on worrying. It is only when new cells are called into activity, when new stars become the lords of the ascendant, that relief, repose, refreshment are afforded."

That's good advice, isn't it? Trying to shut down the mind by turning a mental switch is virtually impossible. But turning it to something new will let the tired part refresh itself. This is why golf, tennis, fishing and other participation sports are important to good health. You can be a spectator at a sporting event and still worry, but you can't play and worry.

The trick—and this is the hard part—is to force yourself to do something else when your mind is full of worry or tired from one kind of work. This knack must be developed, and Winston Churchill developed it. During the darkest days of World War II, when the Allies were losing on every front, Churchill could rest his mind by turning it to some entirely new activity and giving it his complete attention. He did this just as you or I would take the medicine prescribed by a doctor; he did it to keep well. He could then return to the problems of the world with his keen mind rested and refreshed. Doctors have said many times that it isn't overwork that kills people; it's over-worry until the mind becomes discouraged and just gives out.

Dr. Charles Mayo, said, "Worry affects the circulation—the heart, the glands, the whole nervous system. I have never known anyone who died from overwork, but many who died from doubt."

Learning About Thinking

"There is a force—call it what you will—that seems to come to the aid of those who develop a healthy attitude about thinking and getting ideas and moving toward difficult goals. Sometimes we call it 'getting lucky,' but that's not really what it is."

There was an English schoolmaster who made it a point to ask every child coming to his school, "Do you know why you need to go to school?" The children would usually just stare back at him, as overwhelmed by him as by the question. And he would answer, "You go to school so you will learn to think."

My old friend Louis Atkinson of Tooele, Utah, called me recently and told me he had talked to his 3-year-old son, Craig, about that and about the importance of learning to think. The subject of thinking and what it can mean is brought up often between the two of them when they're together, working in the garden or in the evening. And Louis said, "One night we went into Craig's room to get him ready for bed, and little Craig commented, "Thinking helps make you happy. And that's very important!"

There was quick agreement there, and the young philosopher went to bed.

Louis Atkinson is a high school teacher, and he used the story with his students.

Yes, thinking helps make you happy, and that's very important. And the more we learn, the greater our experiences, the more possibilities we put into the thinking raw material pile. And thinking is the father of creation.

Thinking, to the person making plans, is the navigator of his future life. And, yes, that's very important; but there's more there, too.

Louis asked me over the phone if I'd seen the motion picture Star Wars. I said that I had not, but I told him that I had seen, at my son's urging, the two sequels. "Do you remember that bit in there about 'The Force?'" he asked.

I said that I did remember, but more than that, I had been affected by the term as much as he had.

There is a force—call it what you will—that seems to come to the aid of those who develop a healthy attitude about thinking and getting ideas and moving toward difficult goals. Sometimes we call it "getting lucky," but that's not really what it is. It's a momentum—a force—that, like a good wave, will give you all sorts of help once you're really on your way.

It takes a long time to develop sometimes, but when it comes, we seem to be able to feel it. It gives us confidence and at the same time, a sense of appreciation, a sense of gratitude. It is never accompanied by cockiness. In fact, I doubt if it can come to the shallow person.

I'm sure little Craig will learn about that, too, as he gets a bit older. But he's already big where it counts—he's learning about thinking.

Think It Through

Many years ago, there were some very good small books published, written by an Irishman named William T. Reilly, Ph.D. One of them was titled The Twelve Rules for Straight Thinking, published back in 1947.

He reminds us that we cannot stop our minds from jumping to conclusions. Minds tend to do that. And often, in our desire to capture the spotlight in our business or social conversations, to make a good impression on the boss maybe, and prove we're in possession of quick and alert minds, we tend to jump to hasty conclusions which, in more sober consideration, turns out to be the dumbest idea heard in that board room, or conference room, or social gathering, in fifty years.

The trouble is that most of us easily mistake a quick solution as the best or only solution, whereas a quick answer is all too often a poor one and may often be the wrong one which doesn't solve the problem at all. It might create new problems.

Now while we cannot keep our minds from jumping to conclusions, we can protect ourselves from the damaging effects of conclusion-jumping by using a delayed response to any serious question. That is, give ourselves time to think it through, as we should.

The delayed response is actually the first sign of intelligence—the first sign of thought. In fact, any time a person comes to you with a problem you feel you should help with, say, "Let me think about that. I don't like to make quick decisions on important matters." You're bound to make a more favorable impression.

Younger men and women in a company often feel that they have to come up with instantaneous and miraculous solutions to problems posed by their superiors. Nothing could be further from the truth. An executive has a great deal of respect for the person who says, "I want to think about this a while before I give you my best opinion."

Now you have the time to think, to back up and go through the four simple steps in straight thinking. Step one: Separate facts from opinions and analyze the facts. Step two: Define the real problem and consider possible solutions. Step three: Secure evidence on possible solutions. And step four: Weigh the evidence and arrive at a sound conclusion. You're still going to make wrong decisions even with the best system, but you'll make fewer. Ad-libbing your way through life is risky business and I think old Doc Reilly has some excellent suggestions there.

When you consider a problem, think vertically for a while, that is, conventionally. If you can't come up with answers that haven't already been tried and found wanting that way, think horizontally—in totally new directions. That is, instead of just drilling the one hole deeper, look for new ground to drill. You might find just the wonderful solution out in left field. Then your superior will take credit for the idea. No, I'm just kidding. It's really the best way to go about it.

Life presents us with one problem after another, all the days of our lives. Most of them don't require a great deal of thought. When they do, the delayed response is a very good idea.

How to Find New Ideas

If a business firm could find better ways to mine the brains of the people working for it, it could undoubtedly move ahead much faster and do a much better job of cutting costs and improving profits.

I read something in the Wall Street Journal some time back about an electronics firm that stops everything at two o'clock in the afternoon for a think session attended by its top design engineers. The doors are closed, the telephones are shut off in the conference room used for the purpose, and they exchange ideas—spark each other with their thoughts of the day. Knowing the think session is coming up every day, each of the participants tries to come up with an idea or two between sessions.

A shoe company has a private "reflection period" for each company official, plus brainstorming sessions every two weeks. An official said, "It's amazing what comes out of those sessions." And another company takes a dozen top executives out of town every few months to discuss major problems.

Company officials on a business trip are often amazed at the wonderful ideas they get as soon as they leave the routine of their offices and get off together. Companies that worry about their people getting to the office on time, and putting in a full day's work, might be surprised and delighted at the profit-producing ideas these same people might get if they were sent off on a trip to another town for a few days, and asked to get some good ideas.

Rosabeth Moss Kanter tells the story of Clarence Birdseye, the inventor of frozen vegetables. Birdseye had a produce business in New York at the turn of the century. At that time, she says, the conventional wisdom about the best way to manage a business was not so different from the conventional wisdom of today: It was "mind the store;" be there all the time. But Birdseye didn't do that. He was an adventurer, an explorer, as well as an entrepreneur, and on one of his adventure trips, he made an expedition to Labrador. It was there that he noticed that when the Eskimos froze caribou meat in the dry Arctic air, it was still flavorful and tender when thawed and cooked months later. He adapted that idea to his produce business, and, of course, he built a great company.

Kanter says that if we're to be innovative, "We need to make periodic expeditions to Labrador. Get away; go somewhere different; get your thinking shaken up; see something that's different from everyday reality, something that might suggest a creative new twist on the very problem you're trying to solve." She says, "Most organizations have budgets to send people to professional meetings. I've started to recommend that those companies use those budgets to send people to professional meetings in some other field—not their own—so they'll encounter new and different perspectives."

Ideas have a way of coming when we're away from the routine of our jobs. But it takes an awareness of the value of ideas, and the fun of getting good ones. The experts in this field say that most people, even executives, seldom think very much between crises. That is, they use their minds defensively; they use them only when they're attacked with a problem. They seldom indulge in creative thinking between crises. This is a pity. A few minutes a day devoted to deliberate thinking can work wonders for the mind, the person and the business, and the home and family life as well.

You might give it some thought. There are gold mines between all those ears. It costs a lot of money to educate and train a person these days. It's a shame to employ only his physical presence and let all those wonderful brains go to pasture.

Set aside a specific time of day for yourself when you do nothing but collect your thoughts.

Have paper and pencil handy so that you can record your ideas as you discover them.

Every so often, try to remove yourself from your familiar surroundings and everyday routines to gain a new perspective on your life.

The Genius of Daydreaming

A teacher, busy with instructions for the next subject, noticed that one child was gazing out the window. She stopped talking, and the entire class turned to look at the daydreamer. Finally, the child realized everything was too quiet, except for an occasional snicker from another student, and turned to face the teacher.

"What have you been doing?" asked the teacher.

"I was thinking," the child replied.

The teacher snapped back, "Don't you know you're not supposed to think in school!"

Whereupon, after a moment of stunned silence, the children burst into helpless laughter, much to the teacher's embarrassment.

I saw the most interesting little cartoon the other day. It depicted a class of prehistoric children, all dressed in small bearskins, sitting on the floor of a cave. Before them was the teacher, wearing a large bearskin. He had sketched a picture of a deer on the wall of the cave and had drawn a small x where the heart would be. He was apparently teaching a class on how to hunt a deer.

One of the small children, however, wasn't paying attention. He was sitting like the others, but he was turned toward the viewer and was whittling with a small stone knife. The teacher was giving him a bad time about not paying attention and said, "Don't you want to keep up with the other children?" And then you see that the child is whittling an airplane.

When children are thinking, they are performing the highest function of the human creature, and it can happen that they're thinking on a much higher and better plane than they would be if they were paying attention to what is presently going on.

Daydreaming is not necessarily, as popular opinion would have it, a waste of time—far from it. Daydreams have led to many of the benefits we enjoy today—books, motion pictures, conveniences of modern society, scientific breakthroughs. No one knows very much about the human brain, but when it's allowed to fly out the window and come up with what it will, it can occasionally come up with some real winners.

Of course, too much daydreaming, without engineering the good ideas down to earth and putting them into use, can lead to trouble. It might be said that there is a time to daydream and a time to get to work. Certainly, if all the children in a classroom were allowed to daydream at will, nobody would ever learn anything. But we should be careful when we jump on children for thinking instead of paying attention; of the two, thinking is usually the more important, and there's altogether too little of it these days.

It seems that we tend to daydream about subjects that are important to us, and, by so doing, we lay the groundwork for future activity and accomplishment. Daydreaming can also prevent illness from too much negative stress. Every serviceman who has ever gone into combat knows how daydreaming in quiet moments can take one back to one's home and family and friends. For a few moments, the war is blotted out; the anxiety and fear of injury or instant extinction are forgotten; and the world is back in order. There's no doubt that daydreaming has an important therapeutic effect.

Daydreaming is one of our greatest gifts, and we'd be much poorer without it. And when you peek into your youngster's room and find him quietly gazing out the window or at the ceiling, it might be a good idea just to leave him alone for a while.

Keeping Ideas Within Reach

"Once you know what you want to do, what you want to accomplish, you will, if your desire's strong enough, find a way to accomplish it."

An interesting and important bit of information we should keep in mind is that the idea we're looking for is never beyond our reach. I have a little sign near my typewriter that reads, "I've had my solutions for a long time. But I do not yet know how I'm to arrive at them."

It was written by the great nineteenth-century German inventor Karl Goss. "I have had my solutions for a long time. But I do not yet know how I am to arrive at them." It means we know the point at which we intend to arrive. We just don't yet know how to get there.

Thomas Edison knew what he was looking for when he decided to invent an electric light. Once that decision was reached he was able, long and difficult as the solution was, to find the ideas he needed. You might say, "Well, not everyone would be able to do what Thomas Edison did." You'd be right, because not everyone was looking for a way to develop an electric light. In fact, people were quite content with the lights they had, just as they were perfectly happy with the horse and buggy and ridiculed early attempts to produce a workable motorcar. The point that's important to remember here is that once you know what you want to do, what you want to accomplish, you will, if your desire's strong enough, find a way to accomplish it. And the process is not all that difficult to understand.

When you make up your mind to achieve some end, whatever it happens to be, you're excited about the idea. It fills your mind and it's strengthened by your emotional involvement. How to achieve it becomes something of an obsession and you find yourself thinking about it all the time. As you do, you're planting it, charged with the power of your emotion, deep in your subconscious where a great and largely mysterious mental computer goes to work on it. It works on a problem below the conscious level and looks for the solution much, I suppose, like a great electronic scanner, looking at thousands of possibilities, exploring memory, looking at new permutations. From time to time, it sends up a tentative solution. When it does, you shouldn't be too quick to accept it. You should make a note of it always and stick it in the idea file, but keep pushing the problem back down into the big tumbler. From time to time, new solutions or partial solutions will appear. Perhaps you'll try some of them and some won't work.

Finally, if you keep sending the problem back down, the glorious non-collapsible big idea you're looking for will finally be extruded, and that's it, the light works, it's the answer. From then on, it's a matter of refinement and variation.

I think the important thing to remember here, is that you can get the idea you're looking for if you follow this method and stick with it. And it doesn't necessarily mean that the idea will come to you. It can come to someone else, and through him or her to you. That's what happened to Charles Darwin and many other investigators. As long as you find the solution to the problem, you don't care where it comes from. You can get just the idea you've been looking for, for months, even years, from a casual acquaintance at a business luncheon, or from something you see in a magazine or a store window, or read in a good book. But the idea you're looking for is never beyond your reach. Hunting for ideas you need, to reach the goal you've set for yourself, can be an interesting and exciting journey—a journey into meaning and discovery. And it can make living a lot of fun.

The Key to Motivation

People are forever asking, "How do you motivate a person?" People in management, teachers and parents ask, "How does one go about bringing out more of the best in people—for their own good as well as the good of society?"

The answer to that question was given in the seventeenth century by the French scientist and philosopher, René Descartes. I forget in which of his works he said it, but I remember that he said, "Imagination is the key to motivation." And truer words were never put together.

If you would motivate a person, teach him the importance of imagination. You have only to think back to the times in your own life when you've been filled with excitement and interest and enthusiasm. Hasn't it almost always been at times when you've come up with a great idea, when your imagination is all fired up?

Imagination is a sign of youthfulness in any person—young or old. In fact, keeping the imagination active will help a person remain young in everything but years, all his life.

All right—how to stimulate the imagination of others: With some people it isn't necessary; they're just naturally imaginative people who were raised in families in which imagination played a major role. But I think it's safe to say that these people, adults I'm talking about, are rather rare. Every business has people, wonderfully talented, who can take an idea and work wonders with it. But they don't come up with ideas themselves and let's face it: most people don't.

The way to stimulate imagination is to establish the climate for it. It is, simply, to ask for it. One way is to point out to people that their jobs will change remarkably for the better in the years ahead, as new and better ideas come along. And ask them if they can come up with some of those ideas now. Why wait for someone else to come up with the good ideas; maybe we can come up with them first.

Another way is to make sure people are made a part of new plans, that they feel their ideas and contributions are needed and important, that they're vital members of the team.

A few years ago, a large oil company asked its salespeople to give some thought and come up with some answers to this question: What will the service station be like ten years from now? Management was amazed and delighted by the answers. These people calling on service stations everyday were eminently qualified to give some intelligent and exciting answers to that question.

The same sort of thing will work with any group and it will add new interest to the job. Suggestion systems are fine and have made great contributions, but they're largely passive. The best way to stimulate ideas and imagination is to ask questions—to ask for help.

As for management people themselves, studies seem to indicate that they seldom bother to think very much between crises. They, too, need stimulation in the imagination department.

René Descartes was right. The key to motivation is imagination; whether we're motivating others or ourselves. When imagination is working, boredom and stagnation disappear.

Capturing Your Ideas

Ideas, and especially the really good ones, are fragile, evanescent things. They flit into the mind at moments of leisure—while bathing, taking a walk, lying in a hammock, or driving to work and they stun us with their brilliance, with their perfection. They are like one of nature's creatures, perfect in coloration and form. But they are just as wary, too. They can vanish as quickly as they came, to disappear into the incredible and labyrinthine forest of the mind. And they can become inextricably lost, never to be seen again.

I keep paper all over my house, and writing instruments. But what do you do with an idea that comes to you when you're washing your hair, covered with lather in the shower? In my car I have a battery-operated electronic secretary into which I can, in an instant, dictate an idea, a thought. On longer trips, I'll fill an entire cassette. People passing me in their cars see me talking into a small black device and no doubt think I'm a member of the CIA or some other arcane organization—or maybe just out of my mind.

But I have come to learn that ideas are the world's most valuable things. Ideas are the product of the human mind, the world's acknowledged winner in the "most valuable" category.

Ideas are a form of energy and they need to be converted into something productive or useful, or interesting or entertaining, or, like more than 99.9% of the sun's rays, they will stream beyond into the endless void. And to stop and begin the conversion process, the idea must be translated into words, like radio signals, on a piece of paper. Then, the idea must be thought about, studied, and finally formed into physical reality. Everything we see about us was once an invisible idea. I remember thinking about that one time many years ago when I drove my car over the Oakland Bay Bridge connecting San Francisco and Oakland, California. What an incredible structure. And it began as an idea in the mind of a single human being.

People tend to underestimate their own ideas, simply because they have formed lifetime habits of underestimating themselves. Even in the top echelons of business there is a tendency to follow the other guy, because we tend to give the other guy credit for being smarter and more creative than we are.

And, the experts tell us that most people don't get many ideas because they have never learned their importance or the means of developing them.

To develop good ideas, one needs an active, inquiring, creative mind. She needs to develop the habit of questioning everything, realizing that nothing is as good as it will be and that we live in a state of constant change.

Ideas Alone Aren't Enough

I ran across a quotation I like. It reads, "Every time one man puts an idea across, he finds ten men who thought of it before he did—but they only thought of it." There has never been a monopoly when it comes to getting good ideas, but the number of people who will take the raw material of a good idea and from it fashion reality in the world is small, indeed.

We have a tendency to think that when we get a good idea, we have come up with something wholly new. And, of course, this is quite possible. But the odds are that the same idea has flashed across the minds of many others—hundreds, perhaps thousands. And this is not important. An idea that remains only an idea and nothing more is of little or no value. It doesn't do anything and for all practical purposes might just as well have remained unborn.

It's true, as Victor Hugo put it—"Nothing in this world is so powerful as an idea whose time has come." And it's also true that there is nothing in this world of less value than an idea about which nothing is done.

People often write to large companies with unsolicited ideas—which, incidentally, most large companies wish they would not do. The same idea may have been suggested by others, including people within the company, for many years. Finally, let's say the company actually does something about the idea. It spends its brains, time, materials and money to produce the product and immediately is deluged by angry letters each claiming that the idea has been stolen and intimating that the company rose to its present prominence and success by stealing ideas from the helpless "little" people of the world.

It's a funny thing about people and their ideas. Most of the time the idea is the only thing the person is willing to risk. He'll risk that because it didn't cost anything. But ask him to back his faith in his idea with every nickel he can lay his hands on or borrow, and you often find his attitude undergoing a significant change.

This is a good test of ideas; it's also a good test of whether your idea is really the one you've been looking for—your big idea: if you're willing to stake everything you can scrape up and borrow on it, maybe it's a good idea.

Don't be too concerned with trying to come up with an idea nobody has thought of before. Here you're competing with millions. Instead, be concerned with taking an existing, already successful idea and building your good ideas upon it. And don't get in too big a hurry. One of the hardest things to learn is how long it takes to become really, substantially, solidly successful. Ninety-nine times out of a hundred, it takes many years, even when the idea is great.

It is believed that the most fortunate people on earth are those who have found an idea that's bigger than they are, that fills their lives with constant interest, challenge and struggle. It might be growing better tomatoes or kids, doing something for the underprivileged, painting, writing a book or starting a new business. But there's nothing better than an idea we do something about.

If you find yourself running out of ideas, and things in which you can find interest, bestir yourself. Go sit on a rocky ledge and think, or buy a book, or take a long walk. Don't desert the world of ideas, and don't be content with the ideas only. Do something about them.

Do you keep a list of your ideas handy?

When was the last time you acted on them?

Make it a goal to choose one idea a week or a month to investigate, improve or act upon.

See if there are ways to build upon the original ideas you generate.

The Practice of Being Human

Laughter: The Uniquely Human Cure

There's a marriage counselor who has had a lot of success in saving marriages on the brink of dissolution by suggesting that whenever one of the partners starts an argument, the other partner should make him or her laugh. Real trouble begins when laughter goes out of a marriage.

One husband said, "How in the world can I get her to laugh? She hasn't laughed in three years."

"What made her laugh three years ago?" the counselor asked.

The husband thought for a moment and then said, "I fell on the ice in front of the house."

"Then you've got the answer. Whenever she starts an argument, fall down and make her laugh."

This made them both laugh, of course, and the doctor went on to suggest that the husband think of anything that might be silly enough to get them both laughing. "Stick celery in your ears ... anything."

I remember many years ago we were rehearsing a dramatic radio series in Chicago and the rehearsal had been going badly. The script wasn't the best; a couple of the actors and actresses weren't happy with their parts; the director was getting edgy; it was a cold, snowy day. And just as we were about to moodily try to do the dress rehearsal, since time was slipping away from us, one of the actors went out of the studio for a moment and returned suddenly with loud moans, staggering crazily, his eyes crossed and with the ends of a pencil protruding from his ears. He had broken a long, yellow pencil in half, and had stuck the broken ends into his ears; from one ear the end with the eraser and from the other the pointed end. Grisly as the sight was, appearing as it did that someone had pushed a pencil through his head, it threw us—including the director, the engineers, the sound effects people and the musicians—into fits of uncontrolled laughter until we were helpless with tears running down our faces.

From that point on we were all right and the show was one of the best we did that year. Laughter is wonderfully therapeutic. If your kids get into an argument, give them each a cloth, or paper towel and put them on opposite sides of the same window with instructions to clean it. No matter how angry they may have been, just looking through the glass at each other cleaning the window will soon have them howling with laughter, the argument forgotten.

There was a doctor who made it a practice to look for pictures in magazines and newspapers of people laughing—laughing hard. He cut them out and pasted them in a scrapbook. When the book was full, he took it to the hospital and let the nurses pass it around the wards. You can't look at other people laughing without laughing yourself, and the effect on the patients and nurses was wonderful.

Perhaps this is why good comedians are among the highest paid of the world's performers: people need to laugh. You can't feel worried or depressed when you're convulsed with laughter. It seems to have a beneficial effect on the human mind and organs. We're the only creatures on earth who can laugh; and the only ones with enough problems to need it.

I remember reading about a husband who, when he's had a nerve-wracking day at the office, would come home with his hat on backwards. If his wife had had a bad day, she'd wear her apron backwards. In either case, it would start them laughing and clear the air.

The Futility of Criticism

"When we criticize another person, we set ourselves above him; we become the figure of authority and place the other person in an inferior position. The best rule to use when criticism springs to your mind is to wait."

I've got some advice here for you today on how to become hated; how you can stir up resentments and ill will that will simmer and hang on for years. All you have to do is...criticize!

No matter what a person has done, or how he lives his life, he doesn't want nor does he feel he needs criticism. This is why a criminal can fly into a rage against witnesses, prosecuting attorneys and judges. Although he may have committed the most serious crime, and knows full well that he has committed it, he deeply resents those who by their actions are critical of him.

The unfaithful husband or wife will, as often as not, fly into a wounded, self-pitying snit when confronted with evidence of his or her infidelity.

I'm not saying that people should not be criticized for criminal or moral misconduct. But I am saying that criticism makes a person try to justify himself; it wounds his precious pride, hurts his sense of importance and thoroughly arouses his resentment against the person or persons doing the criticizing. When we criticize another person, we set ourselves above him; we become the figure of authority and place the other person in an inferior position. We automatically put the other person on the defensive. And even if he doesn't say anything and accepts the criticism meekly, it rankles.

When the husband at the bridge table says to his wife, "Well, my dear, you bid that hand like a certified moron," she might not say anything—she might not say anything at the moment, that is, but she's secretly praying for a miracle that will deliver a sawed-off shotgun into her hands. The other players squirm in embarrassment and what does it accomplish? As Junius wrote, "It behooves the minor critic, who hunts for blemishes, to be a little distrustful of his own sagacity."

The best rule to use when criticism springs to your mind is to wait. Wait a while and try to look for the reasons behind the act you would criticize. It's also a good time to ask oneself, "Who am I to be criticizing others? Am I really all that great and pure and all-knowing and perfect?" By all means wait until the heat of anger has dissipated. This is one of the world's most difficult things to do and it takes a very mature person to master the wisdom and self-control to withhold criticism. But it's the way to greatness and one of the best-known ways to earn the respect and/or love of others.

People know when they've done something wrong or foolish and they usually know that you know it, too. And when you refrain from being critical, they're grateful; they respect you. Often as not, they'll be much tougher on themselves and make a concerted effort to avoid making the same mistake again. It's been said that the legitimate aim of criticism is to direct attention to the excellent. The bad will dig its own grave, and the imperfect may safely be left to that final neglect from which no amount of present undeserved popularity can rescue it.

As Epictetus put it, "Do not give sentence in another tribunal till you have been yourself judged in the tribunal of Justice." The key to overcoming the urge to criticize others is to wait. Wait a minute, or an hour, or a day, or forever.

Three Gifts to a Newborn Child

Bill Brewer was an especially astute interviewer and caught me completely off guard by his first question. He said, "If you could grant three qualities to a newborn child, what would they be?"

How would you like to be caught off guard early in the morning with that one? And, for that matter, what would your answer be? If you could grant three special qualities to a newborn child, what would they be? I fed the question into my mental computer—thinking of my own children as I did—and I replied that I would grant the child, first, a consuming curiosity about everything... a love of knowledge. Second—I would grant the child a profound love for the earth and everything that lives upon it. And third—I would grant that child the gift of communication so that he or she could pass on to others what was learned during his or her lifetime.

Later, over breakfast, with more time to think about the question, I found I stuck with my original answers. How about you? What three gifts would you confer upon the child? Whatever they are, if your children are still young enough, or not yet born, you can pass them on to them.

With a love of learning, the person would never be bored nor find himself or herself stagnating at a certain level of accomplishment. The more we learn, the more we can do—and, the more we venture to do, the more we learn. It's a self-generating perpetual motion kind of thing, for at least as long as we live. And with deep love of learning, our person would develop a rich sense of humor, because as we learn more and more, the more we tend to pass through stultifying dogma and the lugubrious fearful threats preached by those who would keep us in bondage. Knowledge is freedom—freedom leads to joy and laughter. What was it Pericles said? "The secret of happiness is freedom. And the secret of freedom—courage."

But with a love of the earth and all the living creatures on it, our person would have a deep sense of sympathy for anything or anyone in need. Our person would do whatever he or she could do to ameliorate suffering or the lack of personal freedom wherever it existed. Our person would be a natural champion of the environment, but would understand that the environment is to be used and enjoyed as well as cared for and protected.

And, as our person grew in maturity, he or she would most certainly be helping others to see the wonders and joys and problems of the world about us through one or more means of mass communication. Learning, loving and communicating. Not too bad, I should think. A lifetime of interest, love and keeping in touch with life as we know it here on the planet earth.

With those three qualities, our person would travel all over the earth and get to know this rather small speck of sand in the galaxy we call home and all the people and other living creatures that share it with us.

Think of some of the qualities you value in yourself that were passed on to you.

What are the qualities you value in those closest to you?

Are these qualities you possess or would like to possess? How would they improve your life?

Some of Life's Lessons

The Tale of the Butterfly

There's a story attributed to Henry Miller, the writer, about a little boy in India who walks up to a guru—an Indian wise man—who is sitting and looking at something in his hand. The little boy goes up and looks at it. He doesn't quite understand what it is, so he says to the guru, "What is that?"

"It's a cocoon," the guru tells him. "Inside the cocoon is a butterfly. Soon the cocoon is going to split, and the butterfly will come out."

"Could I have it?" asks the little boy.

"Yes," says the guru, "but you must promise me that when the cocoon splits and the butterfly starts to come out and he is beating his wings to get out of the cocoon, you won't help him. Don't help the butterfly by breaking the cocoon apart. Let him do it by himself."

The little boy promised, took the cocoon, went home with it, and then sat and watched it. Finally he saw it begin to vibrate and move and quiver, and finally the cocoon split. Inside was a beautiful damp butterfly, frantically beating its wings against the cocoon, trying to get out and not seeming to be able to do it. The little boy desperately wanted to help. Finally he gave in and disobeyed the guru's orders. He pushed the two halves of the cocoon apart, and the butterfly sprang out. But, as soon as it got up into the air, it fell down to the ground and was killed. The little boy picked up the dead butterfly and in tears went back to the guru and showed it to him.

"You see, little boy," the guru said, "you pushed open the cocoon, didn't you?"

"Yes," said the little boy.

And the guru said, "You don't understand. You didn't see what you were doing. When the butterfly comes out of the cocoon, the only way he can strengthen his wings is by beating them against the cocoon. It beats against the cocoon so its muscles will grow. When you helped it the way you did, you prevented it from getting strong. That's why the butterfly fell to the ground and was killed."

It's a story every parent should remember, and perhaps pass along to the youngsters when they're old enough to understand. Handing a child the toy he wants instead of letting him crawl across the room for it, or try his best to crawl for it; fulfilling his every whim; loading him down with the shiny, beautiful things of our society before he really needs or desires them; talking about the importance of grades in school instead of the importance of education—all of these things tend to weaken the muscles he should be developing on his own so that when the time comes for him to fly, he will have the strength he needs.

It's a good story to tell at the dinner table—and to discuss. So often, what seems harsh, or cruel in nature is in reality wisdom and kindness for the time ahead.

To Whom We Owe the Most

I remember reading somewhere that we owe the most to those people who make us become what we can become. Whatever little knowledge we have acquired has been because of the knowledge, thoughts and ideas that others before us have managed to piece together. We have taken them as our foundation and have built upon them.

That has not been an unbroken upward movement by any means. There have been times in our history when the light has all but gone out for hundreds of years, and it could happen again. But we owe an incalculable debt to those tireless thinkers and researchers who have added increments of new information to the growing store of total knowledge.

There are those who say, "Why bother with continuing education, continuing to study? Why learn all that, go to all that work and bother, just to carry it to the grave?" But that isn't the way it works. We don't carry it to the grave; we pass it along and often in a new and more enlightened form, sometimes even with a brand new idea that brightens the pathway ahead for those who follow.

I'm sure we don't do it for such noble purposes. We do it, I suppose, because we're curious, because it seems to be a part of us to want to know—to want to know all we can know during our brief turn at life. There is excitement in coming upon new information. It is for the seeker after knowledge what a gold strike is for the prospector. He wants to throw his hat in the air and dance for joy. "Look what I've found," he says as he passes it along to his family, his classroom, his readers. And so they find it too; they can enjoy and use it too, and in their turn pass it along.

And one of them will take the new knowledge and, using it like a piece in a jigsaw puzzle, fit it into a larger picture, so that it contributes to a wholly new idea—an idea that would have been incomplete and impossible without it. And then that new idea contributes to another, and so on, so that new pictures, bigger pictures, continue to emerge.

From time to time there are setbacks. Ideas are not always good in the form in which they're produced. The discovery of dynamite by Nobel was a boon to the construction industry. But it was also a new boom to the sound of war.

We developed thinking, as birds developed wings, in order to survive in a hostile environment. Weak and vulnerable in a world of savage beasts with the need to survive against competition more formidably armed than ourselves, we turned to the cerebral cortex, the thin layer of gray matter that covered the rudimentary brain. And it responded. It resounded so astonishingly that we were able to build a shuttle system to the moon and harness the power and heat of the sun. And it is still responding, growing every day more complex. Most of us never use 20% of our thinking equipment. Some say most idle along at 5%.

If most people realized the fun and profit to be gained from a systematic prospecting of their minds, they would devote an hour or so a day to it, maybe more. But most don't know about it and seldom think from one year to the next.

After You Know It All

"Individuals who remain vital have learned not to be imprisoned by fixed habits, attitudes and routines. We build our own prisons and serve as our own jailers. But if we build the prisons ourselves, we can tear them down ourselves. If we are willing to learn, the opportunities are everywhere."

I received a letter from Douglas Stovall in Danville, Virginia with a copy of a short piece by John W. Gardner that I had never seen before. It's called: The Things You Learn After You Know It All. I found it excellent. See what you think of it.

"Would you bet on the future of this man? He is 53 years old. Most of his adult life has been a losing struggle against debt and misfortune. A war injury has denied him the use of his left hand. He's had several jobs, succeeded at none, and has often been to prison. Driven by heaven knows what motives —boredom, hope of gain, creative impulse—he determines to write a book. The book turns out to be one that has enthralled the world for more than 350 years. That former prisoner was Cervantes, and the book was Don Quixote." And the story poses an interesting question: "Why do some men and women discover new vitality and creativity to the end of their days, while others go to seed long before?"

We've all known people who run out of steam before they reach life's halfway mark. I'm talking about people who have stopped learning or growing because they've adopted the fixed attitudes and opinions that all too often come with passing years. Most of us, in fact, progressively narrow the scope and variety of our lives. We succeed in our field of specialization and then become trapped in it. Nothing surprises us. We lose our sense of wonder and adventure.

But if you're conscious of these dangers, you can resort to countervailing measures. Reject stagnation. Reject the myth that learning is for young people. It's what you learn after you know it all that counts.

Learn all your life, from your successes and failures. When you hit a spell of trouble, ask, "What is it trying to teach me?" The lessons aren't always happy ones. In one of his essays, Ralph Waldo Emerson wrote, "Bad times have a scientific value. These are occasions a good learner would not miss."

Individuals who remain vital have learned not to be imprisoned by fixed habits, attitudes and routines. We build our own prisons and serve as our own jailers. But if we build the prisons ourselves, we can tear them down ourselves. If we are willing to learn, the opportunities are everywhere. We learn from our work and from our friends and families. We learn by accepting the obligations of life, by suffering, by taking risks, by loving, by bearing life's indignities with dignity.

The things you learn in maturity seldom involve information and skills. You learn to bear the things you can't change. You learn to avoid self-pity. You learn not to burn up energy in anxiety. You learn that most people are neither for nor against you but rather are thinking about themselves. You learn that no matter how much you try to please, some people are never going to love you—a notion that troubles at first but is eventually relaxing.

Among your obligations is an appointment with yourself. Self-knowledge, the beginning of wisdom, is ruled out for most people by the increasingly effective self-deception they practice as they grow older. By middle age, most of us are accomplished fugitives from ourselves. Yet there's a surprising usefulness in learning not to lie to yourself.

One of the most valuable things you learn is that ultimately you're the one who's responsible for you. You don't blame others. You don't blame circumstances. You take charge. If you're going to keep on learning, your surest allies will be high motivation and enthusiasm.

Doing What You Love to Do

Many years ago, there was a very successful executive in a financial concern. He was getting along in years when he finally decided he didn't like the work he was in. It was all right—he was successful at it because he was intelligent and hard working—but it wasn't what he really wanted to do.

This particular executive happened to be interested in birds. He wanted to become an expert on birds —an ornithologist. So, in his spare time, he began his studies. He read every book he could find that had anything to do with birds. He studied so steadily that before he knew it he was writing books about birds himself and helping out with the bird displays at the museum. His name was Dr. Frank Chapman. He became curator of ornithology at the American Museum of Natural History. He was doing something he wanted to do—really enjoyed doing, and he was well along in years before he made the decision that gave new direction, meaning and happiness to his life.

The point I want to make is that it's almost never too late to change to work you really enjoy. It's happened hundreds of times that men and women have retired at 65 and with the security of a pension and plenty of time, have turned to the field they should have been in all along. They have accomplished more in 5 years in the work they loved than they had in the 40 years with their previous companies.

So, here's some unasked for advice if you happen to be in work you don't particularly enjoy. First, find out what you'd really like to do. Determine your objective and actually visualize it in your mind. Picture what you want and the kind of person you want to become.

Next, get the facts. Get all the facts about what will be required to attain the objective you've determined upon and visualized. The more information you can get on the subject—the better.

Next, analyze, evaluate and group those facts. Try to put them in the logical order of importance of accomplishment. For example, if a person wanted to become a brain surgeon, she wouldn't just start opening up heads; she'd start with school. Make sure your goal is practical for you.

Then set a timetable for the accomplishment of your objectives and try to stick to the timetable. Don't let people throw you off the track, or tell you you're wrong. You should know what's right for you—what's right for others is their business.

Next, begin! Don't just keep talking about it. Do it! And understand that the time will really never be perfect to start, so start as soon as you're ready. You'll never get to second base trying to keep one foot on first. Take off! If you're tagged out—you can come to bat again.

Be sure your entire plan is written out—a regular blueprint to follow—and you can check, from time to time, to see how you're doing by comparing your progress with your blueprint. And finally, stay with it. Keep your goal firmly fixed in your mind, have faith that you can reach it, and reach it, you will. And, like Dr. Frank Chapman, you'll find yourself happy and excited in work you really enjoy.

What is more important than spending our lives in work we really enjoy? Yet there are millions who don't know it's possible, who largely waste their lives. It's a shame, isn't it?

Take these steps to do what you love to do:

-Find out what you'd like to do

-Get the facts required to gain your objective

-Analyze, evaluate and group your facts

-Set a timetable for your goals

-Begin to work towards your goals

-Compare your progress to a blueprint you create for yourself

-Have faith and perseverance.

Managing Risk in Your life

Look for Opportunity, Not Security

The stoic philosopher Epictetus taught, "Adversity introduces a person to himself. On the occasion of every accident that befalls you, remember to turn to yourself and inquire what power you have for turning it to use.

"Opportunity beckons more surely when misfortune comes upon a person than it ever does when that person is riding the crest of a wave of success. It sharpens a person's wits, if he will let it, enabling him to see more clearly and evaluate his situation with a more knowledgeable judgment."

It's been my observation that people seem to be growing more and more fearful of risk of any kind. They seem bent on an almost frantic scramble for security without taking the time to think it all the way through.

There's only one form of security we can attain during our lives. It's inner security—the kind that comes from courage, experience and the ability and willingness to learn, to grow, to attempt the unknown. Security isn't what the wise person looks for; it's opportunity. And once we begin looking for that, we find it on every side. You can measure opportunity with the same yardstick that measures the risk involved. They go together.

The famous World War II admiral, William "Bull" Halsey, said, "Touch a thistle timidly, and it pricks you; grasp it boldly, and its spines crumble. All problems become smaller if you don't dodge them but confront them." I think we all know that, but we tend to forget it between problems.

I particularly like Epictetus' line, "Adversity introduces a person to himself." That's when we get to really know ourselves; that's when we come face to face with the real person we are and the stage of our maturity or growth to that point.

It does no good at all to worry about times in the past when we've failed to measure up in our own eyes. We weren't ready yet; we hadn't at that point in our lives matured sufficiently; we weren't wise enough. Besides, that's in the past. It's how we stand up to trouble now that matters. And we should keep in mind the truth and wisdom contained in his advice, "Opportunity beckons more surely when misfortune comes upon a person than it ever does when that person is riding the crest of a wave of success."

Most very successful people can remember that their success was discovered and built out of adversity of some kind. It's not the problems that beset us—problems are surprisingly pretty much the same for millions of others; it's how we react to problems that determines not only our degree of growth and maturity but our future success—and, perhaps, much of our health.

It's good to get rid of that word security once and for all. It makes us feel free again, as we felt as children, and we begin to see what this business of living is all about; we begin to really enjoy it.

Innovators and Risk-Taking

People who do well in the world by being creative and willing to take a calculated risk are people who manage to overcome the fear of laughter. Any time you attempt anything in which you risk failure, you run the risk of having people laugh at you. A college professor worked many years on an invention. He tramped all over New England trying to attract capital for his device for making the human voice travel along a wire. The people laughed at him. It was, of course, plumb idiotic they said to suppose that the human voice could be carried along a wire and heard for many miles, or even for a single mile. But our old friend and benefactor, Alexander Graham Bell, could not be laughed out of it. And every time we pick up the telephone we salute the man who stayed on course, despite the laughter.

Millions of people laughing in derision could not hurt us an iota, but we stand in mortal terror of it. Men and women who can prove themselves heroes in great crisis tremble before derision. It's a queer quirk of human nature we probably develop as children. It has cost much. It has changed the history of the world.

Sometimes the price of a laugh has met the slamming of a door to fame and fortune, or even immortality.

Elias Howe invented the sewing machine, but it nearly rusted away before American women stopped laughing about it and could be persuaded to make use of it. With their sewing done so quickly, they argued, what would they ever do with all their spare time? So a biographer paints a tragic picture. The man who had done more than any other to lighten the work of women was forced to borrow a suit of clothes on an occasion of a public appearance.

Men are as bad as women when it comes to resisting new ideas. The typewriter had been a demonstrated success for years before businessmen could be persuaded to buy it. How could anyone have enough letters to write, they argued, to justify the investment of $100 in a writing machine?

Only when the Remingtons sold patent rights to the Caligraph Company and two groups of salesmen worked in competition, was the resistance finally broken down. Xerography faced the same kind of problem when it was first introduced. And other inventions have had similar battles.

Here's an extract from a notebook of Robert Fulton, who invented the steamship which changed the world from sail to steam. He wrote, "As I had occasioned daily to pass to and from the shipyard where my boat was in progress, I often loitered near the groups of strangers and heard various remarks as to the object of this new vehicle. The language was uniformly that of scorn, sneer or ridicule. The loud laugh often rose at my expense—the dry jest, the wise calculations of losses or expenditures, the dull repetition of Fulton's folly. Never did a single encouraging remark, a bright hope, or a warm wish cross my path." And that's about what you can expect when you try something new.

Perversity and built-in envy cause people to think or hope that any new idea or plan that runs counter to established principle will fail. Emerson wrote, "Pythagoras was misunderstood, and Socrates and Copernicus and Galileo and Newton and every pure and wise spirit that ever took flesh. To be great is to be misunderstood."

You know we tend to forget that the greatest people, the greatest writers, the greatest teachers were for the most part in violent disagreement with their times and the way things were being done. We seem to have become so flabby in our acceptance of anything that we fail to do anything personally about what we see about us. Norman Cousins wrote that the biggest issue of all in the years just ahead is not just the squandering of physical resources, but the squandering of human resources.

So what is failure? Failure does not come to a person because he is not recognized by the multitudes during his lifetime or ever. Our success or failure has nothing to do with the opinions of others. It has only to do with our own opinion of ourselves and what we're doing.

The only person that can be called a failure is that person who tries to succeed at nothing. Success, as far as a person is concerned, does not lie in achievement. It lies in striving, reaching, attempting.

Any person who decides upon a course of action he deems to be worthy of him and sets out to accomplish that goal is a success right then and there.

Think about some of the accomplishments you have made in your life. Have you taken your achievements for granted?

Have you done what you set out to do, in spite of the consequences?

Do you give up too quickly?

Reassess those things which were not successful for you and determine whether they are worth a second chance.

Playing It Safe Can Be Risky

"In all walks of life, the most successful believe in something. This has a tendency to make the going a little tougher for a while, but they almost always wind up ahead of the game eventually."

People who play it too safe take the greatest risks. Did you know that? In the long haul, the intelligent risk-takers develop the greatest security. It's a wise person who learns the importance of risk taking.

During World War II, psychologist E. Paulo Torrance made a study of United States aces flying in the Pacific theater of operations. He reported that the most salient characteristic of the ace was his risk-taking ability. Throughout his life, he had kept testing the limits of his abilities. And the life histories of these men showed that they were highly resistant to accidents, and in combat they suffered fewer casualties than pilots who were inclined to play it safe. Dr. Torrance said, "Living itself is a risky business. If we spent half as much time learning how to take risks as we spent avoiding them, we wouldn't have nearly so much to fear in life."

In all walks of life, the most successful people are the risk-takers. By that, I mean they risk believing in their own ideas, striking out toward their own goals, standing up for what they believe to be right. They take the risk of being different when they believe in something. This has a tendency to make the going a little tougher for a while, but they almost always wind up ahead of the game eventually.

Risk-takers realize there's nothing wrong with an occasional failure. The play-it-safers seem to think a failure means the end of the world. The risk-takers are not foolhardy. Getting back to the World War II aces for a moment, it was found that these men were very fussy about their airplanes, armament and equipment. They were painstaking in preparation and highly disciplined in following instructions and what they had been taught. But in an encounter with the enemy, they would immediately take charge and go on the offense. The best defense is often a good offense. The best pass defense in football is to rush the quarterback. When a storm comes up, ships in the harbor head for the raging open sea, unless they're protected in slips. In the harbor, they could drag their anchors and wind up on the beach or the breakwater. So what appears to be risk-taking is often the most intelligent course to follow. It leads to security, while what would appear to be the safest course of action can lead to disaster, or, simply nowhere.

A young woman, whose romance had gone on the rocks, told her mother that she was never going to permit herself to fall in love again. "You only get hurt," she said. "And if you don't fall in love," her mother said, "you don't live." It's another one of those risks the successful person is willing to take.

Everyone runs risks—quite sizable risks—every day of his life, risks he takes for granted or isn't even aware of. But when an unusual situation comes along that involves risk-taking, how do you decide whether or not to go ahead?

When a situation comes along that involves risk, and you don't know whether to go ahead or hold back, reassess your goals. What are you trying to accomplish? What are you working toward? Will taking this risk—if it works out successfully—help you toward your goals?

Advice for the Fearful

Dr. Joyce Brothers has some good advice for the fearful. She points out that everyone is familiar with fear. Normal fear protects us and provides a warning signal indicating the presence of danger. A totally fearless person is probably not too intelligent and can look forward to a very short life. But when fear is inappropriate, it can stand in the way of progress and success. It can destroy love, create failure on the job and interfere with our ability to relate well to others.

Innovation and creativity involve risk, Dr. Brothers goes on to say. The person who's afraid to take chances, who's afraid of failure, is standing in the way of his progress.

In fact, an emotionally healthy person needs challenge in life. Studies show that people who are cautious in the extreme, who are afraid to take risks even when the odds are in their favor, tend to be afraid of life itself—which, of course, is also a gamble. Such persons are not likely to succeed in business or anything else.

Dr. Brothers suggests that such people practice failure. How liberating it would be for the average person to be able to walk into a room, trip over a wastebasket, have all the people in the office laugh and then be able to laugh with them.

Dr. Brothers suggests that fearful people deliberately do such things to discover that an occasional failure is no disgrace but, rather, a perfectly normal part of living.

I remember when I was just starting out in radio, that I managed to get the part of Sky King, the lead in the famous children's radio program of that name. And I would often be asked to make public appearances for schoolchildren. One day, I flew up to Michigan to greet and sign autographs for several hundred children allowed out of school for the event.

I flew there in a small two-seater airplane. I was dressed in my cowboy costume from my hat to my cowboy boots, gun belt—the works. As I was trying to climb out of the airplane cockpit in my unaccustomed costume, while the hundreds of children waited nearby, I caught my heel on the cockpit coaming and fell full-length on the wing. Then I did a slow roll off the trailing edge of the wing to the ground. My guns fell out, my hat rolled away and a deathlike silence fell on the children. There was their hero, sprawled on the grass! He couldn't even get out of an airplane!

I picked up my guns, put my hat back on and with a sheepish grin from ear to ear, walked to the waiting children. We all had a good laugh about it, and I signed the autographs, and all went surprisingly well. As I flew back to Chicago, I thought about how often children fall and that they could easily empathize with me.

Don't lose your sense of humor, and remember that even though they may laugh, people are kinder and more forgiving than we generally give them credit for being. Risks and pratfalls are a part of life; so is an occasional failure in other ways, and so is success—lots of it.

Making the Most of Opportunities

Acres of Diamonds

Some stories are so good; they never grow old. One of them is the old story called "Acres of Diamonds." No one knows who told it the first time. It's supposed to be true, and of course it is in that it's happened thousands of times to thousands of people in thousands of different situations.

But the man who made the story famous, in this country at least, was Dr. Russell Herman Conwell, who lived from 1843 to 1925 and who, by telling the story from one end of the world to the other, raised $6 million with which he founded Temple University in Philadelphia, and thus fulfilled his dream to build a really fine school for poor but deserving young men.

Dr. Conwell told the story "Acres of Diamonds" more than 6,000 times and attracted great audiences wherever he appeared. I'm sure you're as familiar with the story as I am. But it isn't the story that's so important in itself—the important thing is that we apply the principle of the story to our own lives.

The story is about a farmer who lived in Africa at the time diamonds were discovered there. When a visitor to his farm told him of the millions being made by men who were discovering diamond mines, he promptly sold his farm and left to search for diamonds himself.

He wandered all over the continent, found no diamonds, and, as the story has it, finally penniless, in poor health, and despondent, threw himself into a river and drowned.

Long before this, the man who had bought the farm found a large, unusual-looking stone in the creek-bed which ran through the farm and put it on his mantel as a curio. When the same visitor who had told the original farmer about the diamond discoveries stopped by one day, he examined the stone and told the new owner that he had discovered one of the largest diamonds ever found, and that it was worth a king's ransom. To his surprise, the farmer told him the entire farm was covered with stones of that kind. And to make a long story short, if it isn't already too late, the farm which the first farmer had sold so that he could go look for diamonds turned out to be one of the richest diamond mines in the world.

The point Dr. Conwell made was that the first farmer had owned acres of diamonds but had made the mistake of not examining what he had before he ran off to something he hoped would prove to be better.

He would then point out that each of us is like that first farmer. No matter where we live, or what we do, we are surrounded by acres of diamonds if we'll simply look for them. Like the curious appearing stones which covered the farm, they might not appear to be diamonds at first glance but a little study —a deeper examination—and some polishing will reveal our opportunities for what they really are.

The experts say that each of us has deep reservoirs of ability which we habitually fail to use simply because we fail to develop ourselves to our true stature, and there are, lurking in our daily work as well as in ourselves, acres of diamonds.

We See the World We Look For

Among the writings of Henry David Thoreau, I came across this statement, "Many an object is not seen, though it falls within the range of our visual ray, because it does not come within the range of our intellectual ray." In other words, there are many things that exist in our world that we don't see because we are not looking for them or perhaps even aren't capable of looking for them. So in the largest sense, the world we see is only the world we look for.

Show two people the same picture, and each will see a different scene; each will extract from what he sees that which he happens to be predisposed to look for. Different people looking out of a train window as they pass through the outskirts of a city will see the same thing from entirely different viewpoints. One will see a depressing, run-down neighborhood. Another will see an ideal plant site. Still another might see a marvelous opportunity for real-estate development. The passing scene might give someone else the idea for a story or a song or a poem. Another, his face buried in a magazine, will see nothing.

The world presents to each of us, every day, that which we seek. There is not a neighborhood or area that does not offer abundant opportunity to every person living there. That opportunity is limited only by the viewpoint of the inhabitant.

Some years ago, a Wisconsin farmer was stricken with polio and left paralyzed—in an iron lung. Flat on his back, unable to farm his land, he was forced to push back his intellectual horizon; he was forced to think creatively, to take mental inventory of his assets and liabilities. Without moving from his bed, he built one of the country's largest and most successful meat-packing companies. Unable to use his hands and feet, he was forced to use his most precious, priceless possession—his mind—and he found his farm contained all the riches he and his family would ever need. Where before there was only a farm, now there are great packing plants employing thousands.

I am sure that when his friends and neighbors learned of his affliction, they wondered how he would manage to operate his farm and care for his family. He simply looked at the farm with new eyes; he saw what he had failed to see before, even though nothing had changed except his own mobility.

Every one of us lives in a kind of iron lung of his own fashioning. Each one of us has opportunities just as great as that Wisconsin farmer's. But few of us are forced to reach so far into the deep reservoirs of ability within us. And fewer still know the joy of excitement and never-ending interest that can be found in our daily lives when we learn to look at our world as Thoreau looked at his. Surrounded by miracles and limitless opportunity, some people manage to find only boredom and insecurity.

As Thoreau said, we find only the world we look for.

The Value of Maintaining High Expectations

One time when I was in New York City, my plane was canceled because of mechanical difficulties. More than 100 of us, I suppose, were now left to scramble for another flight to our destinations on a busy, crowded afternoon. I went back to the counter, and a woman told me there was another flight in just an hour. "Won't that be filled?" I asked.

"Maybe not," she said.

I thought of all the people on my cancelled flight fighting for seats on the next one, which was already probably completely booked, and I toyed with the idea of staying overnight and making a new reservation for the following morning.

"Why don't you try it?" she said.

The thought of standing around the airport for another hour only to be turned away from a full flight was very unappealing. "Do you think there's any hope at all?"

"Try it," she said.

So I tried it. I wound up with a window seat up front and was only an hour late arriving at my destination. If I hadn't tried it, I would have had to taxi all the way back into the city, register at a hotel, spend the night and repeat the whole process the next day. I'd been saved all that by a woman who suggested that I try it. And I resolved to stop giving up so easily—to keep my expectations alive, to expect more.

This is a small example, but we should never lose sight of the undeniable fact that there is a very thin line, if any at all, between what we expect from life and what we get.

If we're not getting what we'd like, maybe it's because our expectations are too low; maybe we're suffering from the poverty of expectation. Your life will come pretty close to matching your expectations. It can easily exceed them. Higher expectations keep us trying; they keep us pressing upon ourselves; they keep us from giving up.

When I was a kid, I remember hearing the words, "If you don't expect much, you won't be disappointed when you don't get much." But that's just the problem: If you don't expect much, you're ruling out the chance of winning. The world is full of people who don't have much because they don't expect much. They're not trying for more, so how in the world are they going to get more?

We should never be concerned about the opportunities we've missed in the past. There's no way on earth to make the most of every opportunity. It's almost never too late, and there will be just as many good opportunities in the future as there have been in the past.

No one is without hope. Every person has expectations of some kind. But just as we tend to underestimate ourselves, we therefore expect too little. We have expectations, but are they high enough? As Goethe put it, "In all things it is better to hope than to despair."

It might be a good idea to take inventory of our expectations. Maybe we could use a new shipment.

We become what we habitually think about!

Take time to review your own goals and expectations.

Have you set your sights high enough?

Are you giving up on something that deserves more of an effort?

The Fundamental Principle of Human Action

I read a comment in Forbes magazine by Henry George. He said, "The fundamental principle of human action is that men seek to gratify their desires with the least exertion."

There's the rub. There's the difference between what we say we want and what we're willing to settle for. It's like the high-school kid who tells his counselor that he wants to be a physician, and whose grades are C's and D's. Sure, he wants to be a doctor, but only if there isn't too much hard work involved.

I've often thought that therein also lies the crux of the mid-career identity crisis so common among people. You wake up one morning—usually a rainy Monday—look at yourself in the mirror, before you've showered and dressed, and gets a world-record sinking feeling. You're 40, and you suddenly realize those insurance people know what they're talking about when they deal in mortality tables, and that there's one whopping disparity between what you've accomplished and what you used to think you'd accomplish.

"What happened?" you wonder. Where did all those years go?

And what have you been doing all that time? And, more importantly, where are you going? What about all those young dreams? Voilà! Identity crisis— you're not the person you intended to become.

And what happened was that you were comfortable; you had a job you could handle with raises along the way, three square meals a day, a family (these are not in the order of their importance, necessarily), a house—well, actually, it was what the others were doing, too. And then those young dreams had been a bit amorphous—a little fuzzy around the edges. The thing is that while you may not be the person you intended to become, you are the person you settled for. You really have what you wanted after all.

I had a call the other day from an older woman I know, and she said, "You know, when I was a girl, I wanted more than anything to learn to play the piano, but my parents couldn't afford it. And there was a super private school I wanted to go to, but they couldn't afford that, either."

I asked her if she had learned to play the piano later on, after she left home. She said no. I reminded her that she could have learned to play every instrument in the Boston Symphony during the time she'd wasted since then. I told her that blaming her parents was the easy way out. People who would love to play an instrument, or seek a good education, can do it one way or another, even if they have to teach themselves, as countless individuals have proved.

So I won the argument and infuriated a nice woman, I had exploded a myth she'd been clinging to for 40 years. And I reminded her that there was still plenty of time.

I'd Give Anything to Do What You Do

An accomplished woman musician gave a great piano performance for a women's club. Afterward, over coffee, an admirer from the audience gushed to the virtuoso, "I'd give anything to play as you do."

The woman who had given the concert took a sip of her coffee and fixed the red-faced admirer with a cold glare. And then she said, "Oh, no, you wouldn't!"

A hush fell over the group, coffee cups stopped on their way to and from saucers, and the culprit twitched in sudden embarrassment. Looking about her, she repeated—but in a softer voice—her original statement, "I would, too, give anything to play the piano as you do." The virtuoso continued to sip her coffee and shake her head. "No, you wouldn't," she repeated. "If you would, you could play as well, possibly better, possibly a little worse, than I do. You'd give anything to play as I do, except time—except the one thing it takes to accomplish the fact. You wouldn't sit and practice, hour after hour, day after day, year after year."

Then she flashed a warm smile. "Understand," she said, "I'm not criticizing you. I'm just telling you that when you say you'd give anything to play as I do, you really don't mean it. You really don't mean it at all."

In the pause that followed, a napkin falling to the thick rug would have rattled the windows. The women looked at each other and then back at their coffee cups. They realized that this woman had spoken the truth. It would be nice to have her talent now, fully matured and developed, but as for putting in the twenty years of work that went into the fashioning of it, no. That was a different matter.

Soon, the light conversation was resumed, and the incident was glossed over—but not forgotten.

People are forever saying, "I'd give anything..." But the fact remains that they don't; they give very little, often nothing, to do the things they say they'd give anything to do.

The actor who envies the pinnacles reached by the stars, the small-business person, the homemaker, the student, the golfer, the professional person, the aspiring writer, the painter—across the entire spectrum of achievement, the stars are those who have simply given their dedication, their singleness of purpose, their days and nights, weeks and months and years. And when the harvest they have so painstakingly sown and nurtured for so long begins to be reaped, there are others, with the same time, the same opportunity, the same freedom, who come up to say, "I'd give anything to be able to do what you're doing, to have the things you have."

But as the pianist said, "I'm just telling you that when you say you'd give anything to play as I do, you really don't mean it. You really don't mean it at all."

Each of us has the time and the opportunity. If we say we haven't, we're trying to kid ourselves. Everybody ought to become great at something. What is it that you would give anything to become? Then give it, and you'll become it.

Sometimes it seems as though there are far too many spectators and not enough players. Maybe we're so busy watching the world and everyone else, we forget we have one of our own to win.

What Kind of Ship Are You?

"The better prepared, the more skilled and experienced we become, the larger the opportunity we can handle because we've learned to handle the problems that go with it. But at the same time, you can't handle a large opportunity if you permit yourself to be bothered by small problems."

Opportunities and problems come in all sizes, from the very small to the very large. There's no such thing as an opportunity without problems or problems without opportunities; they're two sides of the same coin. But it's how we react to them that determines what sort of people we are and how serene or frustrated, successful or unsuccessful we ultimately become.

Look at it this way: The better prepared, the more skilled and experienced we become, the larger the opportunity we can handle because we've learned to handle the problems that go with it. But at the same time, you can't handle—you might not even recognize—a large opportunity if you permit yourself to be bothered by small problems. If a person is to mature—reach his full stature as a human being—he must learn to sail over the thousands of small, unimportant problems and irritations that beset all of us. If he permits himself to become involved with the numerous small, unimportant vexations, petty arguments, real or imagined personal slights, the interminable minutia of life, he'll spend all the years of his life in the shallows.

As we've said before, a person is only as large as the things he lets bother him; he's only as big as the things he lets interest him.

In discussing this not long ago, I got to thinking that people are like sailing craft, and you can compare life itself to an ocean. Now, think of the people you know—and think of yourself—as vessels. The smallest would be a little skiff that bounces and bobs even in calm weather over the smallest waves. It isn't safe to go to sea in a boat that small; it will be swamped by the first large wave that comes along.

From the smallest vessel, let's go now to the largest ocean liner. It doesn't even feel the small waves in the harbor. Not until it reaches the great swells of the open sea does it begin to compensate for roll and pitch. And even the worst storms find it equal to the task. It might arrive in port a day or two late, but it will get there safely, with its passengers and cargo.

What kind of vessel are you? Are you the big liner that sails serene and confident far out into the deep, open sea—that pays no attention to the small, or even medium-sized, waves that break and disintegrate against its tall sides? Or are you the small rowboat that bobs and rocks in the slightest breeze?

As James Allen so beautifully put it, "The strong, calm person is always loved and revered. He is like a shade-giving tree in a thirsty land, or a sheltering rock in a storm. Who does not love a tranquil heart, a sweet-tempered, balanced life? It does not matter whether it rains or shines, or what changes come to those possessing these blessings, for they are always sweet, serene and calm. That exquisite poise of character which we call serenity is the last lesson of culture; it is the flowering of life, the fruitage of the soul."

Ships and people come in all sizes. We stop to watch and admire the great ships, while the small craft in the harbor attract only a passing glance. What kind of craft are you?

Using Courage to Achieve Success

How to Live Life on Faith

My old friend, Dr. Harold Blake Walker of Evanston, sent me something some time back that I enjoyed tremendously and I think you will, too. He wrote, "We live by faith or we do not live at all. Either we venture or we vegetate. If we venture, we do so by faith, simply because we cannot know the end of anything at its beginning. We risk marriage on faith or we stay single. We prepare for a profession by faith or we give up before we start. By faith, we move mountains of opposition or we're stopped by molehills.

"Faith, however, is not often tranquil and steady. It ebbs and flows like the tides of the restless sea. Normally, like Browning's Bishop, we are forever exchanging a life of doubt diversified by faith, for one of faith diversified by doubt. Yesterday we began the day with confident hope, with trust in its promise. Last night, perhaps after a trying and troublesome day, we were beset by doubt and anxiety."

We grope and fumble in search of certainty, wishing we could escape the doubts that haunt us. The peril is that we shall cease groping on through our doubts and live only on our negations.

What we need, you and I, is faith strong enough to bear the burden of our doubts. No man ever drilled an oil well without being troubled by misgivings as the drill chewed downward toward producing structures. But only a fool would cease drilling halfway to the hoped-for pool. It was William Morris, the painter, who wrote, "I tell you, it's no joke to paint a portrait. Into the painting of every picture that's worth...there comes a period of doubt and despair. The artist, however, goes on with his work, beyond his doubt, to creative achievement."

Faith enough to carry our doubts: It's enough. Perhaps it's all we can manage when fears assail and doubts annoy. Maybe we can do no more than grope on through our uncertainties, pursuing the enterprises of our lives in a grim trust that the end will justify the struggle.

If, despite our gnawing doubts, we can muster faith enough to take a single step on the road to where we're going, we are on the way to creative achievement. Every triumph of the human spirit begins with one step taken in faith. The single step is the small handle to great matters. No man or woman ever won a worthy triumph without faith to keep on and on, always able to last at least five minutes longer.

There's one further thing to be said, namely that worthy triumphs cannot be won without faith enough to maintain our integrity. One of the ultimate tests of faith is our capacity to go on believing that somehow the right is the right, even when right is on the scaffold and wrong seems to be on the throne.

All of the great ventures of our lives require faith enough to bear the burden of our doubts, so that we're able to take the first step in the direction in which we wish to go; enough of faith to keep on going through struggle and strain, and to maintain integrity on the way. I like that. Yes, faith is the assurance of things hoped for, the conviction of things not seen. And we need to exchange a life of doubt diversified by faith, to a life of faith diversified by doubt.

What Do You Believe In?

"It is what you believe in that will determine the course of your life, what happens to you and your ultimate destiny."

When was the last time you were asked the rather personal question: What do you believe in?

It sometimes seems that there is so much doubt, fear and cynicism, so much tongue-in-cheek and wise-guy elbow-rib-poking, that we have come to the place where people don't believe in anything any more. People doubt their own capacity for judgment, for knowing what is right or wrong. They wait to see what others do or say before they'll express an opinion of their own. So what do you believe in?

This is not an unimportant question. It is vital that each of us decides exactly what he does believe in, and here's why. It is what you believe in that will determine the course of your life, what happens to you and your ultimate destiny. The great truth, "As you believe, so shall it be done unto you," seems to go almost unnoticed today, but that's the way it works. What you believe is what will happen to you. For belief is faith, and faith is still the greatest power on earth.

A young medical student was being examined by a board of distinguished doctors to determine whether or not he would receive his license to practice. They asked him, "Why do you want to be a physician?" and he replied, "I've known I was going to be a doctor for as long as I can remember. There is simply no question about it. I'm going to be a practicing physician and a good one."

He didn't beg the question. He told them he was going to be a doctor. They had no choice in the matter. The difference between faith and wanting, or wishing, is that with faith we know what is going to be, but with the others we are only hoping. It is what we believe that makes us the kind of people we are. The greater our faith, the greater we become. People who let others do their thinking for them, who will not venture forth an opinion on any subject until they're sure what they say will be met with approval and acceptance, do not believe. They conform to a picture of what they think others want them to be like. They are chameleons, ready to take on any hue their surroundings demand. They have no deep anchors of belief and drift aimlessly on the surface of life.

So, when asked, what do you believe in, it means what do you have faith in? On what would you be willing to risk everything you have because of the certainty of your belief?

If a person believes he is not much of a person, that's what he is. If he believes that he has value, that there is no other person on earth exactly like him, that he has an important contribution to make, and that he can reach the goals he sets for himself, these things are then true and will come to pass. People remain where they are because they believe that's where they ought to be, and they rise to new heights of achievement and ability because they believe they will.

The greatest teachers who ever lived are men whose minds soared far above those of their times, and whom we still read. They said that according to our faith will it be done unto us. That, my friend, is the way it works. There are no arguments, no exceptions, no hair-splitting. What do you believe? Then that's what you are.

The worst thing that can happen to a person is to lose his belief in something. With belief gone, faith is gone, and when that's gone, there isn't anything left.

The Rewards of Persistence

Sometimes it appears that there's a hidden guide someplace whose duty it is to test men and women through all sorts of discouraging experiences. Those who pick themselves up and keep trying after getting knocked down, arrive. It's an uncanny thing, but it works. And this hidden guide lets no one enjoy great achievement without passing the persistence test, it seems. And those who can't take it simply don't make the grade.

And those who can take it are bountifully rewarded for their persistence. They receive as their compensation whatever goal they're pursuing. And that's not all, because they receive something infinitely more important than material compensation, although they get that. But they get the knowledge that every failure brings with it the seed of an equivalent advantage. There are no exceptions to this rule. A few people know from experience the soundness of persistence. They're the ones who have not accepted defeat as being anything more than temporary. They're the ones whose desires are so persistently applied that defeat has finally changed into victory.

I was reading just the other day about the great Knute Rockne of Notre Dame who believed and applied this very thing we're talking about. He had a blood clot in one leg, and his doctors told him that if that blood clot traveled through his bloodstream to his heart, it would kill him. But the Notre Dame team was playing far from home that day, and he insisted on being taken to the game on a stretcher. So they got him to where the game was to be played and they took him down to the dressing room where his football players were getting ready for the game. And the perspiration was running down his face and he was in terrible pain and he propped himself up on his elbows with a tremendous effort and said, "This team you're playing today beat us last year." And he said, "I want you to get out there and win." And it was then that he said, "The team that won't be beat, can't be beat." And then he fell back on his stretcher, out of breath and suffering terribly, and the team went out and won the game, and they never lost another game as long as Knute Rockne was alive.

Because when they saw the type of courage that he could develop, how persistently he fought to win even though he was flat on his back, it made giants out of men.

And people who stand on the sidelines of life see the overwhelmingly large number who go down in defeat, never to rise again. They see the few who take the punishment of defeat as an urge to greater effort. And these fortunately never learn to accept life's reverse gear. But what we don't see, what most of us never suspected existed, is the silent but irresistible power which comes to the rescue of those who fight on in the face of discouragement. Now if we speak of this power at all, we call it persistence and let it go at that. One thing we all know, if one does not possess persistence, one cannot achieve any noteworthy success in any calling.

When was the last time you gave up without really trying?

When was the last time you persisted in spite of setbacks?

What did you learn from both experiences?

How to Free Your Mind from Fear

Viktor Frankl, a distinguished psychiatrist and survivor of unspeakable atrocities at the hands of the Nazis in one of their concentration camps, says, "The last of the human freedoms is to choose one's attitude in any given set of circumstances." In fact, it was learning this that kept him free and alive even while he was languishing in a death camp.

Attitude, being an inner thing, can keep us free—even fairly cheerful— regardless of the environment in which circumstances may have placed us. The ancient philosophers had discovered this fact. But it seems that each maturing person must rediscover it for himself, if he's to find his own brand of freedom.

Dr. Frankl also wrote, "Fear makes come true that which one is afraid of." Even if it only comes true in the imagination, we must experience the tortures of that which we fear, tortures often as not, worse than those that might actually came to pass in our lives. It's why the old line, "A coward dies a thousand deaths...a brave man dies but once," is really true.

"Fear makes come true that which one is afraid of." If fear of something is held long enough, it may well bring on that which we fear. But it really doesn't make much difference, because experiencing the fear is the same thing—that is, as far as our mind and body are concerned, it's actually happening, over and over again, doing its inevitable damage to our physical bodies.

Ralph Waldo Emerson said that "fear is ignorance." Whenever we're afraid of something—I don't mean the perfectly natural, normal fears that work to keep us alive—but the gnawing, unreasoning, illogical and neurotic fear of something—it's only because we don't know the real truth about it. If we did, the fear would vanish. That would include a neurotic fear of death, the fear that we are not liked or loved, and so forth.

I think the thing to remember here is that when we fear something, it takes its toll on our mind and body, just as if that which we fear had, in fact, come to pass. And we can bring to pass that which we fear, as Dr. Frankl said.

But how does a person change an attitude of fear? Dr. William Glasser, the distinguished psychiatrist and author of Reality Therapy and Schools Without Failure, says, "If you want to change attitudes, start with a change in behavior." In other words, begin to act the part, as well as you can, of the person you would rather be, the person you most want to become. Gradually, the old, fearful person will fade away.

Dr. Frankl learned that by controlling his attitude, the concentration camp fell away. His mind was free to roam where he wanted it to roam, think about what he wanted it to think about; it was as free as the birds—freer, really, for it could fly to the ends of the earth, to the ends of imagination, in an instant. And so can yours.

"The last of the human freedoms is to choose one's attitude in any given set of circumstances." We can let circumstances rule us, or we can take charge and rule our lives from within.

Give Yourself the Gift of Courage

Just as I was boarding my plane in Sydney, Australia to return to the United States, my old friend Roly Leopold of Melbourne handed me a small booklet. He said, "I think you'll enjoy reading this on the flight home."

The title of the little book was The Gift of Courage, written by Paul Speicher. Let me read a part to you:

"If you could have as a gift your dearest wish fulfilled, the wish that lies closest to your heart, the thing that you want most in the world, what would you choose? A million dollars? Abounding health? A magic solution to business worries? A content mind? A devoted family? The privilege of traveling only on the hilltops in the morning sun? Escape from the ills of life which are common to all?

"What gift would be more worthy of you than the fulfillment of an idle daydream? What one thing would help you win through the problems you face today and may face again tomorrow? What gift would enable you to enjoy because you have fought, to rest because you have labored, to reap because you have sown?

"There is such a gift within your grasp, a gift which you yourself can give yourself, a gift which will bring all the things for which you secretly long, a gift which, like magic, will help clear the troubled roadway ahead and set your feet upon the pathway to real happiness.

"And that is the gift of courage."

Emerson wrote, "What a new face courage puts on everything!" And no truer statement was ever written. Wherever it appears, courage changes things for the better. Sometimes it's the courage to be silent when a word or phrase leaps to our mind. It's often the courage to get up on a cold, miserable morning, when it's the last thing in the world you want to do, to go to work. It's the courage to do what needs to be done, when it should be done. It's the courage to discharge a person who should be discharged, and who will probably be better off because of it. And it's the courage to follow the silent voice within you when it means going against the crowd, or speaking out when you know what you're going to say will be unpopular with your listeners. It's the courage to stay with something long enough to succeed at it, realizing that it usually takes two, three or four times as long to succeed as you first thought or hoped.

"There is such a gift within your grasp... a gift which like magic will help clear the troubled roadway ahead and set your feet upon the pathway to real happiness. And that is the gift of courage."

When Laughter Does More Harm Than Good

"When our desire to belong to our crowd is more important to us than to stand up for what we know to be right, we have to admit that we are lacking in the two most important attributes of a human being: courage and maturity."

Do you know what form of punishment people dread more than any other? Well, it's laughter. That's right. As a wise man once wrote, "The deepest principle of human nature is the craving to be appreciated." And the exact opposite of being appreciated is to be laughed at. In fact, among the Eskimos, laughter is the only punishment for thieves. If a person is found to be a thief, all the Eskimos in the village laugh at him whenever they see him. As a result, there is very little stealing among Eskimos.

This is the reason youngsters in school like to dress alike. I drove by a corner the other day where four or five girls who looked to be of high school age were waiting for a school bus. They were all wearing identical coats. It appeared at first that they belonged to some kind of an organization which demanded that its members wear uniforms. Even though dressing like everyone else has the effect of removing our individuality and causing us to disappear by blending in with the crowd, it is much better than taking the risk of being laughed at. And since children will laugh more quickly at an individual who is different than will adults, children are much more conscious of wearing what all the other kids are wearing.

Laughter is the severest form of criticism, and the fear of criticism keeps us from doing a lot of things. It keeps us from doing a lot of things we should not do, and that's good, as laughter keeps Eskimos from stealing; but it also keeps us from doing a lot of things that we would be better off doing.

It is one of the enormous pressures of environment.

Take the worker, for example, who avoids doing an outstanding and conscientious job because of the fear that his more cynical associates might laugh at him. Here, the fear of criticism in the form of laughter could shape a man's life and keep him from the goals and achievements he might otherwise reach, if he weren't so conscious of how his actions will look to others. It is here that a better understanding of what is right and wrong can overcome a person's fear of criticism.

Frequently, being right and doing what is right can bring down upon us criticism and derision, while going along with things, even though we know they are wrong, will keep us "in good" with the crowd and our associates. And it is right here that the men are separated from the boys, the women from the girls. When our desire to belong to our crowd is more important to us than to stand up for what we know to be right, we have to admit that we are lacking in the two most important attributes of a human being: courage and maturity.

Winston Churchill once said, "Courage is the finest of human qualities because it guarantees all the others."

And if there is one vital aspect of living successfully that we should get across to our youngsters, it is this.

If our kids want to dress like all the other kids in their class, fine, that's normal, and we were the same way when we were kids. But they should be told why they want to look like all the other kids in school; that it is their natural desire to belong, to be liked. And that while that is perfectly all right, they should keep constantly in mind that it should end there—that it is also right that we should want to grow into individuals, with individual goals, individual thinking, individual action. And that we will be happiest if we will do our work as best we possibly can, even though it may be the fashion for most of the rest to slide along as easily as possible.

F. D. Huntington wrote, "Conduct is the greatest profession. Behavior is the perpetual revealing of us. What a man does, tells us what he is."

Learning to Fail Through Effort, Not Fear

Here's a question for you. If you came across a plank on the ground— say the plank is 12 feet long, 4 inches thick and 12 inches wide—you'd have no trouble walking from one end of it to the other. Now let's stretch that plank between two buildings that are 100 feet tall. With nothing under you except 100 feet of air and a street down below, would you walk the plank now? Same plank, same distance, but a different, more demanding situation.

And let's say you're telling your family, gathered around the dinner table, about something in which you believe very much—your philosophy of living, for example. Now change the setting to an auditorium; you're standing on the stage before a thousand people. How would you feel about making the talk now? You'd be saying the same thing, in the same way, but the setting has changed.

Walking the plank and making the talk are easy for you in one set of circumstances. Without changing your performance at all but changing the setting, a new element is introduced—one that alters your mental attitude considerably. That element is fear—fear of what might happen. Fear of what might happen under this new set of circumstances turns two perfectly simple and natural performances into occasions of great risk—so great that you might refuse to do either of them.

Since you know perfectly well that you can walk the plank if it's on the ground, it stands to reason you can walk the same plank anyplace else; if you can make a talk under one set of circumstances, you can make the same talk under any other conditions. But fear seems to keep us from taking a formula we know will work under one condition and applying it to a large situation; the fear of what might happen holds us back.

We permit ourselves to fail by default rather than run the risk of failing as a result of having made the effort to succeed. Now, it's not important that we walk the length of the plank whether it's on the ground or high in the air. And it's not too important whether we make our little talk to the people in the auditorium, perhaps. But how many things are there at which we succeed, at which we could be successful on a much larger scale? It's all a mental game. We play the whole thing out in our minds, and it's there—not in actual practice—that we win or lose.

No one can even guess how much is lost by the so-called average person simply because he fears to make the attempt. His fear of failure in his own eyes and in the eyes of his family and friends, and the possible loss of a small stake, raise a formidable wall between his reality and his dream. So he contents himself to peek at his dream over the top of the wall—and wait. Wait until conditions are better, or Uncle Charlie dies and leaves all that money. But waiting just seems to make the wall grow higher. Conditions seem to remain about the same, and Uncle Charlie is going to outlive everybody in the family. And finally, even on tiptoes, you can't see over the wall anymore. It's too high now, and it's too late. Well, so what? It was just an idea—a dream.

Yes, that's all it was—just an idea, a dream. But what could it have been? What might it have been if you'd scrambled over that wall before it got too high?

What are some of the things you've avoided recently, out of fear?

Choose one thing and promise yourself to do it anyway, in spite of your fear. If you fail, try again. What have you learned?

When to Keep Going Even if You Don't Succeed

"When things start to look bleak, remember that you have the power to change them and that you're the only creature on earth with that kind of power."

Here's a line worth remembering. It was written by Balzac: "By resorting to self-resignation, the unfortunate consummate their misfortune."

There's a world of truth, and a world of unnecessary suffering, in that statement. The only thing that can keep misfortune hanging around is self-resignation—giving up. It makes you wonder how many thousands—perhaps millions—of fine people stay on the bottom of the pile because they've formed the habit of saying, "Well, that's the way things are" or "That's the way the old ball bounces."

Now, that would be all right for cows—they have to take life as it comes—but it's the very thing a person does not have to do. If things are going badly for him, he can change things and cause them to become good. If he isn't making enough money, he can find ways of earning more; if he doesn't like his neighborhood, he can move; if he doesn't like his job, he can quit; if he doesn't like being ignorant, he can get an education. He can, as a matter of fact, do anything he wants to do. But, as a rule, he doesn't know this. So he shrugs his shoulders, gets a sad look on his face, stands still, does nothing and says, "Well, that's the way it is." If everybody had said that from the very beginning, we'd still be running around without clothes on, throwing rocks at each other.

Let's go back to Balzac's little epigram. He said, "By resorting to self-resignation, the unfortunate consummate their misfortune." In other words, by wallowing in self-resignation, the unfortunate cause a bad situation to get worse and stay there.

Every human being on earth is going to suffer a setback from time to time; setbacks are a part of life, as are fires, floods, tornadoes, hurricanes and earthquakes. But fortunately, the human being is a builder and a re-builder, and he rebuilds better than he builds. He doesn't sit in the aftermath of the storm and resign himself; he builds better next time so the damage won't be as great or even hurt him at all. This is how skyscrapers evolved from mud huts.

Outside of death and taxes, we don't have to resign ourselves to anything. And if the situation is bad, unfortunate or unpleasant, self-resignation, as Balzac pointed out, will consummate the fact.

To my mind, there are few people to be pitied more than the sighers, resigners and shoulder-shruggers—those who would rather complain than think, who would rather bleat than take action, who would rather ask for help than help themselves. If you know people like that, it's a good idea to keep away from them unless you're very strong. They'll infect you with their virus, splash you with their mud, and they're almost impossible to help. Like rag dolls, they'll flop right back down again the minute you turn loose of them. Just make sure you don't adopt any of their fatal habits.

When things start to look bleak, remember that you have the power to change them and that you're the only creature on earth with that kind of power. Build better and stronger next time; do something about it; change a bad situation into a good one. Don't ask how; figure it out for yourself!

It has been written that it is often better to have a great deal of harm, rather than a little, happen to one. A great deal of harm may rouse you to remove what a little harm will only accustom you to endure.

Treading the Path to Success

Yes, I Will

When the American team of mountain climbers conquered Mount Everest, an interesting bit of information filtered out.

It seems that before the team left the United States, each of the skilled mountain climbers was questioned at length by a psychiatrist. And he made it a point to ask each of them this question, "Will you get to the top of Everest?

As he did, he found each of them answering with enthusiasm with lines such as: "I'm going to do my best" or "I'm going to sure try" or "I'm going to work at it." Of course, each of them knew of Everest's formidable reputation and almost impossible peak. But one of the men, a slightly built man, had a different answer.

When the psychiatrist asked him, "Will you get to the top?" he thought for a moment and then quietly answered, "Yes, I will."

And he was the first one who made it. The people who got near the top and saw him make the final assault on that fabled peak were amazed that he made it because of the poor climbing conditions prevailing at the time.

"Yes, I will." I suppose those three small words, quietly spoken or silently resolved, have been responsible for more human achievement than all the other words in the English language.

At sales conventions, salespeople are sometimes asked to set their own production goals for the year ahead. Sometimes each salesperson is given two cards on which he writes down the amount of business he'll sell during the next twelve months. One card is handed in, and he keeps the other.

In the case of many of the salespeople, the amount they write down is really nothing more than what they would "like" to sell, if everything goes all right, if business conditions stay that way, if they get lucky, and if other interests don't come along to get them off the track.

But for a few in each group, the figure they write on their cards represents what they have made up their minds to really accomplish. It is the irreducible minimum that they will settle for. And by the end of the year, despite economic conditions or anything else, they will have sold that amount or more.

And it often—and I mean quite often—happens that these salespeople are in the smallest, least attractive territories. They're not smarter than their colleagues; they're just people who take the business of being true to themselves seriously. They have determination and endurance, and they wind up winning all the marbles. They also wind up moving ahead in their companies and finally find themselves with the best, highest-paying jobs while the other salespeople are still writing down production figures they don't take seriously and wondering how old Charlie got to be the vice president in charge of sales.

They should learn three quietly spoken words: "Yes, I will." And they would find themselves getting lucky; they would find themselves selling more, making a lot more money and having a lot more fun doing it.

Nothing in the world will take the place of persistence. And there isn't a record in the world that will not be broken by it. And it all comes from an individual's coming face-to-face with himself and saying, "Yes, I will."

What Defines the Successful Person

"To succeed as persons requires that we become highly productive people to whom quality is more important than quantity. Truly successful people are maturing people who grow more productive and more interesting as they grow older. They never run out of interesting and challenging things to do."

Over the year, I've formed a personal opinion or two about who is successful and who isn't. I thought you might like to share these ideas:

An education isn't required for great financial achievement. I know multimillionaires who cannot speak or write a correct sentence. But an education is an absolutely essential ingredient if we are to fully enjoy our success. And, taking people as a whole, it is the educated segment which tends to succeed, while the uneducated, who outnumber the educated 19-to-1, tend to fail, not just financially, but in the other important categories as well.

Successive goals are as important to true success for a person as an education. Unless we have a goal toward which to work and which stretches us to new dimensions in order to achieve it, we tend to become unproductive and unhappy and quite often find ourselves in various kinds of trouble, including poor health.

To succeed as persons requires that we become highly productive people to whom quality is more important than quantity.

Truly successful people are maturing people who grow more productive and more interesting as they grow older. They never run out of interesting and challenging things to do.

Successful people have to continue to develop a sense of humor. They seldom take themselves seriously, but they take their work seriously. They tend to be easy going, easy to talk to, comfortable people who believe that ostentation and putting on airs are signs of mental immaturity.

Successful people make the world go around. They, not the masses who are quick to assume the credit, are the minority that bring us the great innovations and inventions that have helped us cope and adjust to change. They are the innovators, the curious, the questioning, the excited people of the world and without them we would still be walking about naked in the forests and scratching for nuts and roots.

I'm sure you can add important qualifications to that little list. There has long been a crackpot theory that in order to be great, one must be slightly cuckoo—a neurotic, or even psychotic person, and history is replete with such examples which are presented as proof. But such people tend to be seriously crippled and lopsided. They might achieve significant heights in a particular field, but fail in all the other important human categories.

In my opinion, and the opinions of many modem experts such as the late Dr. Abraham Maslow or Carl Rogers, the really successful people tend to succeed in most categories outside their work as well. They tend to be good family men and women, good at sports, with wide-ranging interests and enthusiasm. Maslow called them the self-actualizing people because they have the talent or knack of bringing more of their true capacities to the surface. Far from being neurotics, they are often superbly balanced and happy people. Everyone has his own definition of what constitutes success; these ideas form mine.

Do Unto Others

For the last hundred years, there have been millions of words written about how to succeed. This applies to every department of our lives, personal and professional. They've told us how to walk, how to smile, how to be enthusiastic. Our magazine, newspaper, radio and television media tell us how to smell good, glow with health and keep young looking.

Fine, that's all great. We all want to sell ourselves to those who are important to us—our family, our friends, our boss, our co-workers and our customers.

Over the past years, I've made hundreds of speeches to sales and business groups of all kinds, in just about every state in the union. And I've made it a point to talk with every topflight businessperson or salesperson I've met. I've taken enough notes to fill a good-sized garage, trying to draw a composite picture of the really outstanding, successful person. I've talked to old-timers and young ones, fat ones and skinny ones, extroverts and introverts. (Incidentally, you might be interested to know that a very big percentage of the really successful people I've met are miles from being the hearty, bluff, backslapping, give-me-the-microphone-I-want-to-say-a-few words kind of people. Instead, they're just very nice, warm, friendly people with homes and kids who decided they wanted more out of life than the average person.)

So, as the experts say, I've made a survey, and you'll be a little surprised, maybe, by what I've uncovered. You might say that I took everything I've learned from these people and jammed it into a big wine press, squeezed the whole thing down to its very essence, distilled the essence, and, like Dr. Curie, I was left with a radiating substance of incredible power. But, as maybe you already know, this glowing, wonderful thing I found wasn't new. In fact, it was incredibly old. Like the sun, it's been renewing itself all these centuries so that it's just as bright and warm and life-giving today as it ever was.

It was the golden rule: All things whatsoever you would that men should do to you, do you even so to them.

The so-called secret of the really successful people is treating the people with whom they come in contact as they themselves would like to be treated if the positions were reversed.

Simple, isn't it? It's so simple, as a matter of fact, that it's completely overlooked by the great majority of people. It's the simple, common, every day things we take for granted that we miss seeing. I remember hearing a man on a train once say, as a fly landed on his sleeve, "They call it the common housefly. You think it's common? Try making one some time."

Anyway, that's the secret, if you want to call it a secret, of the world's most successful people. They practice one of the world's oldest and best rules.

What Is Failure?

What is failure? What does a person have to do, or not do, in order to fail—to be designated as a failure? This is an interesting subject. Think about this for a moment:

Herman Melville died in 1891. He wrote the book Moby Dick, the whaling epic with its tremendous metaphysical concept of evil, at the age of 30. The book was published in 1851, sold a few copies, and then was promptly forgotten except by the limited connoisseurs of creative writing.

Melville lived forty years beyond publication of Moby Dick. He considered himself and his book a failure, and from a publisher's point of view, Melville was right. Of his other novels, Billy Budd remained unpublished for 40 years after his death and, like Moby Dick, has since become a literary classic.

Today, sales of Melville's works run into the millions. But there is no retroactive compensation for the author's troubled soul or shoddy purse.

How, then, shall we measure values, assay excellence and compensate for obvious neglect and public apathy? Moby Dick, "the white whale," is dead, but Moby Dick, the novel, lives in imperishable print, and with it, Melville moves into the company of the literary immortals.

This sort of posthumous fame was by no means restricted to Herman Melville. It has happened to a great many men and women. It was true of Henry Thoreau and Edgar Allen Poe.

So, what is failure? Failure does not come to a person because he is not recognized by the multitudes during his lifetime. Our success or failure has nothing to do with the opinions of others. It has only to do with our opinion of ourselves and what we're doing. Getting back to Thoreau for a moment; when he had to take most of his unsold books back home from his publishers, it didn't seem to bother him at all. In fact, he made the comment that he had a library consisting of over 700 volumes, most of which he had written himself.

The only person who could be called a failure is that person who tries to succeed at nothing. Success, as far as a person is concerned, does not lie in achievement. It lies in striving—reaching—attempting. Any person who decides upon a course of action he deems to be worthy of him as a person, and sets out to accomplish that goal, is a success right then and there.

Therefore, failure consists not in failing to reach our goals, but rather in not setting one. Failure consists of not trying. And certainly Melville and all the others who were not recognized until long after their deaths were successful during their lives because of the fact that they strove all their lives, and gave to their work the best that was in them. And for every Melville that we read about, there have been millions of men and women—equally successful—of whom we'll never hear. People who didn't write books or try to save the world but who, in their own quiet way, in their own places, gave to what they had chosen the best that was in them.

Are you working with a specific goal in mind?

Have you ever turned back from trying something because you were afraid to fail?

Set aside time to make a list of all the things you would try to do, if you were guaranteed not to fail. Now try them with a new, positive attitude towards failure.

If You Believe You Can, You Can

Yesterday, I got on the subject of success. I mentioned that only a few people, less than 5%, achieve what the world calls great success. This could cover great success in any field—being a wife and mother, growing a better rose, or building a fortune of several millions of dollars. Success is an individual thing and only the person involved can be responsible for what success is to him.

As long as a person is living within the law, both the spirit and the letter, no one has the right to tell any other human being what success should or should not be.

But, people who succeed are people who believe they can succeed. Success, until it has been won, is a mental thing. A man has only his mental picture and his belief, until he has achieved his goal.

Belief in himself is one of man's most difficult accomplishments. We tend to believe that others can accomplish the things we would like to accomplish, but somehow lack the same faith in ourselves.

Why? Well, it's because we're so familiar to ourselves. We know ourselves, or think we do, and it is human nature to accord more ability to a stranger than to someone we know very well.

As individuals, we're conscious of our shortcomings. We remember, consciously and subconsciously, all our little failings and past failures. We're aware of all the thousands of things we cannot do well, and we underestimate our ability in those areas in which we excel. A man is never a hero in his own home, and the same can be said of how we regard ourselves in our own minds.

We should realize it is no more amazing that we should succeed in the things at which we're good than that others should succeed in their fields.

Succeeding in life is like successfully baking a cake. It's a matter of following a recipe. Any attempts at a shortcut may result in a miserable cake. But any human being on earth can be successful if he will decide, once and for all, what it is he wants to accomplish—and really define it, write it out right down to the last comma and period—and then go after it, relentlessly, day after day, week after week, month after month, year after year until it is accomplished. Once a person has the recipe for success, it doesn't bother him too much if he finds himself with an occasional setback or failure, any more than a good cook would worry too much, or quit baking cakes, just because of an occasional flop. Mature, intelligent people realize that failure is just as much a part of success as success is a part of every failure.

C. W. Wendte wrote, "Success in life is a matter not so much of talent or opportunity as of concentration and perseverance." He's right, but it takes belief in yourself to persevere.

How to Get Rich

"Now, if you want to get rich, you have only to produce a product or service that will give people greater use value than the price you charge for it. How rich you get will be determined by the number of people to whom you can sell this product or service."

I had lunch the other day with a friend of mine who is worth in the neighborhood of $200 million, a fortune which he put together from scratch. If he isn't qualified to speak on the subject 'how to get rich', I don't know many people who are. So for those who feel it would be fun to get rich, here's how you go about it.

To begin with, understand that you don't have to drive sharper bargains, treat people unfairly, or hurt any human being in the process of getting rich. And understand that you won't get something for nothing. What you must do, in fact, is give to every person with whom you deal more than you take from him.

How is this possible? Well, naturally you can't give every person more in cash market value than you take from him, but you can and must give him more in use value than the cash value of the thing involved.

For example, when you buy a good audiocassette program, you receive more in use value by listening to the program and making it a permanent part of your library—to perhaps hear again and share with the members of your family—than the money you parted with in buying it. This means you're happy about the transaction, and so are the publisher and the author of the program. In fact, the cassettes might give you a single idea that could significantly advance your career, or greatly increase your net worth. But if it is simply a good, enjoyable program, it has more than repaid you for its purchase price.

It's the same with your car, your clothes, your home, an education—with the computer and other high-tech equipment at your office. You get greater use value from these things than their purchase price. And yet the people who produced these things are quite content with the profits they received for them. So everybody gets what he wants. This is a pretty basic discussion of what makes the wheels turn, but that's what we frequently need—a return to, a reminder of the basics.

Now, if you want to get rich—and the word rich means something different to everyone—you have only to produce a product or service that will give people greater use value than the price you charge for it. How rich you get will be determined by the number of people to whom you can sell this product or service.

It's here that the hardest part of getting rich comes in: You have to think. You have to find a quiet place where you can go every day and be undisturbed. There, with a pad of paper and a pen, jot down your ideas. Look for things in which you find an intense interest—things you most love to buy and have yourself; perhaps there's something for you here, something you can do better than it's now being done. People vote with their money, and they'd vote for you in a minute if you'll give them greater use value for their money than they're now getting.

Thinking is the one thing everyone has to do on his own. Each of us has a gold mine between his ears —that goes without saying. But digging in it is the world's hardest work. Yet it would richly repay those who go to the trouble to dig in it every day.

People Make the Difference

Some time back I had occasion to do some work with the management of one of the country's largest corporations. A few years prior to my having been called in, the company had been in very serious difficulties and had been losing many millions of dollars. Its stock had sunk to a record low price and many experts felt it to be something of a dinosaur flailing about in its death throes.

Gloom had pervaded the entire organization. The employees, many thousands in number, went about their jobs as though attending a wake, and the company's competitors welcomed its disillusioned customers by the thousands with open arms and racked up new sales records.

Finally, in some desperation, the board of directors fired the company president and hired a new man away from another company, and gave him broad, sweeping powers of reorganization. He brought in a new management team and they rolled up their sleeves and went to work.

In almost no time, a new feeling, a new spirit began to pervade the organization. Slowly the steady downward turn was brought to a halt and the company began to show signs of life. Within three years, the company was comfortably back into a very profitable position. It had a new look, a new spirit and was back into the first rank of world organizations.

The only change had been the management.

The quality, the excellence, the greatness of people had been there all the time, waiting only to be directed, motivated, inspired. This is the job of management, of leadership. It can be an army, a giant corporation, a small business, a classroom, or a family. The people will reflect their leadership and the success of the group, as a unit, will depend upon it.

This is why people in top management in business are so well-paid. It isn't that they're smarter than the people who work under them, or work ten times as hard, or put in ten times as many hours. They are paid, often ten times as much, because they possess that rare gift of being able to successfully direct the efforts of others and to infuse in the minds and spirits of others the belief that the game can be won instead of lost.

I feel certain that when most people see a great company sprawling across the landscape, or see its products at work on every side, they think of it as a giant "thing," an impersonal, mechanical monster that uses human beings much as it uses other raw materials in the shaping of its products.

But that's not the way it is. In reality, it is people that make it work or stand idle, that make it succeed or fail. It is nothing more than a great slave supplying the needs of its customers and under the direction, at every moment, of human minds and hands. And somewhere, in an office with the word "President" on the door, there is a man who is alone responsible for the direction of its destiny.

On the street, or at home, he might look much like any other man, but that's where the similarity ends. He's the person who directs the people who make the whole thing go. People make the difference.

If You Want It, Just Do It

A favorite expression of James F. Lincoln, the man who built the Lincoln Electric Company, is, "You never know what a man can do until he has been given sufficient incentive to strive to his utmost to bring out the God-given abilities within him." How many incipient Fords and Edisons go to their graves unrecognized, the world will never know. The tragedy is, they were never given sufficient incentive—or never met a crisis in their lives, which brought out their hidden powers.

And one of the country's outstanding business executives, A. W. Robertson wrote, "If a man does only what is required of him, he is a slave; the moment he does more than is required, he becomes a free man. We all have work to do in this world; it is the doing of just a little more that leads to happiness and contentment."

It is believed that millions know what they would like to do, but are afraid to begin. They feel inadequate; they're afraid they might fail; they believe they lack the necessary ability.

A man named Clifford Echols had dreamed for years of going into business for himself. All his life he'd worked as a clerk in a grocery store and the highest salary he'd ever made was $45 a week. One day he ran across a quotation by Emerson that got him off dead center. The quotation was this one: "Do the thing and you will have the power; but they that do not the thing have not the power."

He mortgaged everything he had, arranged for some credit from the necessary suppliers, and a few years later was doing $1 million a year in business.

He said later, "As I started to do the thing—the thing I'd been thinking and planning to do—I began to discover that I had hidden talents I had never suspected. Ideas came to me that I was able to turn into more successful business. In short, when I had enough faith to start to do the thing, I did find that I had the power. I had had it all along and hadn't realized it."

There's an important lesson here. It is only when we actually begin, that we find we have the power and the talent to carry it off. As long as we sit and think about it, wish for it and stay where we are, nothing happens.

Even Michelangelo said, "If people only knew how hard I worked to gain mastery, it wouldn't seem wonderful at all."

Somerset Maugham once wrote, "It's a funny thing about life—if you refuse to accept anything but the best, you very often get it."

And that's about it. We get what we expect from life. If we expect more, and plunge in after it, we'll get it. If you want to turn your dreams into reality, you're going to have to take a chance. There's no playing it safe. As long as you keep one foot on first base, it's impossible to get to second. You simply begin and you will find the ability.

Professor Ashley Montagu put it this way, "Be choosy, therefore, about what you set your heart on; for if you want to achieve it strongly enough—you will."

What You Need to Know to Succeed

What Happens When You Don't Do Your Best

"We need only to perform successfully each act of a single day to enjoy a successful day. If you will only do each day the things you know you should do and do them as well as you can, you can rest assured that you will be successful all the years of your life."

A former nuclear-submarine officer tells about an interview he had with the distinguished and formidable Admiral Hyman Rickover, head of the U.S. Submarine Service. Here's the story in his words:

"I had applied for the nuclear-submarine program, and Admiral Rickover was interviewing me for the job. It was the first time I had met Admiral Rickover, and we sat in a large room by ourselves for more than two hours. He let me choose any subject I wished to discuss. Very carefully, I chose those about which I knew the most at the time—current events, seamanship, music, literature, naval tactics, electronics, gunnery—and he began to ask me a series of questions of increasing difficulty. In each instance, he soon proved that I knew relatively little about the subject I had chosen.

"He always looked right into my eyes, and he never smiled. I was saturated with cold sweat. Finally, he asked me a question, and I thought I could redeem myself. He said, 'How did you stand in your class at the Naval Academy?' Since I had completed my sophomore year at Georgia Tech before entering Annapolis as a plebe, I had done very well, and I swelled my chest with pride and answered, 'Sir, I stood 59th in a class of 820!' I sat back to wait for the congratulations—which never came. Instead, Admiral Rickover asked another question, 'Did you do your best?'

"I started to say, 'Yes, sir,' but I remembered who this was and recalled several of the many times at the academy when I could have learned more about our allies, our enemies, weapons, strategy and so forth. I was just human. I finally gulped and said, 'No, sir, I didn't always do my best.'

"He looked at me for a long time and then turned his chair around to end the interview. He asked one final question, which I have never been able to forget—or to answer. He asked, 'Why not?' I sat there for a while, shaken, and then slowly left the room."

The former submarine officer who told that story was Jimmy Carter, former governor of Georgia and president of the United States.

Admiral Rickover made a lot of people nervous in his presence and as a result of his questions. But with regard to the question, "Did you do your best?" how would you stack up these days? In the midst of world competition managed by bright, hardworking people, we must do our best—every day, all over again.

Our job, then, is to play out the role we have undertaken to the best of our ability. Success is nothing more or less than this. We become dull or bored or uneasy with ourselves only when we shirk what we know full well we should be doing. The happiest and most contented people are those who, each day, perform to the best of their ability.

A lifetime consists of years, months, weeks and days. The basic unit of a lifetime is a single day. And a single day in our careers is made up of certain acts that each of us must perform. We need only to perform successfully each act of a single day to enjoy a successful day. If you will only do each day the things you know you should do and do them as well as you can, you can rest assured that you will be successful all the years of your life.

You don't have to run around in circles trying to do a great many things. It is not the number of acts you perform but, rather, the efficacy with which you perform the ones you do that counts. Don't try to do tomorrow's or next week's work today. Just do today's as best you can, and leave tomorrow's for tomorrow. And remember that it's important not to slight a single act during the day, because

144

sometimes we do not know how really important some little act may be.

The Turning Point

On a recent program I mentioned that there must be thousands of people every day who, without realizing they're on the brink of success, give up in failure. It reminded me of something Dr. A. J. Cronin once wrote, so I dug it out. Here's part of it. Because of his health, Dr. Cronin had to give up his career in medicine, so he turned to writing. He took a room on a small farm in Scotland and for months toiled away on the manuscript of a book. When he was halfway through, well, here's what he wrote:

"When I was halfway through, the inevitable happened. A sudden desolation struck me like an avalanche. I asked myself, 'Why am I wearing myself out with this toil for which I am so preposterously ill-equipped? What's the use of it?' I threw down my pen. Feverishly I read over the first chapters which had just arrived in typescript from my secretary in London. I was appalled. Never, never had I seen such nonsense in all my life. No one would read it. I saw, finally, that I was a presumptuous lunatic, that all that I had written, all that I could ever write, was wasted effort, sheer futility. Abruptly, furiously, I bundled up the manuscript, went out and threw it in the ash can.

"Drawing a sullen satisfaction from my surrender, or, as I preferred to phrase it, my return to sanity, I went for a walk in the drizzling rain. Halfway down the loch shore, I came upon old Angus, the farmer, patiently and laboriously ditching a patch of the bogged and peaty heath which made up the bulk of his hard-won little farm. I told him what I had done and why. His weathered face scanned me with disappointment and a queer contempt, and he said, 'No doubt you're right, doctor, and I'm the one that's wrong.' He seemed to look right to the bottom of me. 'My father ditched this bog all his days and never made a pasture. I've dug it all my days and I've never made a pasture. But pasture or no pasture,' and he put his foot on the spade. 'I cannot help but dig. For my father knew and I know that if you only dig enough, a pasture can be made here.'

"I understood. Drenched, shamed, furious, I trampled back to the farm, picked the soggy bundle from the ash can and dried it in the kitchen oven. Then I flung it on the table and set to work again with a kind of frantic desperation."

Well, to make a long story short, that manuscript that A. J. Cronin threw into the ash can and then reclaimed and rewrote was Hatter's Castle. It earned a fortune and made him famous, but far more important, it brought him the greatest triumph anyone can achieve—victory over himself. He went on to produce The Citadel, The Keys Of The Kingdom, and many other popular books—many of which were also made into motion pictures. But nothing gave him the intense satisfaction of that first great success: his conquest over doubt and despair.

What might have happened if he had not come across the farmer that night? The world might have been denied a great author and he would have missed the greatest success and satisfaction possible. It makes you wonder just how many stop too soon, quit too early in the game.

Each of us has a perfectly natural tendency to underestimate our own powers, to feel despair, to want more than anything else to quit. That's the time we should not quit.

The Right to Fail

"Only those individuals who are willing to try again after their failures, those who seem to have some strange inner knowledge that success can be theirs if they just stay with it long enough, finally win their diploma in life."

Has life ever shown you that the right to fail is as important as the right to succeed? If we didn't have bad weather, we would never appreciate sunny days. One hardly ever values his good health until he becomes ill. And I have never known a successful man or woman whose success did not hinge on some failure or another.

There is an old saying that goes, "It is impossible to succeed without suffering. If you are successful and have not suffered, someone has suffered for you; and if you are suffering without succeeding, it is so that you may succeed later or that someone may succeed after you. But there is no success without suffering."

Success in the world, any kind of success, is like a college degree. It can be earned only by following a certain course of action for a definite period of time. It is impossible for substantial success to be easy.

Success also follows a kind of natural selection. Only those individuals who are willing to try again after their failures, those who refuse to let defeat keep them down for long, those who seem to have some strange inner knowledge that success can be theirs if they just stay with it long enough, finally win their diploma in life.

Most men and women who have earned success will tell you that often, just as they felt they were finally reaching the point in life on which they had set their hearts, the rug was pulled out from under them and they found themselves back at the starting line again—and not just once or twice but many times.

Thus, only those of patient persistence are rewarded. But those who do not achieve outstanding success in life are by no means failures. They are successful in their way because they have what they really want. They simply did not want great success enough. They're happy with what they've got, and there's nothing wrong with that.

One day a young man came to my office and told me he wanted very much to make a great success of himself. He asked if I could show him the secret.

I told him to decide definitely upon what he considered success to be for him, and then work at it for 12 to 16 hours a day until he had achieved it—and when he wasn't working at it, to think about it. By doing this, he could reach his goal. However, to achieve success, he must force himself back on the track every time he strayed off, realizing that failures are as necessary to success as an excavation is to a basement.

I never saw that young man again. I wonder if he took my advice. It is an unusual person whose desire is larger than his distaste for the work involved.

Successful people are dreamers who have found a dream too exciting, too important, to remain in the realm of fantasy. Day by day, hour by hour, they toil in the service of their dream until they can see it with their eyes and touch it with their hands.

Growth or Decay

Have you ever wondered why a man keeps growing even after he's what the world considers to be successful? Or a successful business—why does it keep growing long after it has reached great success?

I know of a business firm which each year does several billions of dollars worth of business. If I mentioned its name it would be as familiar to you as your own. At a recent meeting, I gave a talk to the company's management people brought in from all over the country, and from some countries abroad. Afterwards, the executive in charge of the meeting was outlining the company's plans for the coming year. And a part of these plans included some really substantial growth. The company was shooting for sales goals that would have appeared ridiculous a few years before. And they were realistic goals, and they will be reached.

But, you might wonder, why? Why does a company doing billions of dollars worth of business— millions of dollars a month—keep setting higher goals for itself, continue to expand and build and hire more people and get bigger?

Intelligent business people realize that a business is either growing, or decaying. There's no such thing as standing still. You can never reach a place where you say, "This is it. We're as successful as we want to be; now we'll just hold the fort and maintain our present volume and profit." There are too many variables. As Sir Isaac Newton proved in his laws of physics, a body in motion tends to remain in motion. And a stationary body tends to remain stationary. If a business, or a person, stood still, and the rest of the country and the economy and the world continued to advance, it would constitute a situation in which the business or the person would, whether he liked it or not, be going backwards. If everything in the world stood still at the same time, it might be all right, but this is never the case. Our competition is not standing still; the times are changing, tastes and likes and dislikes of the customer change. And we must change and grow with them, or die.

If a successful man should consider himself to be as successful as he wants to be, and if he would collect his marbles and quit—what then? What happens to his habits of hard work, of creative thinking and activity that he's devoted many years to develop? What happens to his enthusiasm for an exciting project?

Unless he soon throws himself into something challenging and interesting, he will begin to retrogress, to shrink, to die. He can't stand still even if he wants to. Nor can anything in nature. A tree, any tree at any time, is either growing or decaying, and a business or a man works the same way.

This is why the successful small business tends to grow into a successful large business, and successful large businesses tend to grow larger. It's good for everyone concerned; more jobs, more wealth, more productivity, more growth, and a higher standard of living for everyone.

If you find yourself standing still, watch out.

When Opportunity Knocks, Are You Ready?

"Succeeding in life is not a matter of luck or chance or circumstance, but only a matter of preparation—of doing what they are given to do each day they bet they can, and holding firm to the certain knowledge that their time will come and that they'll be ready for it when it does."

A young and aspiring actor once asked Eddie Cantor for advice on getting ahead in show business. The veteran comedian thought for a moment and then answered him in one word: "Prepare."

Opportunity comes to most people many times, in many ways. The question is not so much when and how it will come, but whether we'll be ready for it when it does come—whether or not we'll even recognize it.

People today who complain about a lack of opportunity are generally the kind of people who have the mistaken idea that the world owes them a living. They're generally the people who sit around waiting for something wonderful to happen to them, with no particular effort on their part. In fact, many people still hold the mistaken idea that it's not what you know, but who you know. They couldn't be more wrong, and as long as they cling to this worn-out, old alibi, they're their own worst enemy.

If you'll examine the lives of men and women people call lucky, you'll find that their luck consisted of painstaking preparation and indefatigable persistence. They are, almost without exception, men and women who had something they wanted very much to do and who somehow knew they could do it, if they'd only stay with it long enough.

That's what Eddie Cantor meant when he gave his success formula for show business in one word: prepare. Because if a person will prepare, he can do so in the calm certainty that his opportunity will come and that he'll be ready for it when it arrives.

It's all a matter of doing certain things a certain way, every day. That's all there is to it. I think our young people in school should be taught this fact: that succeeding in life is not a matter of luck or chance or circumstance, but only a matter of preparation—of doing what they are given to do each day the best they can, and holding firm to the certain knowledge that their time will come and that they'll be ready for it when it does.

Giving a person an opportunity when he has not prepared for it makes him look ridiculous. And the people who complain about the lack of opportunity are only indicating to the world that they are not prepared, not qualified, for opportunity, because it is all around them every day of their lives.

The Turks have a proverb that goes, "The devil tempts all other men, but idle men tempt the devil." I wonder how much dissatisfaction in the world could be traced to not having enough to do, or not doing enough of what we should be doing.

The Drowning of Mr. And Mrs. Elbert Hubbard

"Dear Sirs:

"From the latest intelligence that I can get from the Cunard office, I fear that Mr. and Mrs. Elbert Hubbard on the Lusitania are not amongst us who were more fortunate, and as a fellow passenger on that boat, and as one who has known Mr. Hubbard for years, may I express to you my deepest sympathy in your sudden and terrible bereavement.

"It may be some satisfaction to you to know that Mr. Hubbard and his wife met their end calmly and serenely, together. I am confident of this, for I was standing talking to them, by the port rail directly near the bridge, when the torpedo bit the ship on the starboard side. I turned to them and suggested their going to their stateroom on the deck below to get life belts, but Mr. Hubbard stood by the rail with a half smile on his ace and with one arm affectionately around his wife. She was quietly standing beside him, and no sense of fear was shown by either of them.

"I went to my stateroom and got several life belts and came back to the place where I had left them, but I did not see them, nor did we meet again on the boat.

"These are poor words of consolation at a time like this, but I trust they will be acceptable to you. I never saw two people face death more calmly or almost happily, for they were speaking together quietly, and each seemed to have a happy smile on his and her face as they looked into each other's eyes.

"Yours very sincerely,

"C. E. Lauriat, Jr."

And that was the way it ended for Elbert Hubbard, writer, editor and printer, who, at the time, was one of the world's most famous men, and his wife, Alice. They were never seen again. One of the last things Elbert Hubbard had written was his definition of a successful person.

Elbert Hubbard's definition of a successful person, "He has achieved success who has worked well, laughed often and loved much."

Finding Happiness in Life

Understanding Discontent

A person can go a long way toward alleviating and understanding his discontent if he will understand the perverse nature of the human being. When a person works too hard, or just works steadily for a long time, he becomes discontented and wants rest and relaxation. When he relaxes too long, he seeks work. When he is around too many people for too long, he longs for solitude; when he's alone too long, he longs for human companionship.

The young envy the older person and long for the years to quickly pass; the older envy the young and often wish they could somehow turn back the clock of time.

You'll be a lot happier and have a much better sense of humor if you'll understand that it is an integral and indissoluble part of human nature to become dissatisfied, to want what you don't have at the moment. Moments of complete and blissful satisfaction are wonderful but rare and soon give way to a nagging desire for something else. And that's good.

If we understand this part of ourselves, we can avoid frustration. It is this godlike discontent that lurks in the growing person that is responsible for all human progress. That our discontent is also responsible for a great deal of pain and unnecessary suffering is simply the other side of the coin.

Do you remember the old fable about the fisherman who caught a magic prince in the form of a fish? The fish told the fisherman that if he'd let him go, the fish would grant any wish. The fisherman let him go, talked it over with his wife, and they started wishing. Each time their wish was granted, they'd then wish for something greater. Finally, they lived in a great, gleaming castle, with hundreds of servants, but it wasn't enough. The wife wanted then to control the sun, to make it obedient to her whim. When the fisherman asked for this wish, the finny prince was disgusted and took away everything. They were once again in the simple shack.

Like so many old fables, it's a commentary on human nature, and it comes uncomfortably close to the truth. We say, "If only I had such and such, I'd be completely happy for the rest of my life." It isn't true. As soon as we have such and such for a while—a surprisingly short while—we then want something else. Discontent comes with the territory; it comes with being human.

Are you discontented? If you are, that's good. That's why we're not still squatting in a filthy, drafty cave and grunting and scratching. Divine discontent: to understand it is to use it properly.

The Smell of Horses

I was staying at a resort hotel—the Grand Hotel on Mackinac Island in northern Michigan. One evening after dinner, I settled myself comfortably in a chair on the porch that runs the entire length of the old frame hotel—supposedly, it's the longest porch in the world—just to relax and enjoy the delightful evening. There was a light breeze and a good moon. The lake was beautiful, and the lights of the passing ships could be seen. The evergreens stood out clearly in the moonlight, and it was altogether one of those really great nights you remember.

Before long, a young couple came strolling down the long porch. They were walking arm-in-arm, and I thought that they were all that was needed to make the picture complete. They walked slowly by me and then took seats not far away. They were silent for a moment, and I naturally thought that they were enjoying the remarkable beauty of the scene and the night as much as I was, when the young woman spoke. I know these were her exact words, because I wrote them down as soon as I could stop laughing. She said, "I hate the smell of horses."

There are no automobiles on Mackinac Island. Horses are the only method of transportation, and they naturally lend their own unique flavoring to the island's atmosphere. I found it charming and a lot less irritating than the noise and fumes of cars, taxis and trucks.

But what made me laugh, of course, was that in the midst of all that beauty, on one of the most beautiful evenings of the year, in so romantic and charming a setting, the only thing the young woman noticed that was worth mentioning was the faint odor of horses.

They looked at me in surprise when I laughed, so I had to explain why—which neither of them found to be amusing at all. In fact, the young woman seemed somehow offended, and they soon moved away from the strange character who not only eavesdropped but also laughed at them.

The sad thing about it all was that the attractive young woman belongs to that vast army whose members make it their business to spend their lives focusing on the wrong things. I'll bet if the young man gave her a string of pearls, she'd busy herself with a minute inspection of the clasp. On a beautiful day, such people can spot that tiny cloud on the horizon. They don't appreciate the good qualities in people but complain about their defects. If their children bring home report cards with five B's and one C, it's the C that will get the comments and the attention.

They do not look for what's right but what's wrong. In a world of miracles and beauty, they see only horse droppings. If you mention this to them, they will usually say you have your head in the sand and they have it all backward.

There is nothing in the world that is perfect, and it's our job to eliminate as many defects as we can. But pity the poor people who go through life seeing only the flyspecks on the window of the world.

How to Be Happy

Would you like to know how to be happy? The answer, believe it or not, is known, and it took one of the most brilliant minds ever to appear on the earth to come up with the answer. His name was John Stuart Mill, who lived from 1806 to 1873 and became an outstanding philosopher and economist. He is believed to have had perhaps the highest I.Q. of any person who has ever lived. So, unless you think you're smarter, pay attention. John Stuart Mill said, "Those only are happy who have their minds fixed on some object other than their own happiness: on the happiness of others, on the improvement of mankind, even on some art or pursuit, followed not as a means, but as itself an ideal end. Aiming thus at something else, they find happiness by the way."

To my mind there is no doubt whatever that this is the true and only path to lasting and meaningful happiness. The definition is so excellent, and people so often seem to be so confused as to what happiness is all about, let me repeat it:

"Those only are happy who have their minds fixed on some object other than their own happiness: on the happiness of others, on the improvement of mankind, even on some art or pursuit, followed not as a means, but as itself an ideal end. Aiming thus at something else, they find happiness by the way."

I wonder why that isn't taught in school. I believe it's safe to say that not one person in 5,000 could give you as intelligent a definition of what true happiness is all about. We must have our minds fixed on something other than happiness, in order to find it. If we seek it directly, it will elude us forever. People say, "I want to be happy," as though it's something that can come to them whether they do anything about it or not. Such people can never know happiness until they break out of the tiny world of themselves. "Those only are happy who have their minds fixed on some object other than their own happiness."

Therein lies the secret. The happiest people are usually the busiest people, and almost always those whose business consists of serving others in some way. By losing themselves in what they're doing and where they're going, happiness quietly joins them and becomes part of them. The miserable, unhappy people who cause such misery and unhappiness to others are the self-centered people, people who worry constantly about what they're getting, rather than what they're giving; and the world is full of them, unfortunately. We see their harried, unhappy, furtive, ferret-like faces everywhere, pushing, their grasping hands extended. They fear life; they fear death. They are the pitiful caricatures of humanity. And they pay a terrible price for their ignorance.

A Mistake in Waiting for Happiness

"The fact is that most of the ingredients necessary for happiness are present in the lives of most people everyday. They are things and conditions for which we need not wait. And most of them are things we're so used to, we take them for granted."

Have you ever noticed how most people seem to be waiting to be happy
in the future? They seem to be so intent on getting through the day they forget to enjoy it. It's as though happiness is a distant city to them—a city they're striving to reach. But happiness is something that must be learned and practiced if we're to become skilled at it. Pushing it out into the determinate future involves running the risk that we won't know how to be happy when we get there. It's like saying, some day when I can afford to buy a piano, I'll sit down and play beautiful music. It doesn't work that way. Owning a piano doesn't confer the knowledge of how to play. And arriving at a particular stage of life, whether it's measured in terms of age or income, doesn't mean that we'll suddenly become happy people.

A reporter interviewing J. Paul Getty, who could, at that time, have cashed in his chips for several billion dollars asked, "Mr. Getty, what is it that money cannot buy?" And he replied, "I don't think it can buy health and I don't think it can buy a good time. Some of the best times I have ever had didn't cost me any money."

The fact is that most of the ingredients necessary for happiness are present in the lives of most people every day. They are things and conditions for which we need not wait. They are ours today. And most of them are things we're so used to, we take them for granted. They're the people with whom we live and work, our children, our hopes; there's the anticipation of the day and what it will bring; the opportunity to work well and honestly so that we can take pride and satisfaction from it and by so doing enjoy our leisure and our rest. There's the happiness that should come from being with our friends and neighbors. And the thoughtful person finds happiness in just being alive. He enjoys walking on a sunny day, but he likes to walk in the rain, too. He can find happiness from the sound of the surf, or the crackling of a fire.

How to Be Miserable

Let me give you some tips on how to be miserable.

Don't laugh—there are literally millions of people who wouldn't trade their daily misery for all the gold in the world. You may know some of them. In fact, if you know ten people, you probably know several of these misery-lovers. (This may be an exaggeration—and it may not be, either.)

The first step to real, professional-type, solid, unremitting misery is to get all wrapped up in yourself and your problems—real or imagined. Become a kind of island, surrounded on every side by yourself. By turning all of your thoughts inward, upon yourself, naturally you cannot spend much or any time thinking about others and other things. And so, finally, the outside world—the real world—will disappear into a kind of Hitchcock-type fog. You'll know the world is there because every once in a while you'll bump into it; but for the most part, it will be murky and indistinguishable.

And it's right here that you have to understand an important, but little known fact: The type of person who turns inward upon himself doesn't have much in the wisdom department, or he'd never do it; and as a result, he doesn't have much to turn inward upon. He finds a kind of vacuum, and he must then invent things.

He invents things like "the world is against him"—which is the worst possible kind of conceit. The world isn't against him—it doesn't even know he exists—and as a result, it ignores him completely.

So, since this person doesn't get too much attention from this attitude, he tries to get attention through various other means. One is to hunt for illness of some kind. If he looks long enough, and it doesn't take long, he can find symptoms of any condition or disease known to man—and some that are unknown—ranging from yaws to rabies. With his newfound illness, he has something with which he hopes to make everyone else as miserable as he is.

So he tells them all about it. They don't particularly want to listen, but he tells them anyway, and watches for signs of sympathy. And at first he gets it, so he thinks he's got it made, and he keeps it up, with new and interesting medical problems. He wakes up every morning feeling rotten, and he lets the world know about it!

But soon he detects a change. People begin to walk away as he approaches—they don't want to hear his deadly recitation any more. Even his family turns an uninterested, deaf ear to his protestations of being on the brink of a slow and painful death.

This makes him angry, so childlike, he cries out that nobody cares whether he lives or dies, and by this time he's pretty close to the truth. So the bitterness deepens, the misery thickens, and he draws farther and farther back into his cave, shouting imprecations at the world, throwing an occasional stone at a passerby and, in general, making a complete ass of himself.

Well, there you have it: One of the best, and most common formulas for being miserable, and making those around you miserable, as well. And it all starts with becoming too wrapped up in yourself, feeling that you're important, somehow.

Samuel Johnson wrote, "Many of our miseries are merely comparative; we are often made unhappy, not by the presence of any real evil, but by the absence of some fictitious good." And a Hindu proverb says, "The miserable are very talkative." And they are... aren't they?

The Master Word

I ran across something interesting called "The Master Word." It's about a word that will work wonders for a person regardless of his age, or what he does with his days. Man, woman or child, the master word will bring meaning and usefulness into his or her life, new clarity and self-respect and satisfaction into the passing days.

This was written by the great physician, Sir William Osler:

"Though little, the master word looms large in meaning. It is the 'open sesame' to every portal, the great equalizer, the philosopher's stone which transmutes all base metal of humanity into gold. The stupid it will make bright, the bright brilliant, and the brilliant steady. To youth it brings hope, to the middle-aged confidence, to the aged repose."

Do you know what the master word is? Guess. I used it in the second sentence. Did you recognize it? Well—the master word is—WORK!

I've talked about this before, but it's been said that we need reminding as much as we need educating. Human beings have the strangest and most perverse tendency to take the best parts of life for granted. In fact, the human being has the capacity to take anything, no matter how great it might be, for granted—once he becomes used to it. The actor in front of the cameras, the captain of a great ocean liner, the man at the controls of a giant earth-moving machine, the writer, the painter, the mother, all seem to let the charm and excitement of their work fade after a while until it becomes as humdrum to them as candling eggs.

The By-Products Of Life

Dr. Paul Scherer, speaking of Job's impatience to get immediate and direct answers to his questions, said, "Greatness and peace and happiness are simply not proper ends for any human soul to set for itself. They are the by-products of a life that has held steady like a ship at sea to some true course worth sailing."

In other words, if the course to which you're holding is right, everything else you want will come as by-products. How does a person find "some true course worth sailing?"

I remember some time back a man came to me for advice on how he might become a popular, sought-after platform speaker. He told me he enjoyed making speeches and wanted to make a career of it. I asked him what he wanted to say, and he drew a complete blank. It became clear that he was ready to speak on any subject the entertainment committee wanted him to speak on. It wasn't the subject—it was just that he wanted to make speeches. I told him that he would never become a great and sought-after speaker until he had something he wanted very much to say; something inside him that burned to get out, that he felt needed telling. Speakers become great because of what they want to say; greatness follows the zeal of their subject.

And it's the same with some true course worth sailing. A person needs to find the course in which he can lose himself—dedicate himself. Then the greatness and the peace and the happiness will come to him naturally as the bee comes to the blooming flower, or a child runs to its parents.

People who find their lives filled with confusion and uncertainty, with boredom and unhappiness, need to find a meaningful vehicle for their lives, something in which they can lose themselves completely. It need not be some great cause, although it can be. It can be found in our present work as a rule; it needs only to be ferreted out.

We need to become, in the words of Dr. Abraham Maslow, "self-actualizing." We need to become people who are steadily moving toward fulfillment, toward personal enrichment.

Dr. J. Wallace Hamilton puts it pretty well when he asks and answers his own question. He writes, "What then are the basic laws of happiness, and how do we learn them? I suppose the clearest law upon which there is fundamental agreement is that this inner music of the soul, which we have named 'happiness', is essentially and inevitably a by-product, that it comes invariably by indirection. To pursue it, to pounce upon it, to go directly after it, is the surest way not to obtain it."

People who make a mission of seeking happiness miss it, and people who talk loudly about the right to be happy seldom are. It's a by-product, an agreeable thing added in the pursuit of something else.

Are you doing something with your life that offers you a sense of fulfillment?

What do you love to do most that allows you to forget yourself?

Use this self-knowledge to cheer yourself up, next time you're feeling low.

Plant Your Roots in a Great Moving Current

"A person should have his roots deep in a great, moving current—a moving stream of conscious direction—which will keep him sailing steadily toward the destination he has chosen regardless of the economic and social winds which blow first this way and then that on the surface."

Way back in the days of sailing ships, sailors who entered into Antarctic waters would occasionally see a strange and awe-inspiring sight. They would see a great iceberg towering high out of the sea, moving against the wind. Since they depended upon the wind to drive their ships, they were keenly aware of its direction, and to see this great, shining, apparently inanimate monolith of ice moving mysteriously into the teeth of the wind was, to them, uncomfortably curious.

It was not until much later that students of the sea learned of the great currents which, like titanic rivers, moved their mysterious ways through the body of the sea.

These icebergs—some so huge that it took days to sail past them—had their roots, 90% of their bulk, caught in these great currents. They moved majestically along their way regardless of the winds and tides on the surface.

I like this story because to me it's a wonderful example of the way a person should have his roots deep in a great, moving current—a moving stream of conscious direction—which will keep him on course, sailing steadily toward the destination he has chosen regardless of the economic and social winds which blow first this way and then that on the surface.

In such a life, there is no great hurry, no frantic running about, no doubt or confusion. Instead, each day he moves a little way along his course—steadily, unrelentingly. In one day, he doesn't seem to make much headway to the casual observer, but like the iceberg—if you come back in a week, you will no longer find him at the exact latitude and longitude of a week ago. And in a year, he will have covered a really marvelous distance, while most of those about him will still be moving in circles and by fits and starts. They'll go tearing past him one day like the hare sped by the turtle (if you don't mind my mixing my metaphors) but he plods steadily on, never looking back, thoroughly enjoying the trip. Above all, he has the wonderful calm knowledge of his destination, and knows that each day finds him closing the distance that still separates him from it.

Sometimes in his life, as in all lives, there are storms which tend to throw him off course and obstacles which, for a time, may delay him. But soon, he's right back on course again, moving ahead. This is the life of the strong, serene person, the person of wisdom. The person who knows that he cannot do or become everything in his lifetime calmly chooses that which he desires and which best fits his proclivity, pushes everything else from his mind and begins his life's journey.

The life of such a man or woman always demonstrates the almost unbelievable cumulative effect of time well spent. His steady, unswerving use of time seems to make it compound until in a very few years he is miles ahead of all but the few who live as he does.

He's like the great iceberg; his roots are firmly held by the steady stream of his belief.

Ralph Waldo Emerson taught, "A point of education that I can never too much insist upon is this tenet that every individual man has a bias which he must obey, that it is only as he feels and obeys this that he rightly develops and attains his legitimate power in the world."

Serendipity

There are few things more interesting than words. Here's one you can add to your vocabulary and to your way of life, if you want to. The word is SERENDIPITY. The meaning of serendipity, according to the Oxford Dictionary, is "the faculty of making happy and unexpected discoveries by accident." And it means, also, the good things that almost always happen to a person following a bold course of action—serendipitous things.

The word was coined by the British author Horace Walpole, who based it on the title of an old fairy tale, "The Three Princes of Serendip." The princes in the story were always making discoveries of things they were not in quest of.

Let's say you're trying to invent something. Frequently, you will stumble onto something entirely different, and wonderful, that you had no idea of discovering. That's what serendipity means. Now the point I want to make is that you wouldn't have made the serendipitous discovery if you hadn't been looking for something else.

I'll bet you've heard people say of someone, "That's the luckiest guy in the world." But if you'll get to know the man, you'll usually find he's a busy, positive kind of individual who's always looking for new and interesting ways of doing things. Someone once defined luck as something you find when preparedness meets opportunity; it just won't happen, usually, unless a person's prepared for it. There are lots of interesting and pretty wonderful things that would be happening all the time to a lot more people, if people weren't such stick-in-the-muds, as a rule.

Take the person who hates his work, for example. There are millions of people, I suppose, who actually hate—loathe—the work they're doing. But they stay with it because of some warped sense of security. Now, if they'd find out what it is they'd really love to do, and prepare themselves for it, they could cut loose of what they're doing now. The minute they did, this word "serendipity" would come into action—the good things that happen to a person following a bold, positive course of action.

It is frequently true that a lot of the boredom and frustration in a job comes from not knowing enough about it. You'd be surprised at the number of people who know only their own job, and that in a limited way, and who have no idea what's going on in the rest of the business. Frequently, a person in any given line of work can find interest, challenge, and just the job he's looking for—right in his own business or industry, if he'd just take the time to find out more about it.

One of the greatest explorers who ever lived, Captain James Cook, began as an ordinary seaman. In four years he had learned enough to become a master of his own ship, and later made the discoveries that made him famous—a happy, successful, serendipitous life—beginning as a common seaman. Another common seaman, named Joseph Conrad, studied and worked his way to become a ship's captain. He later wrote the wonderful stories of the sea that made him loved and famous.

There isn't a single line of work where this hasn't happened. I just picked a common seaman as an example. The same applies to anything. Serendipity: quite a word. And it'll apply to whatever you do for a living.

Thoughts on Existence

Reminders of Mortality

Back in the days of ancient Rome, during the years of the Caesars, there was a person whose only job was to hold a laurel wreath over the head of Caesar and from time to time intone the words, "Thou art mortal."

The purpose of this was to remind the man in whom such great powers resided that he, too, was, after all, only a man, and as such, mortal.

When we're young, we tend to think of life as never-ending. Time for us stretches off limitlessly into the future. But as we get older, even in our forties—which should be a time of vigor, interest and activity, really a time of young maturity—we begin to get, from time to time, small reminders of our mortality. It might be a sudden shortness of breath, or a perfectly normal twinge in the chest, a bit of back trouble. But we get these occasional reminders that time is not, after all, standing still for us. That we, like the Caesars of old, are indeed mortal.

To the neurotic, this sort of reminder fills him with dread and plunges him into even deeper depression. But to the fairly normal, reasonably well-adjusted person this comes as a reminder to enjoy to the fullest the time that is remaining; that days are not things to be waited through until Saturday, or a birthday, or Christmas, but rather to be savored and enjoyed one by one, hour by hour. We come to an understanding that to kill time, as we so aptly put it, is really nothing more than to kill a little part of ourselves since time is all we have.

It reminds us too, or at least it should, to be more patient, more tolerant of others, particularly those we love. If we're mature enough to love everyone, it means exactly that. And it reminds us to follow our hunches and obey our sudden impulses, especially those which involve a kind word, or a pat on the back or a sign of tenderness. Those we love, as well as ourselves, are only passengers for the journey's duration; let's let them know we enjoy sharing it with them. And if we don't always enjoy it, let's fake it, let's pretend we do. After all, the trip really isn't all that long.

I saw a newspaper picture not long ago of a woman 75 years old who was ice-skating. It reminded me that 75 is only old to people under 60 years of age. To people who are 75, it's a good, thoroughly enjoyable age. And maybe we'll all live to be 85 or 95. And maybe we won't. In any case, there is a limit and there should be or it wouldn't be there. And since there is, why not relax a little? Don't take things too seriously. And, as an old friend of mine once said, "In a life where death is inevitable, never worry about anything!"

Sure, it's easier said than done. I remember reading a story about an old man who was planting a young tree in his yard. His neighbor hailed him and said, "What are you planting the tree for? You'll never live to see it grown." And the old man calmly went on with his planting and said, "I believe you have to plan on dying tomorrow or living forever. I'm not planning on dying tomorrow."

Yes, the smart people of the world—the really mature people—are those who know the length of the journey is limited. They don't dwell on this. But they make certain they enjoy every day of the trip as much as they possibly can.

Enjoy the Interval

George Santayana once wrote, "There is no cure for birth and death save to enjoy the interval." It's being reminded of something like this which can really shake a person.

Have you ever thought about how much time we waste, and unhappiness we bring upon ourselves by worrying about the future, and reliving in our minds the mistakes of the past?

One of the neatest tricks in the world is to learn to enjoy the present, since the present is the only time we will ever own. Distance is no longer a serious obstacle due to modern means of travel. But time remains unconquerable. It cannot be expanded, accumulated, mortgaged, hastened or retarded. It is the one thing completely beyond man's control. And while the supply of time is certainly limited for anyone, generally it is squandered as though there is no end to it.

The man on the commuter train, bored, waiting to get home, then waiting for dinner, then waiting to go to bed or for a particular television program, thus spends his time slightly behind reality, waiting for something that's coming up. And while it will keep him going, he never, or seldom, learns to enjoy the time he is using right now. What it takes is an awareness of living. It means being aware that you are alive at this moment, and that the world and people are interesting enough at any time so that we need not waste so precious a thing as time in boredom.

If we know where we're going in the future, we can do our work to the best of our ability, give it everything we have, and have no need to worry about it or the future. And as for reliving our mistakes of the past, this is the easiest advice on earth to give and probably the most difficult to follow. Everybody knows it's perfectly useless to relive in our minds the foolish stunts we've pulled in the past, but this doesn't keep us from doing it. Again, according to the experts, the solution may be found in living for the present and enjoying it as much as we can. This does not mean that we should not plan for the future. We should! But once our plans are laid, work on them, but don't stew and fret over them.

All we will ever have is today. Yesterday is gone forever. It can never be recalled, and tomorrow never comes. If we find it difficult to enjoy the day in which we're living, we should remember that what we're waiting for will be made up of the same kind of days we're getting now.

Frequently a person who is unhappy by nature will believe that when something happens in the future such as marriage, a better job, more money, or whatever it happens to be, he will suddenly be a happy person. The facts don't bear that out. If we're living in the past, or worrying, or hoping for happiness in the future, the best thing we can do is ask ourselves, "How am I doing with the days I'm getting right now? How am I doing today?" It is not how much we have but how much we enjoy that makes happiness. Try the business of being aware of the present and its possibilities, and the chances are you'll enjoy it.

The Greatest Gift on Earth

"Millions of people with the miracle of sight never really see the world about them until it's practically too late; millions with the inborn capacity to love, and to know the joy that loving brings, wait too long to express it."

In interviews with very old people—people who realize that their remaining time is drawing to a close—you frequently hear them say, "I waited too long to start living."

When the researchers—or others who hear this kind of response—are young, they find it strange. But what these older people mean is that they often failed to enjoy life even during the years that they were living it most fully. And it seems that most people, during the richest and fullest years of their lives, fail to develop an awareness of living, an enjoyment of living.

It's like the person who puts the best china and silver and linen away for some future, or very special time, and dies before any of it is ever used. Or it's like the person who puts seat covers in his car and thus, passes on, to the second person to buy it, brand new upholstery that he himself never used or enjoyed.

And so, millions of people with the miracle of sight never really see the world about them until it's practically too late; millions with the inborn capacity to love, and to know the joy that loving brings, wait too long to express it. They live through the passing years without really being aware of their days, of the riches that are passing through their hands.

Few people, it seems, develop an awareness of daily living. In possession of the miracle of life, they pass through their days like automatons. In possession of the greatest gift on earth—life itself—they tell us by their actions that they don't even know they have it and haven't the slightest conception of its value, let alone an awareness that it is to be enjoyed to the fullest every day.

I remember reading an account of a famous show-business personality—a woman of great talent—who, as she made the announcement of her impending fourth or fifth marriage, said, "After all these years, I am finally going to be happy." She thought another husband could somehow give her something she should have been enjoying all along. She obviously had no idea as to what happiness is, where it's to be found, or what living is all about. And she belongs to a big club.

It is only when life is threatened that a conception of its value begins to dawn on the average person.

A man plotted a kidnapping for months. His mind was filled with the thought of the million-dollar ransom he was going to get—more important to him, he thought at the time, than anything else on earth. Yet, when he was surprised by the police, he dropped the suitcase containing the ransom and ran for dear life. Ran for dear life. It took the sudden threat of death to put things in their proper order for this poor, stupid person.

It's amazing, isn't it? Most people place the greatest value on the cheapest things in life, while the greatest gift of all—life itself—goes unnoticed.

The most fortunate people in the world are those who have the wisdom to place value where it belongs—those who have an awareness of life.

It Alone is Life

Same 4,500 years ago, one of the most inspiring thoughts the world has ever produced was written in Sanskrit. Here's its translation: "Look well to this one day, for it and it alone is life. In the brief course of this one day lie all the verities and realities of your existence; the pride of growth, the glory of action, the splendor of beauty. Yesterday is only a dream, and tomorrow is but a vision. Yet each day, well lived, makes every yesterday a dream of happiness and each tomorrow a vision of hope. Look well, therefore, to this one day, for it and it alone is life."

With that one bit of ancient philosophy and little else, a person could live an ideal and richly successful life. It applies to everyone in every walk of life—certainly the student, the teacher, the businessperson, the worker (whatever his task may be), the housewife, the politician, the clergyman.

I remember reading somewhere about a businessman who visits his barbershop every morning for a half hour. He doesn't want a shave or haircut. He lies stretched out in the chair with a hot towel on his face, not just because it is soothing and relaxing but so no one will recognize and speak to him. And during that half hour, he gets himself organized mentally for the day ahead. It sounds like a good idea. But I think everyone could accomplish much the same thing by sitting quietly and slowly reading that great piece of wisdom from the Sanskrit.

"Look well to this one day, for it and it alone is life." It's true.

Today, right now, is all the life there is for any person on earth. We can look toward and plan for the future, certainly. But if we pass up living and enjoying today, we're passing up all we've got for something we hope to get.

"In the brief course of this one day lie all the verities and realities of your existence; the pride of growth, the glory of action, the splendor of beauty." In reading and thinking of this at the beginning of each new day, we would remind ourselves of these points: the truth and reality of our lives, in themselves a miracle. And we would remind ourselves of our duty to grow a little as persons, to rise above the petty and the trivial, to become stronger and more serene. And we would remind ourselves to take some action calculated to move us a notch closer to our goals and toward fulfillment as persons, and to recognize and be aware of the beauty around us.

The proof of the greatness and truth of this piece of writing is in the fact that it has successfully withstood the test of time and has endured for more than 4,500 years. It is as modern and important today as it was the day it first flashed across the mind of some person whose name has long been forgotten. And it will be just as important to thinking men and women 4,500 years from today, for real truth is as ageless as the mountains, as enduring as the sea.

The Wish to Be Like Someone Else

"When a person finds himself, when he stops imitating and envying others, there is something in his nature that says to him, "This is it. You've found your road at last."

Ralph Waldo Emerson wrote, "There is a time in every man's education when he arrives at the conviction that envy is ignorance, that imitation is suicide, that he must take himself for better or worse as his portion; that though the wide universe is full of good, no kernel of nourishing corn can come to him but through the toil bestowed on that plot of ground which is given him to till. The power which resides in him is new in nature, and none but he knows what that is which he can do, nor does he know until he has tried. Trust thyself: Every heart vibrates to that iron string."

There is a bit of advice that a person would do well to reflect upon every morning of his life. No one can even estimate the number of people who live nervous, anxious, unhappy lives because they daily attempt the impossible, which is to be like someone else. They are people who don't realize the truth of Emerson's words that envy is ignorance, that imitation is suicide. He must have used the word suicide because we have to kill that which is natural in ourselves when we attempt to be like someone else.

They need to recognize the truth, also, that the power that resides in them is new in nature, that it has never appeared before in just that way, on earth; that if they'll learn about and develop their own powers, they'll have no need of envy or imitation.

Envy is ignorance because it means a person is ignorant of his own powers and abilities, his one-of-a-kind natural talent. He has never looked within himself for his own road to greatness but, instead, seeks it in the lives of others. And when he fails to succeed as do those he envies—as fail he must because he cannot possibly be exactly like them—his image of himself shrinks. Not understanding that he is unlike those he envies, he does not realize that this simple fact lies at the bottom of his failure. Nor does he understand that he can be as successful as anyone on earth if he will build upon that power that resides in him.

As Emerson put it, "The power which resides in him is new in nature, and none but he knows what that is which he can do, nor does he know until he has tried."

This is why a parent is off-base when he says to a child, "Why aren't you like so and so? Look what he's doing." The parent doesn't understand that it's a human impossibility for the child to be like so and so, and to do what he does in the same way.

Instead, a parent would be wise to say, "Don't worry about so and so. He's found his strength, and he's building on it. You have strength of your own, and when you find it, you can build just as high."

And then those great words, "Trust thyself: Every heart vibrates to that iron string." When a person finds himself, when he stops imitating and envying others, there is something in his nature that says to him, "This is it. You've found your road at last."

Every person is born to be a star at something. The purpose of his life is to discover it, and then to spend his years building upon that plot of ground it was given to him to till.

The Identity Trap

What makes you happy will depend upon your own personal nature— which is different in many ways from that of any other human being. To try to find happiness by doing what seems to make others happy is to fall head first into the Identity Trap. So writes Harry Browne in his book, How I Found Freedom in an Unfree World.

He believes that there are two Identity Traps: (1) the belief that you should be someone other than yourself; and (2) the assumption that others will do things in the way that you would. These are the basic traps, of which many others are variations. In the first trap, you necessarily forfeit your freedom by requiring yourself to live in a stereotyped, pre-determined way that doesn't consider your own desires, feelings and objectives.

The second trap is more subtle but just as harmful to your freedom. When you expect someone to have the same ideas, attitudes and feelings that you have, you expect him to act in ways that aren't in keeping with his nature. As a result, you'll expect and hope that people will do things they're not capable of doing.

Others can suggest what you "should" do, or what "ought" to make you happy, but they will often be wrong. You have to determine for yourself who you are, what makes you happy, what you're capable of doing, and what you want to do. Be open to suggestions, but never forfeit the power to make the final decision yourself. Only then can you act in ways that will bring you happiness.

You're in the Identity Trap when you let others determine what's right or wrong for you—when you live by unquestioned rules that define how you should act and think.

You're in the Identity Trap, says Mr. Browne, when you try to be interested in something because it's expected of you, or when you try to do the things that others have said you should do, or when you try to live up to an image that others say is the only legitimate, valid image you're allowed to have.

You're in the Identity Trap if you allow others to define labels and impose them upon you—such as going to PTA meetings because that's what a so-called "good parent" is supposed to do, or going to visit your parents every Sunday because a "good child" would never do less, or giving up your career because a so-called "good wife" puts her husband's career first.

You're in the Identity Trap if you feign an interest in ecology to prove your civic interest, or give to the poor to prove you aren't selfish, or study dull subjects to appear to be "intellectual."

You're in the Identity Trap if you buy an expensive car to prove you're successful, or a small foreign car because your friends are anti-Detroit; or if you shave every day to prove you're respectable, or let your hair grow long to prove you don't conform. In any of those ways, you allow someone else to determine what you should think and be. You deny your own self when you suppress desires that aren't considered "legitimate," or when you try to appear to be having fun because everyone else is, or when you settle for a certain life because you've been told that's all you should expect in the world.

The Power of Reason

Most of the earth's creatures have been given the gift of concealment through protective coloring. In fact, all of them that need concealment blend in so well with their natural surroundings that, when they're motionless, they become virtually invisible. This, of course, protects them from the sight of their enemies or their quarry. They, through the endless ages of evolution, have conformed to their environment; they have copied the appearance of their natural surroundings.

But what of man? He is among the weakest, physically, of all creatures. He can be killed by a leopard one-fourth his weight, or by a germ or virus that's totally invisible. He has no protective coloring at all but can easily be seen in any kind of environment. He can't run fast enough to escape any animal bent on catching him; he can't swim very far; he has no claws or sharp teeth, and can hardly climb a tree. His vision is weak and he can't even catch a puppy that doesn't want to be caught.

But he was given the greatest gift of all—reason! He can think! Because he can think, he doesn't need to blend in with his surroundings—his environment. He can make his surroundings and environment change to match him! In fact, just as you can tell what kind of country an animal comes from by looking at the pattern of its coloring, you can tell what kind of reasoning a person is doing by observing his surroundings—his environment, because environment fits the person, just as an animal fits its environment.

To the exact extent that a person uses the greatest gift on earth, the gift of reasoning—of thinking—which belongs to him alone of all the creatures on earth, will he determine the kind of environment in which he will live. Only man can make the scenery change to match him.

By changing himself, he changes his surroundings. If a person understands this, he understands, at the same time, why he is king over everything else.

Because of this, he solves the riddles of the invisible germs, travels with the speed of two hundred hurricanes, swims to the bottom of the sea, and will one day visit the farthest planets of the universe.

And yet, it is here we find the greatest paradox: With this greatest gift of all, the great majority of people neither know they have it, nor use it, but spend most of their time aping those about them—playing a silly kind of copycat game that you'd expect to see in a tribe of baboons cavorting on the forest floor. No two of them are exactly alike, and yet they pretend they are, and they let a handful of their brothers do their thinking for them. Each of them has been given the greatest gift on earth and he doesn't even open the box.

I think from time to time it would be good for all of us to remember Archibald MacLeish's great line: "The only thing about a man that is a man... is his mind. Everything else, you can find in a pig or a horse."

The Lives We Imagine

Here's something worth keeping in mind: "If one advances confidently in the direction of his dreams, and endeavors to live the life which he has imagined, he will meet with a success unexpected in common hours." It was written by Henry David Thoreau. And it contains a truth most people do not even dream exists. If they did, the entire country might be turned into total chaos.

The truth most of us miss in that great quotation is that success—beyond anything we might now imagine—lies in wait for those who can put together enough courage to actually live the life they imagine.

Most people live in two worlds: There's the real world, the world in which they move and work and live, the world of the nitty-gritty; and there's the world of the imagination, the world in which they would secretly like to live. And what keeps them from moving from the world of reality into the world of their imagination is habit, and the fear of falling flat on their faces in the attempt, and losing even the little that they presently have, and perhaps looking ridiculous in the eyes of their loved ones and friends. They are like the character Walter Mitty, created by James Thurber. They are the people who dream their whole lives instead of living their dreams. We're all Walter Mittys to some extent.

What we fail to realize is what Thoreau discovered: that if one advances confidently in the direction of his dreams, and endeavors to live the life which he has imagined, he will meet with a success unexpected in common hours.

Thoreau knew this because he did it. So have thousands of others who have found to their delighted surprise that life pays off most handsomely when we are doing that which we most want to do, when we are actually living the life we have imagined for so long.

That doesn't mean that we run off after every vagrant whim. But it does mean that we should live the life that we know deep down in our very being, we would most like to live. It means that we should be doing that which every indicator of our makeup, every fiber of our being, tells us we should be doing—and has been telling us for some time. Even Thoreau didn't go to live at Walden Pond the first time the idea struck him to go off by himself, and meditate and think and write and try to discover for himself what was important and what wasn't.

But when an idea tugs at us day after day, year after year, when we think about it as we lie awake in bed or the first thing when we wake up—when it worries our consciousness like a puppy with a slipper—then it's time to do something about it. And even though making the move might seem to jeopardize everything of order in our lives, it is very likely as Thoreau suggested, that we will meet with a success unexpected in common hours. The most commonly voiced thought after taking such a step is, "Why didn't I do this years ago?"

Emerson said, "A man should learn to detect and watch that gleam of light which flashes across his mind from within, more than the luster of the firmament of bards and sages. Yet he dismisses without notice his thought, because it is his."

When was the last time you allowed yourself to nurture your imagination?

Do you take the time to write down your dreams and thoughts?

If the idea of taking a big risk to pursue your dreams frightens you, consider taking smaller steps first and watch your success grow!

The Man, the Seashore and the Four Prescriptions

Once upon a time, there was a man who felt he'd reached the end of his rope. It seemed that all the interest had suddenly vanished from his life; his creative wells had seemingly dried up. He still had his work, but it suddenly seemed meaningless to him. Even his family and his home receded darkly in his mind.

Finally, nearing the point of desperation, he went to see his old friend, the family doctor. The doctor listened to his story, saw the depth of his depression, and then asked him, "When you were a child, what did you like to do best?"

"I liked to visit the seashore," he said.

"All right," the doctor said, "you must do exactly as I tell you. I want you to spend all day tomorrow at the shore. Find a lonely stretch of beach and spend the entire day there from 9 o'clock in the morning until 6 o'clock in the evening. Take nothing to read, and do nothing calculated to distract you in any way. I'm going to give you four prescriptions in order. Take the first at 9 o'clock, the second at noon, the third at 3 o'clock, and the last at 6 o'clock. Don't look at them now. Wait until you arrive at the shore tomorrow morning."

The man promised he would take the doctor's advice and the next morning, a little before 9 o'clock, he parked his car on a lonely stretch of beach. There was a strong wind blowing in from the sea and the surf was high and pounding.

He walked to sand dune near the seething surf and sat down. He took out prescription number one, opened and read it. It said: "Listen." That was all that was written on it, the one word, "Listen!" And so for three hours that's all he did. He listened to the sound of the buffeting wind and the lonely cries of the gulls. He listened to the sound of the booming surf. He sat quietly, and he listened.

At noon, he read the second prescription. It said, simply, "Reach back." And so for the next three hours he did just that. He let his mind go back as far as it could go and he thought of all the incidents of his life he could remember: the happy times, the good times, the struggles and the successes.

At 3 o'clock, he tore open the third prescription. It read: "Re-examine your motives." And this took so much intense thought and concentration that the remaining three hours slipped quickly by. For 3 hours, he re-examined his motives, his reasons for living and moved closer to fulfillment. He clarified and re-stated his goals.

And at 6 o'clock, under a gray, darkening sky and with a taste of salt spray on the wind, he read the fourth and final prescription. It read: "Write your worries in the sand."

There had been one thing that had been worrying him particularly, so he walked to the hard sand and with a stick wrote this worry in the sand and stood looking at it for a moment. Then, as he walked toward where his car was parked, he looked back and saw that the incoming tide had already erased his worry. He got in his car and drove homeward.

My old friend, Norman Vincent Peale, told me that story some years back about the man, the seashore and the four prescriptions: Listen, reach back, re-examine your motives, and then write your worries in the sand.

Life Comes Full Circle

The head of a great corporation died in his New York office of a heart attack. Later, when it came time to clean out his desk and collect his personal effects, a hand fishing line, wrapped on a stick, complete with bobber, sinker and hook, was found in his bottom desk drawer. It was probably the one he had used as a small boy on the family farm in the Middle West.

Had that relic of younger, carefree days represented his real dream of what living was all about?

He had gone to school, found a job, got married, worked hard, purchased a home on the installment plan and won the other niceties of living. Children had come along and there was their education to think about. There were the promotions that had come from hard work and native ability and the passing of the years. There were the clubs and civic things, the professional associations—the crises on the job and at home. And finally, the top job with a company that had grown very much larger with the passing of 30 years; the top job—with its responsibilities to stockholders, employees, customers, research and development, and finance. The kids were out of school and married now. It had all happened so fast, and with no real plan of any kind. It had been school, then job, then work, then promotions and family and income problems and suddenly there he was, on top of the pile.

And rummaging in his things in the attic or the basement one day, he had come across that old, worn-out fishing outfit, with its tiny hook for bluegills and the red bobber with the paint all peeled off. The string had almost come apart in his hands. And he had sat there and remembered that cool little creek with the summer smell of it, the green moss along the bank, the frogs plopping into the water, the water bugs skimming and the willows along the bank. He remembered the excitement of seeing that bobber suddenly disappear, and the frantic tug of the fish on the line and finally a nice string of them for dinner.

And suddenly he had wanted to go back. He had realized that that had been living—that had been real, and elemental and satisfying. And somehow, he hadn't done enough of it; he hadn't had the time to just go sit on a bank and fish for a while and chew on a twig and feel the sun on his back and wait for the bobber to disappear; the time and the leisure to listen to the voice inside and get things straightened out in his mind as to what was important and what wasn't. Things like goals and roles.

So someone had called him, and he'd put the fishing outfit in his jacket pocket. And he thought about it the next morning, too, when he took the outfit to the office and looked at it again and then finally put it down in that bottom drawer. Out of sight, but not out of mind. And then there'd been the coronary, and that had been the end of that. The fishing outfit was still in the bottom drawer. And when his wife went through the effects they sent home from his office, she sat with the fishing outfit in her hand for a long time. She saw him as a little boy, too, and wondered why he had followed the course he'd chosen.

Mentoring

We live by example. As youngsters, our parents set our example. As we grow older, examples are set for us by our parents and the people with whom we habitually associate—relatives, the friends of our family, our neighbors, and the school we attend.

We take our cues from those about us. It's all we can do. We are born not knowing how to survive in the world. We must learn how, over a period of many years. So we watch and we listen to those about us, and we conduct ourselves as they do. What they take for granted as part of living, we learn to take for granted. We devote 17, perhaps 18 years or more to living at home with people who are, in every sense of the word, our teachers. And the quality of our lives and our learning will, of course, depend on the quality of their habit-knit, automatic response to living. We live and learn by example.

Peter Drucker wrote, "The best prescription for achievement is to have an achieving father or mother—better yet, an achieving milieu." High achievement seldom accrues to a man or woman who has not been inspired by a mentor; the word mentor means "wise and trusted counselor." This counselor can be a schoolteacher, a manager, a parent, a friend—anyone who represents what we most want to become.

The Harvard Business Review said that, "Everyone who makes it has a mentor." And Lee Iacocca said, "You've got to have mentors along the way."

If every young person could have a wise and trusted counselor to lead him step-by-step onto the wise and rewarding pathways of the world, all would be well.

My old friend, the late Eric Hoffer, said, "Those who invest themselves in becoming all they can become and, more important than that, those who invest themselves in helping others become all they can become, are involved in the most important work on the face of the earth. That is, they are helping to complete God's plan."

We should never forget that we are setting an example for others—example is the school of mankind—and that the flame of a candle is not diminished when it is used to light another. Consider, for example, what is believed to have been the greatest intellectual succession in history: Socrates was the teacher of Plato; Plato, in turn, was the teacher of Aristotle; and Aristotle, in turn, was the teacher of Alexander the Great. We might not have had the great works of Plato had it not been for Socrates and his questioning method of teaching. And the only reason we know anything about Socrates is because Plato wrote down his words; Socrates never wrote down anything at all.

As adults, we tend to be mentors—or, at least an example—to others as well as protégées of the person or persons who manage us and who set examples for us.

Can you think of someone who really is your mentor?

Are you in some ways patterning your life after this individual?

If you became exactly like your mentor, would you be content?

Do you feel you can transcend—go beyond—your mentor to new levels?

The History Of The Parish Of Garstang In The County Of Lancaster, Part 1...

Henry Fishwick, Chetham Society

Chetham Society,

ESTABLISHED   M.DCCC.XLIII.

THE CHETHAM SOCIETY

FOR THE PUBLICATION OF

HISTORICAL AND LITERARY REMAINS

CONNECTED WITH THE PALATINE COUNTIES OF

LANCASTER AND CHESTER.

Council for the year 1877-78.

President.

JAMES CROSSLEY, Esq., F.S.A.

Vice-President.

THE REV. F. R. RAINES, M.A., F.S.A., Hon. Canon of Manchester, Vicar of
Milnrow, and Rural Dean.

Council.

JOHN E. BAILEY, Esq., F.S.A.
WILLIAM BEAMONT, Esq.
THE VERY REV. BENJAMIN MORGAN COWIE, B.D., F.S.A., Dean of Manchester.
THE WORSHIPFUL RICHARD COPLEY CHRISTIE, M.A., Chancellor of the Diocese
of Manchester.
LIEUT.-COLONEL FISHWICK, F.S.A.
HENRY H. HOWORTH, Esq., F.S.A.
WILLIAM LANGTON, Esq.
THE REV. JOHN HOWARD MARSDEN, B.D., F.R.G.S., late Disney Professor.
THE REV. JAMES RAINE, M.A., Canon of York, Fellow of Durham University.
FRANK RENAUD, Esq., M.D., F.S.A.

Treasurer.

ARTHUR H. HEYWOOD, Esq.

Honorary Secretary.

R. HENRY WOOD, Esq., F.S.A., F.R.G.S.,
Mem. Corr. Soc. Antiq. de Normandie.

RULES OF THE CHETHAM SOCIETY.

1.   That the Society shall be limited to three hundred and fifty members.

2.   That the Society shall consist of members being subscribers of one pound annually, such subscription to be paid in advance, on or before the day of general meeting in each year. The first general meeting to be held on the 23rd day of March, 1843, and the general meeting in each year afterwards on the 1st day of March, unless it should fall on a Sunday, when some other day is to be named by the Council.

3.   That the affairs of the Society be conducted by a Council, consisting of a permanent President and Vice-President, and twelve other members, including a Treasurer and Secretary, all of whom shall be elected, the first two at the general meeting next after a vacancy shall occur, and the twelve other members at the general meeting annually.

4.   That the accounts of the receipts and expenditure of the Society be audited annually, by three auditors, to be elected at the general meeting; and that any member who shall be one year in arrear of his subscription, shall no longer be considered as belonging to the Society.

5.   That every member not in arrear of his annual subscription, be entitled to a copy of each of the works published by the Society.

6.   That twenty copies of each work shall be allowed to the editor of the same, in addition to the one to which he may be entitled as a member.

Applications and communications to be addressed to the PRESIDENT, *Stocks House, Cheetham, Manchester, or to the* HONORARY SECRETARY, *Penrhos House, Rugby.*

PUBLICATIONS OF THE CHETHAM SOCIETY.

First year (1843–4).

We Have Book Recommendations for You

- The Strangest Secret by Earl Nightingale (AUDIOBOOK and Paperback)

- Acres of Diamonds (MP3 AUDIO) [UNABRIDGED] by Russell H. Conwell

- Think and Grow Rich [MP3 AUDIO] [UNABRIDGED]
  by Napoleon Hill, Jason McCoy (Narrator)

- As a Man Thinketh [UNABRIDGED]
  by James Allen, Jason McCoy (Narrator) (Audio CD)

- Your Invisible Power: How to Attain Your Desires by Letting Your Subconscious Mind Work for You [MP3 AUDIO] [UNABRIDGED]

- Thought Vibration or the Law of Attraction in the Thought World [MP3 AUDIO] [UNABRIDGED]
  by William Walker Atkinson, Jason McCoy (Narrator)

- The Law of Success - Napoleon Hill [MP3 AUDIO]

- The Law of Success, Volumes II & III: A Definite Chief Aim & Self -Confidence by Napoleon Hill (Paperback)

- Thought Vibration or the Law of Attraction in the Thought World & Your Invisible Power (Paperback)

- Automatic Wealth, The Secrets of the Millionaire Mind - Including: As a Man Thinketh, The Science of Getting Rich, The Way to Wealth and Think and Grow Rich (Paperback)

ONLINE AT:
www.bnpublishing.com

keep Ithaka always in your mind.
Arriving there is what you're destined for
But don't hurry the journey at all.
Better if it lasts for years,
so you're old by the time you reach the
island.
wealthy with all you've gained on the way,
not expecting Ithaka to make you rich.

Ithaka gave you the marvelous journey
without her you wouldn't have set out.
she has nothing left to give you now.

And if you find her poor, Ithaka won't have
fooled you.
wise as you will have become. so full of experience
you'll have understood by then what these
Ithakas mean.

Lightning Source UK Ltd.
Milton Keynes UK
UKHW031046160321
380445UK00007B/1219

9 789562 915731